Allai

Sex: Male / Gender: Masculine

READINGS IN MALE SEXUALITY

SEX: MALE
GENDER: MASCULINE

READINGS IN MALE SEXUALITY

Edited by JOHN W. PETRAS
Central Michigan University

ALFRED PUBLISHING CO., INC.

Library of Congress Catalog No.: 74-32335

Printed in the United States of America

LIBRARY OF CONGRESS CATALOGING IN PUBLICATION DATA

Petras, John W   comp.
Sex/male—gender/masculine : readings in male
sexuality.

Includes bibliographies.
1. Men—Sexual behavior—Addresses, essays, lectures.
2. Sex role—Addresses, essays, lectures. 3. Mascu-
linity—Addresses, essays, lectures. 4. Men—
Psychology—Addresses, essays, lectures. I. Title.
[DNLM: 1. Sex—Collected works. BF692.P493s]
HQ2.P48   301.41'1   74-32335
ISBN 0-88284-019-3

Alfred Publishing Co., Inc.
75 Channel Drive, Port Washington, N.Y. 11050

CONTENTS

Acknowledgments

To Lynne and the students of my "society and sex" class, who provided a forum for discussion and a critical re-thinking of the concept of masculinity; to Nancy J. Woodfield who, as a student co-facilitator in the sex class, never failed to point out to me and the class the masculine biases in my presentations; and, finally, to John Stout who, as editor, shared, from the beginning, my enthusiasm for the project.

Sex: Male / Gender: Masculine

READINGS IN MALE SEXUALITY

Introduction

*T*he long range impact of women's liberation is yet to be felt in American society. That impact, for the most part unrecognized, is not restricted to females. The sex role revolution which began almost a decade ago has diffused into the male domain, and, for the first time in history, males are being forced to reexamine their sexual status relative to females—a status which, especially in the power dimension, has remained virtually unchanged for centuries.

Social processes play an essential role in determining human behavior. One way to gain a better understanding of that role is to examine the system of sex role relationships in society. For, it is through the impact of social and cultural influences that we have come to define a biological given (sex) and socially learned phenomenon (gender) as being one and the same. That such a learning process begins early can be seen in children who first learn and distinguish *sex* differences with gender (socially acquired) credentials, e.g., women wear makeup, men drive trucks, boys play in Little League, girls play with dolls, etc. It is hardly surprising, therefore, that we have grown up to take the socially derived constructs (feminine and masculine) as part of the biological given (female and male).

In part, our belief in a direct tie between the biological given and the socially learned has severely limited social change in the cultural definitions of masculinity and femininity. Not only have our beliefs regarding the socially learned and the biological dimensions prevented a critical evaluation of the concepts and the role they play in determining relationships between the sexes, but a greater inhibiting pressure is felt because our identities are so firmly rooted in the basic gender distinctiveness as defined by the culture. Thus, change is often perceived as a threat to our individual selves.

Changes, however, are taking place. These changes were first recognized with respect to the growing assertiveness of women regarding their status in society. More and more, males are having to reevaluate their relationships with women. Also, our society is experiencing, at the present time, a rise of interest in the body, feelings, and emotions. Re-sensitizing experiences are being advocated as necessary in a technocratic, de-personalized world. With the developing concern for expressiveness, affective responses are now characterized as appropriate for members of both sexes, and the traditionally learned gender distinctiveness with respect to emotionality vs. non-expressiveness is rapidly changing.

Some writers, in unsuccessful attempts to explain these changes, have viewed them with alarm. They foresee a "neuter" society populated by "feminine men" and "masculine women." Such interpretations only serve to illustrate the degree to which social scientists have adopted the cultural mythology which defines the biological and social as inextricably linked. To believe that men become more or less masculine through time (or women more or less feminine) is to believe that there exists a static configuration of unchanging factors that constitute masculinity or femininity. Such an assumption ignores the fact that these socially constructed concepts have little reference to a time dimension. When American males in the 1970's construct their identities on the basis of a masculine/feminine dimension, they do not use indicators of 5, 10, 50, or 100 years ago; they use current cultural definitions. The socially constructed concepts of masculinity and femininity have reference to the culture of a particular society at a particular time and place. As society changes, the bases of the definitions change.

The selections in this book were chosen to represent the varying ways in which gender and sex distinctiveness, individual differences, and social conditions have combined and operated in the past and present. The readings have been grouped into four areas, each of which represents a particular perspective that can be applied in attempting to understand masculinity.

Part One includes selections which view masculinity from an individualistic perspective. Here, the emphasis is upon understanding the gender dimension in terms of the biological or personal structure of particular individuals, rather than social pressures. Perhaps most basic to the individualistic perspective in the study of sexuality has been the idea that men, by nature, are sexually aggressive. In addition, there is a tendency for such explanations to see male/female interaction in terms of the "nature" of men and women.

The selections in Part Two emphasize a socio-cultural perspective in defining the concept of masculinity. For the most part, these articles deal with the influence of socio-cultural conditions, e.g., peer, economic and structural pressures, upon the definition of masculinity, as well as ways in which changes in these conditions influence social and personal changes in the gender definitions.

Part Three looks more explicitly at masculine/feminine differentials. Hence, the perspective tends to define understanding the varying gender definitions between the sexes in terms of their relationships to one another. Studies utilizing such a perspective are inclined to incorporate a socio-cultural dimension, but analyze prevailing definitions in the same fashion. More often than not, the relationship is seen as being expressed in power terms which have been supported by both traditional as well as current definitions of masculinity and femininity.

The articles in Part Four continue the idea of power, in one form or another, as an important variable in understanding the relationships between the sexes. For the most part, these articles have been written in response to the changing definitions that have, in a sense, been forced upon men with the advent of the women's movement. In this perspective, the authors are inclined to develop ideal or improved definitions of masculinity from an analysis of the wrongs of previous and current male/female relationships. Thus, an especially common concern in the growing literature of male liberation is the conscious construction of new definitions, set forth as improvements on definitions which had functioned as tools in the oppression of women in society. The "new male," as perceived by many of these writers, is the man who is first of all able to recognize the injustices of the past and present system with respect to women, and, then, on the basis of this newly acquired consciousness redefine himself in terms of a shared concept of "personhood."

Finally, the selections contained in this book are seen as helping to play a role in the current re-evaluations regarding the concept of masculinity in American society. In this sense, it is one of the first publications to compile the scattered sources which are available. Once the women's movement became organized, women's literature, writings which pointed to and offered new styles of self-definitions in a male dominated society, followed at a rapid rate. We are now at the stage of recognizing and examining the source of the "woman problem"—males and masculinity.

John W. Petras
Mount Pleasant, Michigan

Part One

THE INDIVIDUALISTIC
PERSPECTIVE

*T*hose who use an individualistic perspective in giving explanations
to human sexuality have a tendency to perceive males as primarily
motivated by an inborn sexual impulse. While socio-cultural conditions
may be seen to play a role, more often than not, these social
phenomena are seen as merely shaping or directing a basic drive.

In studies of males and masculinity, this perspective is most often
expressed in some form of the observation that men, by nature, are
sexually aggressive. Rosenberg and Sutton-Smith report an overview
of those materials which have looked to the biological distinctiveness
between males and females as the basis for masculine and feminine
differentiations.

The selections from Stout (1886), Shannon (1913), and Hall (1913)
are illustrative of the individualistic perspective as applied to male
sexuality at the turn of the century. In these works, and numerous
similar ones, males were seen as grappling with an almost
uncontrollable sexual desire. The lack of self-control was seen as
turning back upon the individual and creating physical, in addition to
psychological, damage. Also, males were defined as deriving a
sense of masculinity from the social conditions imposed upon them
by the nature of women, who were seen as passive, naive, and
in need of male protection.

The selection by Tiger represents a currently popular application
of the individualistic perspective. In this selection, Tiger argues that
despite the role played by social learning, the concept of masculinity

*reflects a sense of "maleness" which he believes to be inherent
in the species. Although updated social characteristics are used as
examples, the underlying assumption regarding the nature of males
is the same as that used by Stout, Shannon, and Hall.*

*Duffy represents a position held by many in American society.
Sex is seen as a drive underlying most human behavior. In his
selection, Duffy attempts to demonstrate that sex often causes most
crime, even though such recognition is often lacking in both the
criminal and society.*

*As Rosenberg and Sutton-Smith note in their overview of the
literature examining constitutional bases for gender definitions, the
exact roles of the social and the biological are unknown. Money and
Ehrhardt provide evidence for the fact that, perhaps, the influence of
the biological is more a function of our expectations than a direct
influence. They provide specific evidence for the prominence of the
social over the biological in establishing a sex and gender identity.*

*Is there an inborn sense of maleness? Is sex a drive that
motivates men to engage in certain non-sexual activities? What
role does our body play in determining a sense of masculinity?
These are questions that arise from the individualistic perspective.
And, since we are from all time social beings, they are questions
that may never be answered.*

The Language of Biology

By B. G. Rosenberg and Brian Sutton-Smith

*I*t is likely that man's sex role development and sex role behavior are, in part, explicable in biological terms, but the extent to which this is the case is not at all clear. It has been argued that man possesses an inherent somatic sexuality which organizes his psychosexual development. However, it has also been argued that man is essentially psychosexually neutral or undifferentiated at birth, that he is mentally neither male nor female. These arguments define the territory of the present chapter.

The notion that masculinity and femininity have constitutional origins has been accepted for thousands of years. As recently as the last century, major theorists held that there were two basic constitutional types with minor variations. Krafft-Ebing (1922), for example, believed that there were male and female brain centers, though there was little evidence to substantiate this theory. This biological line of reasoning is argued in the more recent work of Broverman and his co-workers (Broverman, Klaiber, Kobayashi, & Vogel, 1968), who maintain that known sex differences in cognitive abilities reflect sex-related differences in physiology. The authors survey evidence indicating that sex differences are reflections of divergencies in relations between adrenergic activating and cholinergic inhibitory neural processes, which in turn are said to be sensitive to the sex hormones, androgens and estrogens. These basic biological gender differences, they say, influence performance of simple perceptual-motor tasks like typing (at which females are superior) and inhibitory restructuring tasks like problem-solving (at which males are superior).

Another presumed demonstration of biological substrata are the studies showing sex differences existing at birth. The work of Moss (1967) with neonates reveals that the sexes possess differential patterns of reactivity at birth, girls being more susceptible to comforting than boys, and mothers, in turn, tending to spend less time nurturing the more irritable males. The relationship between females and mothers is thus more mutually rewarding than that between males and mothers. Several investigators have shown sex differences in neonates, including the demonstration that male infants are, on the average, larger in every dimension and have relatively more muscular development (Garn, 1958), are more active (Knop, 1946), and seem to have a higher pain threshold than do female infants (Lipsitt & Levy, 1959). Garn and Clark (1953) have also shown that males have higher basal metabolism rates than do girls, suggesting different energy levels. A series of studies by Bell (Bell, 1963; Bell & Costello, 1964; Weller & Bell, 1965) indicate that infant females are more reactive to tactile stimulation than are males, and exhibit higher skin conductance.

We proceed now to review briefly other evidence suggesting that genetic and hormonal influences do establish a tendency for sexual behavior and thus for gender role development.

Chromosomal Level

As a rule, sex determination in higher animals occurs as a result of chromosomal mechanisms. In man, for example, the female normally has two X chromosomes and the male one X and one Y chromosome. Use of new cytological techniques has led to the discovery of abnormal numbers of chromosomes (normally forty-six) in certain individuals. It is only since 1959 that scientists have been certain that the presence of a Y chromosome makes a fertilized ovum develop into a male, and that its absence causes the ovum to develop into a female. Of the twenty-three pairs of chromosomes, only one pair, referred to as the sex chromosomes, determines the child's sex. It was through the efforts of Barr and Bertram (1949), who developed a simple buccal (of the mouth) smear technique, that sex chromatin was shown to be present in female cells and to be absent in male cells. The technique involves microscopic examination of skin biopsy materials, mucosal scrapings, or blood films, and, as Kallman (1963) points out, allows normal individuals to be readily assigned to their correct genetic sex through microscopic determination of their nuclear sex.

Anomalies in sex chromosome structure, due to the loss or addition of a sex chromosome, result in such variants as females who are chromatin-negative and males who are chromatin-positive, when the opposite case (females are chromatin positive) is normal. An example of a chromosomal deviation would be the Klinefelter's Syndrome, in which forty-seven chromosomes, including an XXY sex-chromosome complex, are found. An individual possessed of this syndrome is distinguished by small testes after puberty as the most salient feature, and he is sterile. Because of the presence of the male-determining Y chromosome, the individual tends to be pheno-typically male, but is also chromatin-positive due to the possession, typically characteristic of females, of two X chromosomes (Barr & Carr, 1960). In Turner's Syndrome, there is disturbed sex development in the female as a result of the loss of a sex chromosome (XO). These women are chromatin-negative, have only one X chromosome (Money, 1962), and are characterized by retarded growth, no development of secondary sexual characteristics at puberty (breasts, pubic hair), and intellectual subnormalcy.

Kallman (1963) maintains that the X chromosome is indispensable for fertility in females, while sex determination in males depends on the presence or the absence of the Y chromosome. Thus, irrespective of the number of X chromosomes present, one Y chromosome carries a sufficient number of strongly male-determining genes for male sex determination.

As we have shown in the previous chapter, there is much agreement that animals are subject to inherited tendencies in relation to their sex roles. For humans, the evidence is less compelling. Some of the most relevant work is found in the studies by Kallman (1952a, 1952b), who examined forty pairs of monozygotic twins (identical, having developed from a single fertilized egg) and forty-five pairs of dizygotic twins (fraternal, having developed from two separately fertilized eggs) in which one member of each pair was a known overt homosexual. In the monozygotic twins, he found 100 percent concordance in homosexuality (that is, in all cases where one twin was a homosexual, the other was as well), while for the dizygotic twins, the frequency was similar to that of the general male population. In addition, the mode and extent of deviance were dramatically similar in the monozygotic twins. Kallman concluded that such evidence casts considerable doubt on the validity of purely psychodynamic theories of adult homosexuality. The evidence, he argues, places great weight on genetically determined maleness and femaleness (Kallman, 1952b). Schlegel (1962) examined the histories of 113 pairs of twins and found 95 percent concordance in homosexuality among monozygotic twins and only 5 percent agreement among dizygotic twins, confirming the findings of Kallman.

This brief summary suggests the coercive influence of inheritance upon the development of sex role. What is lacking is knowledge regarding the mediators of such influence, whether they are genetic effects on the developing central nervous system or hormonal influences.

Hormonal Level

It has long been known that hormones have significant effects on human behavior. A summary of recent evidence (Hamburg & Lunde, 1966) indicates that the secretion of sex hormones is stimulated by gonadotrophins, which originate in the anterior lobe of the pituitary gland. These gonadotrophins are hormones that prompt development and secretion in the ovaries and testes and regulate the female menstrual cycle. The pituitary action, in turn, is controlled by the brain through the hypothalamus. The onset of puberty apparently involves an interaction between the sex hormones and certain cells of the brain. In normal children, androgenic (male) hormones in the urine occur in almost undetectable amounts until the child's eighth to tenth year of age, at which time the amounts present show a sharp increase in both sexes (Tanner, 1962). Similarly, estrogenic (female) hormones exist in minute amounts in children of both sexes, showing a marked increase at about the eighth or ninth year of age. At this time, the excretion rate of hormones for girls shows a remarkable increase and it becomes cyclic at about the eleventh year, accompanying the acquisition of secondary sexual characteristics and a growth spurt.

A great deal of information regarding the specific influences of the sex hormones on behavior derives from cases in which there exist alterations of the normal state, that is, where hypo- (under) or hyper- (over) function of the endocrines results in abnormal states. These conditions are a result of chromosomal or congenital dysfunctions, and may necessitate surgical removal of the sex glands and hormonal therapy, with significant effects on the individual.

In men the male hormones, androgens, originate in the testes, while in women they derive from the adrenal gland and the ovaries. The bulk of evidence indicates that androgens activate sex drive and that castration or other loss due to some pathological condition reduces sexual impulses, though the latter is directly related to the developmental stage at which castration occurs. The earlier the operation, the more marked the effects on the sexual behavior (Ellis, 1936). Whereas prepubertal castration or removal of the ovaries predictably results in lessened sexual impulse, postpubertal castration or ovariectomy leads to highly variable results. For example, Bremer (1959) and Money (1961a) show that men castrated after puberty continue to have erotic sensations, desires, and fantasies, and do masturbate and occasionally have intercourse. Habits, in the absence of hormones, presumably can mediate some sexual expression. However, it should be acknowledged that the absence of androgenic hormones in males does generally lead to a reduction of sexual arousability. When females are castrated postpubertally, the effects are varied, as in the study by Filler and Drezner (1944) of forty-one females, where thirty-six showed no change, three dropped in arousability level, and two exhibited increased sexual expression. We can see that these varied results travel the entire range from heightened sexuality to an abrupt cessation of sexual motivation (Hardy, 1964).

Thus, females, too, are influenced by their endocrines. Several studies (Filler and Drezner, 1944; Waxenberg, 1963; Sopchak and Sutherland, 1960) show the significant role played by androgens in contrast to the female hormones (estrogens and progesterone) in the activation and maintenance of erotic feelings and sexual desires in the female. Further, androgens, which are antagonistic to feminized genital maturation in women, may be found in excess in some females producing virilizing hyperadrenocorticism in some girls suffering from this condition (Money, 1961b). These girls have a precocious and exclusively virilizing (masculinizing) puberty. Their ovaries fail to mature and the clitoris becomes hypertrophied (enlarged) to resemble a penis in size.

As we can see, then, there are some highly dramatic alterations in sex role behavior that are clinically widespread; these disorders of hormone secretion presumably are initiated by a congenital abnormality, or hypo- or hyperfunction of the sex glands and the adrenals, which may be toxically induced, spontaneous, or may derive from several other possible causes. A ready example is precocious sexual development which involves the acquisition by a young child of pri-

mary and secondary sexual characteristics, including the capacity for
ejaculation. Its cause may be a disorder of the hypothalamic region
of the brain, of the sex glands, or of the adrenals.

While these examples clearly demonstrate the power of hormonal
factors in extreme cases, they do not tell us what occurs under normal
conditions, and here discussion varies to a greater degree.

In several comprehensive reviews (e.g., Jost, 1958; Burns, 1961),
evidence has been advanced to show that sexual differentiation of
the normal male and female is contingent upon the presence of tes-
ticular substances. If these are present, masculine differentiation
occurs; if absent, feminine differentiation takes place. The mech-
anism appears to operate as follows: genetic forces induce gonadal
development, and gonadal development is usually followed by the
elaboration of the fetal or neonate gonadal substances responsible
for the sexual differentiation of the nervous system (Diamond, 1965,
p. 161). It is possible to conclude from this description that at some
early point in development where humans are possessed of quanti-
ties of hormones of both sexes the human being may be described as
a bisexual entity. If one accepts this conclusion, we suggest, however, that in the adult this assumed bisexuality is *unequal* in both the
neural tissues and the genital tissues. The capacity exists for giving
behavioral responses appropriate to the opposite sex, but the response
pattern is variable and, in most mammals that have been studied and
in many lower vertebrates as well, the response appropriate to the
opposite sex is elicited only with difficulty. It is likely, then, that
hormones can be viewed as directional as well as activational, and at
birth the individual may be considered to be neurally inclined by
genetic and hormonal means toward one sex or the other (Diamond,
1965).

However, there are many subtleties involved in hormonal effects.
As was indicated in the previous chapter, recent work with monkeys
suggests that the masculinizing effects of male hormones lead to
sexual behaviors different from those exhibited by normal females
(Goy, 1965; Hamburg and Lunde, 1966). Administering androgens to
pregnant females resulted in masculinized female offspring which
exhibited behavior more typical of males: threatening, initiating
activity, and rough-and-tumble play. Such a relationship between
androgens and aggressive behavior may exist in more subtle form in
humans. Hamburg and Lunde suggest that androgen effects which
take place during critical phases of brain development may influence
central nervous system differentiation and the subsequent ease with

which patterns of aggression are learned; in addition, large-muscle movements so critical in agonistic encounters might be generally experienced as highly gratifying and therefore be frequently repeated (1966, p. 14), actions intrinsic to the behavior complex referred to as aggression.

To this point, we have examined evidence suggesting the profound influence of genetic and hormonal factors on the development of sex role and behavior. It has been possible to demonstrate with a degree of conclusiveness that in the extreme case, direct outcomes in sex role behavior evolve as a result of genetic and hormonal anomalies. Thus, both seem to provide a powerful influence on sex role behavior and development. Indeed, though more tentative, subtle chromosomal and hormonal forces dispose to alterations in sex role behavior even in the normal developing individual. Though the means of critically determining this latter notion are lacking at present (i.e., we have not the "hardware" necessary), the evidence we do have suggests that many sex behaviors and their correlates may have their basis in poorly understood chromosomal-brain-endocrine activities in early, critical periods in development. The argument from the chromosomal-hormonal position is that inherent sexuality provides a built-in bias influencing the way an individual interacts with his environment.

References

Barr, M. L., & Bertram, E. G. 1949 A morphological distinction between neurons of the male and female, and the behavior of the nucleolar satellite during accelerated nucleoprotein synthesis. *Nature*, 163, 676-677.

Barr, M. L., & Carr, D. H. 1960 Sex chromatin, sex chromosomes and sex anomalies. *Canadian Medical Association Journal*, 83, 979-986.

Bell, R. Q. 1963 Some factors to be controlled in studies of behavior of newborns. *Biologia Neonatorum*, 5, 200-214.

Bell, R. Q., & Costello, N. S. 1964 Three tests for sex differences in tactile sensitivity in the newborn. *Biologia Neonatorum*, 7, 335-347.

Bremer, J. 1959 *Asexualization, a follow up study of 244 cases*. New York: Macmillan.

Broverman, D. M., Klaiber, E. L., Kobayashi, Y., & Vogel, W. 1968 Roles of activation and inhibition in sex differences in cognitive abilites. *Psychological Review*, 75, 23-50.

Burns, R. K. 1961 Role of hormones in the differentiation of sex. In W. C. Young (Ed.), *Sex and internal secretions*. Baltimore: Williams & Wilkens, pp. 76-160.

Diamond, M. 1965 A critical evaluation of the ontogeny of human sexual behavior. *Quarterly Review of Biology*, 40, 147-175.

Ellis, H. 1936 *Studies in the psychology of sex*. Vol. 1. New York: Random House.

Filler, W., & Drezner, N. 1944 The results of surgical castration in women under forty. *American Journal of Obstetrics and Gynecology*, 47, 122-124.

Garn, S. M. 1958 Fat, body size, and growth in the newborn. *Human Biology*, 30, 265-280.

Garn, S. M., & Clark, L. C., Jr. 1953 The sex difference in the basal metabolic rate. *Child Development*, 24, 215-224.

Goy, R. 1965 Unpublished paper presented at Conference on Sex Research, University of California, Berkeley.

Hamburg, D. A., & Lunde, D. T. 1966 Sex hormones in the development of sex differences in human behavior. In E. E. Maccoby (Ed.), *The development of sex differences*. Stanford, Calif.: Stanford University Press, pp. 1-24.

Hardy, K. R. 1964 An appetitional theory of sexual motivation. *Psychological Review*, 71, 1-18.

Jost, A. 1958 Embryonic sexual differentiation (morphology, physiology, abnormalities). In H. W. Jones, Jr., & W. W. Scott (Eds.), *Hermaphroditism, genital anomalies and related endocrine disorders*. Baltimore: Williams & Wilkins.

Kallman, F. J. 1952 Comparative twin study of the genetic aspects of male homosexuality. *Journal of Nervous and Mental Diseases*, 115, 283-298. (a)

Kallman, F. J. 1952 Twin and sibship study of overt male homosexuality. *American Journal of Human Genetics*, 4, 136-146. (b)

Kallman, F. J. 1963 Genetic aspects of sex determination and sexual maturation potentials in man. In G. Winokur (Ed.), *Determinants of human sexual behavior*. Springfield, Ill.: Charles C. Thomas, pp. 5-18.

Knop, C. A. 1946 The dynamics of newly born babies. *Journal of Pediatrics*, 29, 721-728.

Krafft-Ebing, R. 1922 *Psychopathia sexualis*. New York: Physicians and Surgeons Book Company.

Lipsitt, L. P., & Levy, N. 1959 Pain threshold in the human neonate. *Child Development*, 30, 547-554.

Money, J. 1961 Components of eroticism in man: The hormones in relation to sexual morphology and sexual desire. *Journal of Nervous and Mental Diseases*, 132, 239-248. (a)

Money, J. 1961 Sex Hormones and other variables in human eroticism. In W. C. Young (Ed.), *Sex and internal secretions*. Vol. II. Baltimore: Williams & Wilkins, pp. 1383-1400. (b)

Money, J. 1962 Chromosomal sex incongruent with gender role and identity. In *118th Annual Meeting, American Psychiatric Association*, Washington, D.C.: American Psychiatric Association, pp. 38-39.

Moss, H. A. 1967 Sex, age, and state as determinants of mother-infant interaction. *Merrill-Palmer Quarterly*, 13, 19-36.

Schlegel, W. S. 1962 Die konstitutionsbiologischen grundlagen der homo-sexualitat. *Zeitschrift fur Menschliches Vererberung: Konstitutions-lehre*, 36, 341-364.

Sopchak, A. L., & Sutherland, A. M. 1960 Psychological impact of cancer and its treatment. VII. Exogenous sex hormones and their relation to life-long adaptations in women with metastatic cancer of the breast. *Cancer*, 13, 528-531.

Tanner, J. M. 1962 *Growth at adolescence*. (2nd ed.) Oxford: Blackwell Scientific Publications.

Waxenberg, S. E. 1963 Some biological correlatives of sexual behavior. In G. Winokur (Ed.), *Determinants of human sexual behavior*. Springfield, Ill.: Charles C Thomas, pp. 52-75.

Weller, G. M., & Bell, R. Q. 1965 Basal skin conductance and neonatal state. *Child Development*, 36, 647-657.

Masturbation (Onanism)

By H. R. Stout

*T*his is a very degrading and destructive habit, indulged in by young people of both sexes. There is probably no vice which is more injurious to both mind and body, and produces more fearful consequences than this. It is generally commenced early in life before the patient is aware of its evil influence, and it finally becomes so fastened upon him, that it is with great difficulty that he can break off the habit.

The symptoms produced by this vice are numerous. When the habit begins in early life, it retards the growth, impairs the mental faculties and reduces the victim to a lamentable state. The person afflicted seeks solitude, and does not wish to enjoy the society of his friends; he is troubled with headache, wakefulness and restlessness at night, pain in various parts of the body, indolence, melancholy, loss of memory, weakness in the back and generative organs, variable appetite, cowardice, inability to look a person in the face, lack of confidence in his own abilities.

When the evil has been pursued for several years, there will be an irritable condition of the system; sudden flushes of heat over the face; the countenance becomes pale and clammy; the eyes have a dull, sheepish look; the hair becomes dry and split at the ends; sometimes there is pain over the region of the heart; shortness of breath; palpitation of the heart (symptoms of dyspepsia show themselves); the sleep is disturbed; there is constipation; cough; irritation of the

Pp. 333-334 in H. R. Stout *Our Family Physician.*
Peoria: Henderson and Smith, 1885.

throat; finally the whole man becomes a wreck, physically, morally and mentally.

Some of the consequences of masturbation are epilepsy, apoplexy, paralysis, premature old age, involuntary discharge of seminal fluid, which generally occurs during sleep, or after urinating, or when evacuating the bowels. Among females, besides these other consequences, we have hysteria, menstrual derangement, catilepsy and strange nervous symptoms.

General Treatment

First of all, the habit must be abandoned; this is the first and most important thing to be secured, for unless this is done, every other treatment will be without avail. Everything should be done to strengthen the moral nature of the patient, and to raise his self-respect. He should cultivate the society of virtuous and intellectual females. Everything of a lascivious character must be avoided. His mind should be directed to some employment or amusement, that will engage his attention without causing fatigue. He should avoid solitude and never be left alone more than is absolutely necessary, and above all he should never be permitted to sleep alone. The patient should sleep on a mattress, and be lightly covered with clothes. Frequent bathing and washing of the private parts should be employed, as well as sitting baths, and bathing the whole body. The treatment of this disease should be undertaken only by a skillful physician.

The Boy's Relation to the Home

By T. W. Shannon

The Boy Problem

The boy problem is becoming one of unusual interest to writers, teachers, lecturers, ministers and parents. Books, teaching, lecturing and preaching can aid some, but the real problem of the boy must be solved in the home.

The Boy Should Be Treated Differently From His Sister

The mental make-up of a boy, his superior strength, his natural aspirations and his duties in life, require that some of his training should differ from that of the girl.

He Should Be Taught To Work

One of the most important steps in the solution of the boy problem is to have the boy actively engaged in some wholesome, pleasant and rational way. He should be given work that is worth doing well and that will be of use to him in future life. This training should

Pp. 34, 36, 37, 38 in T. W. Shannon *Self Knowledge.*
Marietta, Ohio: S. A. Mullikin Co., 1913.

begin in childhood and continue until he is matured. Every day he should have some task to perform and he should never be allowed to neglect his work.

Boys Enjoy Making Money

A boy should be given a chance to make some money. Rarely should money be given to a child. It is far better for him to earn it. He will in this way learn the value of a dollar. He should be encouraged to deposit his money in the bank, to loan it, on interest, or to wisely invest it. It is a great deal better for a boy to invest and lose than to spend his earnings for candy or a ticket to a ten cent show. A boy had as well be allowed to swear, drink and steal as to waste his money. If started right most boys would take pride in saving their money. Usually when parents wish their children to have candy or some other luxury, it would be wiser for them to pay for it, than for the children to do so. A child should be encouraged to give, out of his own money, to the needy, Sunday School and church.

Boys should have their own room in the house, their own things in the room and their property rights should be respected. When he fails, he should be encouraged; when downhearted, he should be boosted and when he succeeds, he should be praised and commended. Give the average boy a chance and he will make a man.

His Future Vocation

Very early, boys show aptitude toward special vocations. When they do, they should be encouraged in every way possible. However, they should not be nagged and forced to follow any vocation for which they may have shown interest and natural skill. Furnish them helps and books and allow them to develop their own individualities. Parents should not choose the boy's vocation for him. They should not interfere with his choice, unless it be pernicious.

Morally, His Training Should Be the Same As That of His Sister

Parents, who hold to two sets of morals, do right for the girl and do as you please for the boy, are not qualified to train a boy. A boy should be trained to believe that whatever is morally wrong for his sister and mother is equally wrong for him; it is just as ungentlemanly for him to swear, as it would be unladylike for his mother and sister to swear; that it is just as wrong for him to use vulgar and obscene language as it would be for his mother and sister to do so; that if he can drink and be sexually impure and remain a gentleman, his mother and sister can indulge in the same vices and remain perfect ladies. If parents believe in the double standard of morals, that the boy must sow his "wild oats," most likely he will. There is no sane reason why a boy should swear and his sister should not, why a boy should use tobacco and his sister should not, why a boy should drink and his sister should not, or why a boy should be sexually impure and his sister should not. The boy, with the single standard of morals instilled in his mind, is incomparably more likely to make a useful, successful, great and good man than the boy trained to believe in the double standard.

Boys Should Play With Girls

Boys are, by nature, inclined to be rough, rude, coarse and untidy. They need to associate with girls who naturally have just the opposite tendencies. It is refining for boys to learn to enjoy the games of girls.

A girl's ambition is to be beautiful; a boy's ambition is to be strong. These preferences are natural and should be encouraged in them. All boys delight in displaying their physical powers. Thus, they are led to test their strength with their sisters and often display roughness and rudeness. They should be carefully instructed that it is natural for girls not to be as strong as boys, and that for this reason they should protect girls and never be rude with them. Boys should have a place and the proper means of taking exercise.

Father's Fifth Talk–
The True Young Knight

By T. W. Shannon

The True Young Knight

A true young knight is a boy, or young man, who is strong, brave, ambitious, intelligent, gallant and pure. The knights of the Middle Ages were strong men. They practiced athletics, took their outdoor sports and were proud of their physical strength. In those days, one with a weak, defective body could not be a knight. They were also, brave men. They would die for what they believed to be right. They were very gallant toward women. They would offer every courtesy and respect to girlhood, womanhood, wifehood and motherhood. They had to be pure men to be strong, brave, gallant and manly. A knight would die in defense of womanhood.

The purpose of this chapter is to inspire you to become a true knight in your social relations with girls and ladies. The proper social relations of boys and girls, men and women, is one of the best ways of developing the social side of our lives, of improving the mind and strengthening our moral natures. God has made us social beings. He wants us to enjoy life.

Pp. 211-217 in T. W. Shannon, *Self Knowledge.*
Marietta, Ohio: S. A. Mullikin Co., 1913.

Treat All Girls as You Would Have Boys Treat Your Sister

Until girls are sixteen and boys are eighteen, when thrown together, it is wisest and best for them to engage in plays and games as children without any thought of being sweethearts. Small boys could learn that it is not manly for them to squeeze the hand of a girl, tease, pinch or pull a girl's hair and he should not think of such an ungentlemanly thing as to try to kiss a girl. The reason for this advice is, these relations tend to create in the mind thoughts that a true knight will not entertain. You would not want a boy to treat your sister in this way. A boy who would treat another boy's sister as he would not want her brother to treat his sister, it not a true knight. Nature and God teach that man is woman's protector.

The Truest Bravery

The boy who would expose himself to danger and death to save a girl from drowning or being crushed by a street car, is brave and deserves much praise. But he is not as brave and does not deserve as much praise, as does the boy who defends the honor and purity of a girl, not his sister. To positively refuse to allow a boy to talk about a girl in your presence in a way that you would not allow him to speak to your sister, is the courage of a knight. The good name of a girl is worth more to her than money, houses, and lands. It is so easy for boys, who engage in obscene language about girls, to invent and tell some story about some girl who is perfectly innocent, and, in this way, start others to talking about her. This is called slander. It is one of the most unmanly and cowardly deeds a boy can be guilty of. This is a very common sin among a class of boys. A boy cannot become a true knight who allows himself to have wrong thoughts about girls, much less to talk about them. All vulgar men were once vulgar boys. If you will cultivate a hatred for vulgarity while you are a boy, you will hate it when you're a man.

Bad Company

When hundreds of prisoners were asked, "What brought you to this"? they replied, "Bad company brought us to this". No doubt that more boys go wrong through bad company than through any other agency. When a boy keeps bad company, it will be very hard for him not to do as they do. Many times he will do wrong rather than be called "baby". A true knight will be interested in helping a bad boy to overcome his temptations, but he cannot run the risk of being injured by making a bad boy his companion. If he associates with the rude, listens to vulgarity long, he will become rude and vulgar.

Boys Should Protect Girls

The very thought of a boy's insulting your sister causes a feeling of great hatred to rise in your breast. Why is this? Girls are not as strong as boys. They need protection. That feeling comes to you because you know that you are your sister's protector. This is bravery. But the knightliest young knight, is the boy who will not speak an unmanly word about another boy's sister and will bravely and kindly rebuke the boy who does.

The True Knight Has One Standard of Morals

No young knight would play and associate with a girl who uses cigarettes, vulgarity or swears. Then, if he is brave, a true knight, he will not ask for better company than he is willing to give. The true knight of the twentieth century will have but one standard of morals. Ever since the days of savagery, when man could sway, exchange or sell his daughters in the same way that he could his property, society has been accustomed to a double standard of morals—purity and temperance for woman, do as you please for boys and men. In the days of savagery, the value of a girl on the marriage market was determined by her being pure. If she had been impure, no man wanted to buy her to become his wife, but she was stoned to death or forced to become a slave. Man was free. No one owned him. He could live just as he pleased. Woman could not do as she pleased. Her very life, the privilege of becoming a wife and mother all depended on her being pure. Is it not strange that people have allowed this relic of savagery to pass down the centuries without correcting it? People take what is customary to be right. They do not try to decide whether a custom is fair, just and right or not. It is hard to rid our minds of this old custom. If you should see a girl or woman walking along the street of a city smoking you would condemn her as a bad woman. But there goes a man doing the same thing. Is he as bad as the woman? We judge that he is not. Unless we know him as a gentleman. On a street corner or in a hotel you hear a girl or woman swearing and using the most obscene language. You do not hesitate to believe that she is bad. You would frown upon her in society. You would scorn her association. Even the guilty man would not respect such a woman. This is because custom has biased our very thinking. The very best people are unfair to the girl and the woman. They forgive in man what they condemn in the girl and woman.

Will You Enlist In The New Knighthood

There was never an organized effort to break down and destroy the double standard of morals until some twenty years ago. In England there are several hundred organizations of young men, in some of these are several hundred members, and they have pledged themselves to live as pure lives as the girls they expect some day to marry. Every one of these boys and young men is a knight. These organizations are being formed throughout Canada, and there are some being formed in the United States. The world has never offered such a grand and great opportunity for boys to become knights as it does in this century. In the days of chivalry, the young man who gave his life to protect the honor of a lady was a truer knight than the man who gave his life on the battlefield to protect his country. It takes a higher form of bravery and manhood to protect the virtue of girlhood and womanhood than it does to face whizzing bullets, booming cannons, and exploding shells. The great purity movement of this age, with its ever-increasing army of brave, determined and self-sacrificing authors and lecturers, is enlisting and marshalling an army of knights destined to overthrow this monster of savagery. All over this country thousands of brave boys and men are enlisting. This great twentieth century crusade against vice is summoning to its ranks every chivalrous boy and man and every good girl and woman. Here is the chance to be a true knight. Will you enlist? We invite you. We welcome you to become a true knight.

Sexual Hygiene of the Man

By Winfield Scott Hall

*F*rom what has preceded, it must be evident that from the early months of the period of puberty, through the adolescent and adult period, even until some progress is made in the senile period, every normal male will experience sexual desire. It has been shown that these particular experiences are linked more or less intimately with the condition of the sex apparatus. But, whatever the cause, we are confronted with the question, What shall be done about it? When a man experiences a sexual desire, does it necessarily follow that the desire must be satisfied? Some have reasoned that the muscles of the arm, if not exercised, wither and become weak. Therefore, by analogy, the sexual apparatus, if not exercised, will become weak; and if its function is not repeated at comparatively regular periods, the apparatus will eventually become withered and atrophied. While this course of reasoning is absolutely sound, so far as it applies to the muscular system, and while the reasoning may seem rational, and the conclusion may seem tenable in its application to the sexual apparatus and sexual function, it is well known to physiologists and sociologists that the reasoning is fallacious. The fallacy rests in the premises. It was assumed above that the activity of the sex glands is comparable with that of the muscles. We must not lose sight of the fact that the sex glands are continuously active; and, in this continuous activity, they get their exercise. This activity develops them and keeps them physically perfect after the onset of the period of puberty.

Pp. 123-129 in Winfield Scott Hall, *Sexual Knowledge.*
Philadelphia: The International Bible House, 1913.

Their activity consists very largely in the formation of the internal secretion, the function of which is to develop in the male the highest possible state of virility, as fully described above.

In this connection, we might call attention to the fact that the muscles are kept in a perfect physical condition by two or three hours of active exercise in each twenty-four hours; but the sex glands are working more or less continuously. Hour after hour, seven days in the week, three hundred and sixty-five days in the year, nights, Sundays and holidays included. They are almost as continuously at work as the heart.

We must also note the fact that every procreative act is performed at a sacrifice of some of the vital fluid on the part of the male. A wanton sacrifice of vital fluid, either in the act of self-abuse or excessive indulgence in the sexual act, is not justifiable under any consideration. In the light of these facts, every normal man will admit that frequent masturbation or excessive sexual intercourse, in wedlock or out, would certainly not be recommended as a method of developing the sex apparatus.

Most men, however, raise the question: "Is any indulgence or any artificial means for satisfying the sexual inclination to be discouraged?" This inclination comes to us in the course of nature. Man, in a primitive state, would seek a mate as soon as he felt this inclination, would fight for the possession of her as soon as he had reached a sufficient stage of muscular development, and, once in possession of his mate, would take her to his lodge in the trees or to his cave in the rocks. In his primitive home, he would follow his sexual inclination, impregnate his wife, and protect her against all dangers. Under our present social conditions, the young man experiences all these desires the same as his primitive ancestor, but, as a rule, he is not able to choose a mate and begin with her the building of a home for at least five years, and perhaps ten or fifteen years, after he experiences the desire to do so. What is the solution? It must be evident that the solution lies in the acceptance of one or another of three alternatives. Either the young man will seek illicit intercourse with women to satisfy his sexual desire, or he may take some artificial measure, such as masturbation or self-abuse; or, finally, he will lead what is known as a continent life. By "continent" we mean to adopt neither one of the first two alternatives mentioned, but to leave the sex apparatus wholly inactive, so far as external activities are concerned, subjecting them to no artificial stimulation whatsoever, and indulging in no illicit intercourse whatsoever. This is the continent life.

We may now consider these three alternatives in turn.

By "illicit intercourse" with women, we mean sexual intercourse out of wedlock. The term applies either to intercourse between any man and a prostitute, between an unmarried man and a married woman, between an unmarried man and an unmarried woman, or between a married man and a married woman not his wife. The term "illicit intercourse" applies to all sexual intercourse that is illegal.

In our discussion of the young man's problem, we may confine our consideration particularly to intercourse with professional prostitutes and the clandestines, or women who are willing to accept the sexual embrace for money, or for their own gratification.

In this phase of sexual gratification, it is assumed that the woman has these relations with various men. We purposely eliminate from this discussion the deliberate seduction of pure girls for the purpose of sexual gratification, as such seduction is a heinous crime against the victim and against society, for which offense the man is legally responsible. We are here discussing not the crimes of men, but their vices.

The question that the young man naturally asks is: "Why should society hold these relations as a vice when the woman, who is party to the act, gives her free consent, perhaps even soliciting the relation, and has given herself up to this sort of life, either as a sole occupation (prostitute), or as an auxiliary occupation (clandestine) to supplement a wage on which she may not be able to live in luxury?"

The answer to this question is not far to seek. Women so occupied, have, as a rule, made themselves incapable of maternity. They are outcasts from society, unfortunately exerting a most harmful influence on all those who come into relation with them. Furthermore, they are centers for the dissemination of venereal diseases, which wreck the health of all those who become infected. But for the uncontrolled passions of men, there would be no such women. So while the reader may not be responsible for the ruin of any woman, we must confess that men as a class are responsible for this condition of prostitution and clandestine intercourse. An overwhelming majority of women would, if following their inclinations, seek these relations in wedlock only and for procreation only. But many a young woman, under promise of marriage, sometimes even under a bogus marriage, is brought into a condition of hypnotism or into a mental state that puts her in the power of the man whom she loves and respects. If he deceives her and betrays her, continuing such betrayal until the victim becomes pregnant, he will, in the average case, leave her to bear her child in shame, while he slips away to other scenes of activity. We cannot wonder that the girl,—deserted, humiliated, crushed, by the one in whom she reposed absolute confidence, cast out of society, perhaps thrust from the protection of her own father's roof,— gives up the struggle and says, "What's the use?"

A vast majority of such poor girls make their way to houses of ill-fame and give themselves over to a life of prostitution. Hardly one of these women, if married by the man who brought her to this condition, would have failed to make a true and loving wife and mother. So society, while it casts these women out, has come to recognize that men are the real sinners in such cases.

It may be added here, that an occasional girl goes wrong through temperamental shortcomings in herself,—perhaps she may even be a degenerate; but the proportion of women who would willingly and deliberately sacrifice their virtue is vanishingly small as compared with the proportion of young men who seem to be willing to sacrifice their virtue. This is probably in part due to their training. Mothers, as a rule, instruct their daughters carefully regarding their relations with boys and men. It is in part due to the instinctive and inherent purity of mind of the normal woman.

Man, Aggression, and Men

By Lionel Tiger

*T*ypically, maleness involves physical bravery, speed, the use of violent force, etc.[1] While there are enormous inter-cultural variations in the definitions of maleness and femaleness, some core characteristics remain widely attached to males and females in most cultures. Males more than females incline to tough mastery of the environment and a creative rather than reactive interference with physical and social realities. When the masterful activity is undertaken by a group of men, the pressures for bravery, toughness, self-proof, etc., are normally increased. The dares which young boys issue each other and their effort to achieve decisive drama in their play foreshadow the patterns of mastery which in part comprise the adult manly style. Clearly the socialization of boys differs among cultures in the encouragement given to aggressive and violent display, and there are great variations between individual boys as well as between social classes.[2] But the generalized conception of maleness, represented in such projective materials as films, advertisements, literature, and in the sexual composition of the controlling organizations of societies—especially obvious aggressive and/or violent ones—suggest that the central concern and capacity of males for toughness, bravery, confident assertion, violence, and related phenomena is probably species-specific.

This is understandable in phylogenetic terms, as well as through

functional analysis of contemporary societies.[3] Carveth Read saw the
development of the hunting life as a superposition of wolf-like gre-
gariousness upon a basically primate pattern of consciousness and
society (see his pp. 48-61). Though we now know that human hunting
and separation from the other primates occurred much earlier than
Read thought, there remain sufficient physical similarities to see behavioral similarities as representative of divergence from a common
original pattern. Read did not stress sexual differences in behavior,
though his conception of human evolution and contemporary behavior does not appear to permit the interpretation that males and
females can interchangeably perform social roles other than explicitly reproductive ones. Margaret Mead notes the possibility that
human warfare has a direct biological basis and that warring is a
male occupation, stimulated when most intense by

> . . . protectiveness toward women, children, land, and ideals. . . . It is prob-
> ably . . . that the young male has a biologically given need to prove himself
> as a physical individual . . . in the past the hunt and warfare have provided
> the most common means of such validation.[4]

Young males seek self-validation. In addition I am suggesting:
(1) that validation involves a process of attachment to specific male
peers and superiors who become defined as the "significant others"
with respect to whom the individual seeks validation; (2) that the
process of attachment itself facilitates the effort of validation and in
fact leads to a demand that satisfactory evidence of maleness by pre-
requisite to group membership; and (3) that the combination of the
process of attachment and the need for validation leads to a cumulative group "feeling" which—particularly under the stimulus of external threat or the perception of a possible advantage—tends to become
an increasingly bold and effective activity. The latter characteristic, as
much as misinformation, prejudice, inertia, etc., may lead to "escalation" of conflicts between groups of males for whom conciliation
without triumph means invalidation of their maleness. "Honor must
be served," even though the escalation involves danger and the loss
of property, time, and opportunities for other rewarding activities.
And validation does not occur only once. The need for validation
recurs throughout the different stages of the male career, and is expressed by the different symbols of success, achievement, power,
goodness, etc., which are appropriate to the various age categories as
defined by individual cultures. Ceremonies of initiation or *rites de
passage* chiefly signify changes in criteria by which individuals are

judged and ranged, not the cessation of the process of validation altogether.

Thus I am relating the control of human aggression—at the level of schoolboy fights and barroom brawls as well as possibly on the international scale—to the control of the dynamics of male groups and the maintenance of male self-respect and confidence. With only half a whimsy I suggest that one reason for the removal of women and children from the battlefield is that, as well as protecting them, the absence of women and children permits males to fight without the inhibition they might experience were children to cry and wander about, were women to complain about the danger to children, themselves and their men, or all the participants. In addition to Lorenz's notion that bonding evolves as a concomitant of aggression, it may be necessary to assume that the process occurs primarily and most significantly among males, and that the control of aggression is essentially a question of the extent to which males with power and sense of their manly status may retain their self-esteem and maintain their positions without recourse to actions which involve destruction and pain for some other group, and probably their own as well.

This phenomenon is connected not only with defense and politics, but also with a propensity for men to engage in hunting or hunting-type activity. This makes the management of aggression considerably more complex than the fairly straightforward, rather mechanical model sketched above may suggest. The focusing of a group on a specific goal—which is functionally equivalent to a prey animal in the dynamics of the group—suggests that perhaps male bonding requires a consummatory stimulus. Such a stimulus "cuts off" the aggressive impetus, as does the killing or escape of a prey animal.[5] Outright victory is one consummation, loss is another. Possibly the drinking of alcohol by groups of men is somehow associated with triumph or consummation rituals. Dart has noted that certain fossil remains among Australopithecine settlements suggest that the skulls of the defeated were used for the drinking of blood by the victors in con-specific battles.[6] (It is also to be noted, for what such an observation may imply, that the prelude to much Scandinavian drinking, the word skol, translates into "skull.")[7] The significance of drinking to men's groups, the importance of inscribed personal drinking mugs, etc., may be taken as one index of the relationship of drinking to male affiliation. In some cultures, where a variety of inhibitions prevent the warm expression of male-affiliative sentiments, the role of drinking may be unusually important in permitting affiliation to occur at all. Drinking certainly functions as a means of validation. Rules governing entry of minors to places of public drinking are fairly widespread. But perhaps it is most markedly in North America, and possibly in Scotland, that there is such a strong popular correlation between manliness and the ability to drink a great deal of alcohol. Why the ingestion of a mild poison should be regarded as the test of the manly virtues is curious, except insofar as response to alcohol may belie an individual's response to other circumstances involving noxious food, odor, sights, etc. A comparable situation is the smoking of cigarettes and the frequent association of smoking with manliness, both in life and in projective materials such as advertisements and films. It is particularly interesting that smoking is so frequently depicted in advertisements in association with hunting or fishing, or with some "tough" enterprise. The derision may be recalled which greeted one company's attempt to characterize its product as "the thinking man's filter." The implication was that manly men do not think. On the other hand, there is a clear popular association between pipe-smoking and intellectualism.

The relationship between cigars and the concept of manliness is intriguing also. Is it simply because cigars are expensive and prized that they are handed out by new fathers to their male friends? Or lurks there some deeper if obvious significance in the gift of a rigid phallic-sized object to be orally enjoyed? Is this a symbolic celebration by the male group of a man's virile success, in the absence of cultural patterns which permit men with manly self-conceptions to enjoy the activities of each other in the tender sphere of women and babies? Walter Pople has speculated that conceivably the pleasure humans derive from smoking reflects an evolutionary history in which the smell of smoke meant security, warmth, and possibly food.[8] That we should seek to re-create this pleasure by means of little portable fires which yield much fragrant smoke is not wholly improbable. Of course, there are a vast array of cultural differences with respect to smoking, but the persistence of the habit despite its now certain potentially disabling effects may indicate something about the role of smoke in human evolution and consequently of fire.

Another curiosity is the special willingness of males to cook on an outdoor barbeque grill which involves charcoal smoke, heat, and a sense of the rich reality of the culinary operation underway. Barbequing appears to present no threat to men who might avoid cooking boiled cabbage in their wives' kitchens. Neither does cooking in hunting or fishing camps. While I have no data to support this beyond the observations I have made, it seems that men prefer steaks while women prefer salads—rather than the other way round. Perhaps women enjoy steaks more than men appear to enjoy salads. Have we here a reflection of the hunting-gathering dichotomy, even in a supermarket culture? Incidentally, does the relationship between fire, food, hunting, and success have anything to do with the popularity of restaurants and occasions in which the cooking fire is visible and nearby? Is this also why *flambé* dishes particularly connote festivity and well-being? And why dining by candlelight or dim light is regarded as "romantic."[9] In some situations, drinking may be more closely related to consummation—to the hour of triumph or feast (among Orthodox Jews, for example, drinking is associated only with feasts). Carveth Read regards the feast as a direct relative to early man's hunting, and even suggests that "the origin of laughter and the enjoyment of broad humor . . . may be traced to these occasions of riotous exhilaration and licence."[10] Lorenz describes the adaptive value of gluttony among hunting peoples after a large kill; it is clear that among persons with secure food supply this is now an ill-adaptive behavior.[11]

What is of interest here is the possible connection between feasts, drinking bouts, stag parties, etc., with consummatory features of processes of male affiliation after aggressive or violent enterprise. The literal or symbolic sacrifice of animals or other humans may also function as consummation of a process of bonding and exercise of power and mastery. Typically, of course, religious sacrifices result from the decisions of male leaders. Where sacrifice and/or torture (of either humans or animals) have political implications, these are necessarily a function of male-dominated systems. The catalog of bloodletting, cruelty, sadism, and cavalier disregard for the suffering of others is so extensive as to suggest that these crudities may result not from something private as "instinctive cruelty" or the fact that man is "evil," but as a direct consequence of a process of male bonding which is deeply related to the *social* nature of human beings and which is linked both to political structure and the hunting method of ecological exploitation. Again, if hunting is indeed the master pattern of the species, one may presumably expect that, like all biological patterns, some consummatory stimulus must be available. Perhaps sacrifices and various other forms of killing-the-prey provide this consummation. Thus the argument about the concept of pseudospecies and its relationship to the use of animals for totemic purposes can be seen in this context as an additional clue to under-

standing the otherwise perplexing and apparently profitless ceremonies in which ritual tasks are sanctioned—tasks which in other
circumstances would be condemned as heinous and unnecessary. I
am suggesting, then, that the phenomena of human cruelty, blood-
craving, sacrifice, and pseudo-specific killing and abuse are directly
related to the sense of personal manly validation individual men feel
in terms of their male groups, and that perhaps the chief effect of
inter-cultural difference in this matter is to specify object, instrument, and mode for the validation of individual maleness and group
power in different cultures. While it is clear that females may participate in the situations I am concerned with and may, in some
cases, act more cruelly and viciously than males, females do not often
contrive, manage, and justify the social structures surrounding the
violent and aggressive violation of the rights and health of coerced
persons.

Hannah Arendt's term "the banality of evil," used in her description and discussion of the trial of Adolf Eichmann, implies
inter-cultural differences in moral order and the essentially routine
prosecution of policies once they are clearly stated. Evil becomes an
incidental by-product of a process of activity involving personal repu-
tations and corporate bonds. If only because they sought to destroy
the records of genocidal activity, it appears many Nazis were aware
of the illegality (if not immorality) of what they were doing. But the
social pressures of the military machine were such that even individuals who could withdraw from the more flagrant violations of
war law were loath to do so. Again, it is presumably significant that
the Nazi movement was an essentially male organization. While a
substantial number of infamously cruel women presumably took
their cue from the male structure, even their behavior seemed to be
more private and arbitrary than the relatively smoothly bureaucra-
tized male variety.

A visit I made to Dachau made clear the tidiness, regularity, and
internal logic of the concentration camp and crematorium system.
That the system involved human destruction of a fantastic and monu-
mental order at the same time as it was genteelly orderly and self-
justifying suggests that the term "inhuman" cannot be used to describe it. If anything, this was a devoutly human feat; the photos of
the genial faces of the officers in their mess alongside the faces of the
prisoners propose a contrast different only in degree from the legion
examples of minor or gross human invidiousness. That the degree of
difference is great is a comment on the specific people and set of

events in question rather than on the process of social differentiation between captors and sacrifices which was most bewilderingly reflected in the German camps in our time. Even in the camps of U.S. troops, clear and superior conditions for officers caused U.S. soldiers bitterness and distress to the point where some reflected on the similarity of U.S. and German military conditions.[12] There is no question of equating the two types of camp. But what is of interest is the effect of social permissiveness in creating social divisions within communities of two cultures which differed dramatically in—and indeed were fighting about—their central approach to equality and human fellowship.

References

1. Margaret Mead, *Continuities in Cultural Evolution*, New Haven, Yale University Press, 1964, pp. 96-7.

2. Robert R. Sears, et al., *Patterns of Child Rearing*, Row, Peterson and Co., Evanston, Ill., 1957, pp. 252-9.

3. Carveth Read, *The Origin of Man*, Cambridge Univ. of Press, New York, 1925.

4. Margaret Mead, Introduction to *Male and Female*, Penguin Books, Harmondsworth, 1962, p. 23.

5. Berkowitz calls this "the competition tendency." See his very useful article, "The Concept of Aggressive Drive: Some Additional Considerations," in L. Berkowitz (ed.), *Advances in Experimental Social Psychology*, Vol. 2, Academic Press, New York, 1965.

6. Raymond Dart, "The Minimal Bone-Breccia Content of Makapansgat and the Australopithecine Predatory Habit," American Anthropologist, 60, 5 (October, 1958).

7. Alex Comfort, personal communication.

8. Personal communication.

9. See John Pfeiffer's article, "When Homo Erectus Tamed Fire, He Tamed Himself," *New York Times Magazine* (11 December 1966). I am grateful to Pfeiffer for the observation about steaks, salads, and sociosexuality.

10. Read, op. cit., pp. 60-1.

11. Lorenz, On Aggression, New York, Harcourt, Brace & World, 1966, p. 253.

12. See Samuel Stouffer, et al., *The American Soldier*, Vol. 1, Princeton University Press, 1949, pp. 364-79.

Sex As the Cause of Most Crime

By Clinton T. Duffy

Sex is the cause of nearly all crime, the dominant force that drives nearly all criminals. After thirty-five years of correctional experience as warden of San Quentin prison, a member of the California Adult Authority and executive director of the San Francisco Council on Alcoholism, I'm convinced that it is a rare crime that can't be traced to a sexual inadequacy of some sort.

Sex causes men to commit all manner of misdeeds, obvious and otherwise. Rape, for example, is obviously a sex crime. Arson doesn't appear to be, yet it is. Lewd and lascivious behavior is obviously a sex crime. Purse snatching doesn't appear to be, yet it is. Child molesting is obviously a sex crime. Burglary doesn't appear to be, yet it is. Incest is obviously a sex crime. Forgery doesn't appear to be, yet it often is. A homosexual advance is obviously a sex crime. Kidnapping doesn't appear to be, yet almost always is. Exhibitionism is obviously a sex crime. Murder doesn't appear to be, yet more often than not it is. Thievery, pocket picking and car stealing are as much motivated by sex as voyeurism, sodomy and attempted rape. Assault with a dangerous weapon may be as sexually inspired as an unhealthy fascination for women's underwear.

Criminals are plagued and puzzled and upset by sexual tensions, doubts, fantasies, anxieties and hungers. In my opinion 90 percent of the men in our nation's prisons are there because they couldn't come to grips with the problem.

I know some experts don't agree with me and I respect their right to their own opinions. Mine are based on years of long, intimate discussions with men in confinement, the guards who watched them, the doctors who treated them, and on my own close observations. When I was at San Quentin I talked at length to thousands of convicts, and I talked to thousands more after joining the Adult Authority, the state parole board. Sooner or later, most of them admitted a fundamental lack of sexual control which led to disaster.

This is something which must be recognized if we are to keep our prisons, already overcrowded, from overflowing, for we can't solve the problem without first admitting its existence. To say, for example, that a crime of violence stems from anger is not enough. We must learn the source of the anger. This, of course, is a job for the psychiatrists, psychologists and counselors, but I strongly suspect the deeply imbedded roots are sexual.

The armed robber has a sensitive feeling of general inadequacy. He may be short, or weak, or stupid, or inferior in some other way. So he carries a gun, which makes him stronger in his own mind than the man without a gun, and that means stronger sexually as well as in his ability to overpower his unarmed victim. Time and again, convicted gunmen have told me that they got a physical thrill from the prospect of firing their weapons. And in many cases, these men have a criminal history that includes sexual misbehavior of some kind.

The same is true of forgers, counterfeiters, bad-check passers and embezzlers. They nearly always have a background of sexual problems. These people suffer the same feelings of sexual inadequacy that gunmen do. Only their method of seeking satisfaction is different. Instead of overpowering victims, they seek to outsmart them. The attempt alone is sometimes physically stimulating, success even more so.

Burglars get a charge out of entering a place where they know they shouldn't be. The presence of a man will drive them away, but they go in hoping to find a woman alone, preferably in bed. Sometimes they'll "case the joint," checking ahead of time to make sure. Age and appearance have no bearing. Men of this type will settle for a child or an elderly adult, a bearded woman or one with warts, just so long as she's female. They intend to rape, not to look. The darkness which is their only protection will prevent them from observing the features of the victim anyhow.

A small-time thief and purse snatcher who, although a veteran convict, had never picked up more than a few dollars on any of his forays, once came into San Quentin on a $30,000 robbery rap. I heard him tell some other inmates about it in the big yard.

"I'm going through a dresser in the bedroom hoping to get a little money," he said, "and I find the thirty thousand under some clothes. I was so surprised I almost left the money there."

"No wonder you were surprised," somebody said. "You went in there looking for a dame."

"There wasn't anybody home," the robber said. "So I had to settle for the money."

I have never known a purse snatcher who simply grabbed the purse and ran. Always, whether he thought it necessary or not, he wrestled his victim to the ground, roughing her up and touching her wherever he could in the process. This was his real reason for taking the purse, not the few dollars it might contain. He wanted the physical contact. If he got that, the insignificant amount of cash he collected was no disappointment to him.

Narcotics users almost invariably are victims of sex frustrations. They're inadequate, or clumsy, or sexually small. Often, they are the object of ridicule because of their failure to complete the sex act. So they turn to dope and become addicted. It reduces their sex drive, and they seem to be happy in their own little world of fantasy. Sex no longer means very much to them, but of course they're still in trouble because they have swapped a bad problem for a worse one. Drug addicts almost never get involved in direct sex crimes, although they are often picked up for pandering. The crimes they commit are more likely to be robbery, blackmail or peddling, because they'll do anything to raise money for the support of their habit.

Active homosexuals will also do anything to raise money. A homosexual in love is one of the comparatively few burglars who prefers an empty house to one with a woman alone in it, for all he wants to do is steal. He will involve himself in anything from shoplifting to robbing a bank, stopping at nothing to get what he wants. Some of the toughest thugs I knew were men with male mates to support. There seemed no relation whatever between their crime and their sex problems, yet sex was all that drove them.

There are, of course, thousands of active homosexuals who support their mates by legitimate and peaceful means. Except for the peculiar features of their kind, they are as law-abiding as normal folks, and, even in states where homosexual activity itself is considered a crime, the authorities generally leave them alone. At that stage of their lives little can be done to change them—as long as they don't bother anyone else there is no point in harassing them.

But our prisons are full of homosexuals, both active and latent, who have landed there for other offenses. The latent ones almost invariably become active while in confinement, which is a tragedy because they probably never would have on the outside. There are hopes of rescuing these people, but some are too far gone by the time they leave prison. Their sex drive is so great that they violate paroles to get back into prison in hope of being reunited with the object of their affections.

One of the bloodiest affairs in San Quentin history, the murder of two guards and the mutilation of two others about twelve years ago, was reported as an escape attempt, but in my opinion it was actually the result of a homosexual attachment between two inmates. Eugene Burwell and James A. Rogers were evidently at the height of their love-making in the prison library when they were interrupted by officers making a routine check. Both men went berserk, and it took half a dozen more officers to subdue them. They ended in the gas chamber.

Because of their frustrations, many prison inmates turn to homosexuality. Others, unable to stand a life without women, try to escape. Sex is the dominant force behind these breaks. The pressures of a celibate existence boil over and often result in brutal riots which I believe can be avoided. A system of conjugal visits, such as I will discuss in detail, would cut homosexuality appreciably and eliminate prison breaks almost entirely.

The man who performs illegal abortions usually has sex problems of his own. He gets sensual pleasure from this type of surgery. In most cases he is a sadist who likes to intensify and prolong as long as possible the pain he inflicts on his victim. Sometimes he even demands sexual relations with her before operating.

A convicted abortionist is rarely a licensed physician. I know of very few who ever had more than a smattering of medical training. Most of them had an extraordinary interest in playing doctor as children and never outgrew it. Their little knowledge, truly a desperately dangerous thing, was acquired from books and talk. A woman seeking help from an abortionist would be fortunate indeed if she got a person with any medical-school background. She'd be far more likely to get an amateur thrill-seeker who never saw the inside of a hospital except as an orderly, a janitor, a patient or a visitor.

Child molesters, voyeurs and exhibitionists have sex problems of another sort. In them, according to psychiatrists, the sex maturation was arrested at an early age. They progressed to a certain point and stuck there. In most cases, these men were deprived of the normal sexual stimulation a child receives from his mother.

And, of course, a child gets a great deal. A little boy will paw his mother from head to foot, instinctively reaching for the parts of her body that will excite him the most. Her reaction can be the key to his future behavior. If she responds with loving warmth as most mothers do, she is, without knowing it, preparing him for normal behavior when he grows up. If she rejects him in one way or another, she may be laying the groundwork for a lifetime of problems. And if she recoils in horror, as sometimes happens, she makes it even more difficult for him to develop normal sex urges. He is likely either to withdraw into the shell that spawns child molesters or break out into the aggressiveness that spawns rapists. Molesters either like or hate children, fondling them in misdirected affection or murderously assaulting them. As a doctor once pointed out to me, it is much like a person who has had religion crammed down his throat from childhood. He ends up either a fanatic or an atheist. The well-balanced in-between is more the exception than the rule.

Many child molesters are elderly men who have lost their ability to perform the sex act. In their frustration they turn to children, since mature women will have nothing to do with them. Lonely and deprived of the enjoyments of their younger days, these men want only to look, touch and fondle, but most of them are otherwise harmless. Of course, there's no knowing what psychological scars they leave on the children they approach, or perhaps I should also say on their parents. I'm sure young children wouldn't be half so upset emotionally by these experiences if it weren't for the horrified reactions of their elders. To some little girls, the old man is like an affectionate grandfather or elderly friend who becomes a frightening ogre in retrospect only after her mother tells her he is one. In many cases the incident is best forgotten unless the child has suffered physical or mental harm.

Sexual inadequacies cause men to commit such crimes as the Boston stranglings, which have been baffling the police there for some years. The pattern is generally the same. The victim, raped, and strangled by her own stocking, is middle-aged or even elderly, lives alone, and has or had some connection with hospital work. It is probable that a young and beautiful girl would be safe from such attacks. Whatever else he is, the strangler is no Don Juan. He's afraid of attractive women and unable to cope with them sexually.

Here in the United States we have the highest incidence of sex crime in the civilized world. Some experts feel that this is caused by our British heritage with its strict Puritan code of morals. Sex has generally been looked upon as something bad except in the normal marital situation. Despite the more liberal thinking of modern times, it is still soft-pedaled in the home.

In our tradition it has tended to be a private, poorly expressed thing, and there has been an appalling ignorance on the part of our young people concerning it. The vast majority grow up not really knowing what is and what is not acceptable sexual practice, or what is good and what is evil in the whole area. Nowhere else is there such anxiety, such confusion, such a mass of guilt complexes regarding sex. And nowhere else are there so many sex offenders.

In other countries sex is accepted as a natural and human fact of life which very young children take as much for granted as their elders. There is nothing evil or sordid about sex, no backstairs whispering, no dirty jokes as we know them. In other countries sex jokes have a sophistication that most of ours lack. They can be written as well as told, for there is nothing offensive about them. Conversation about sex is open and untrammeled in front of children, who grow up with none of the guilt feelings or unhealthy curiosities that so many of our children have.

A Japanese psychiatrist visiting the California Medical Facility at Vacaville was amazed at the number of overt sex offenders he found there. It was hard for him to believe that we have thousands more in prisons and mental hospitals all over the country. In Japan, a nation of nearly one hundred million people, only three or four rape cases a year is about average and other sex crimes are practically unheard of. He attributed the difference to the difference in attitude about sex in the presence of small children.

The secrets we keep from our children fan emotions that are accentuated rather than offset by our crass lack of sex secrecy in public. This stimulates hidden urges that should never have been hidden in the first place. The sights and sounds and smells and literature designed to excite the emotions hold no attraction for the adult who as a child never thought sex was a dirty word. The streets of Paris are still full of peddlers of "feelthy pictures," designed almost solely for the American trade. If your tourists would stop buying them, those peddlers would go out of business.

All our talk and display of sex is general, but our horror of sex as it relates to any of us in particular is so deep-seated that most of our rape victims would rather drop charges than testify against their attackers. They refuse to accept the fact that rape is a disgrace only for the perpetrator so they won't publicly identify themselves. They are not alone. Witnesses often won't testify and parents often won't permit their children to testify in sex cases. Because of this reluctance it is very difficult for prosecutors to get rape convictions. Instead, they have to try to make deals with obviously guilty offenders, offering, for example, to drop the rape charge if a man will plead guilty to burglary. The defendant almost invariably accepts, so he goes to prison under false colors and usually serves less time.

This leads to ridiculous secondary problems. Once in prison, a man forgets what he's there for. Refusing to acknowledge his actual crime, he admits only to the simulated one. This doesn't make him any the less a rapist or any the less dangerous when he is released, but he considers himself entitled to refuse treatment as a sex offender. "Hell," he says, "I'm not a rapo. I'm a burglar. Go look at the record."

Kidnapping is sometimes used in the courts as a substitute for rape. This is not by the choice of the defendant, however, for kidnapping is a more serious charge and carries more serious consequences. It was a capital crime under California's "Little Lindbergh Law" until a few years ago. Caryl Chessman, the so-called "red-light bandit," went to the gas chamber on a kidnap conviction, even though the law under which he was sentenced had been repealed before his execution. Chessman was a rapist in fact, a kidnapper only by technical definition.

One of the strangest of all sex crimes is incest. Why does a man violate his own daughter? Usually, the answer is a desire to get even with a wife who has rejected him. I have known of cases where the wife deliberately steered her husband to it. Unable or unwilling to meet his sexual needs, she set up the daughter as a foil, operating on the preposterous theory that it was better to keep it in the family than to have him go off to a mistress.

Men convicted only of incest are among the best bets for rehabilitation, provided the daughter has left home by the time they return. They are harmless to others and highly unlikely to get into trouble again. Wives, realizing their own guilt, usually are willing to take them back and everyone lives more or less happily ever after. A doctor once told me that if he wanted to make a perfect record as a therapist he would handle nothing but incest cases.

On the other hand, men with a preference for young boys are among our most dangerous criminals, almost impossible to cure or rehabilitate, and a constant threat while at large. These men hate and fear all females and adult males, and no one, even the boys they seek out, is safe with them.

The hardest crime to categorize is murder, because the motives are so different. Men kill in anger or jealousy or fear or greed or frustration. They kill for money, or for a woman, or for revenge. Few kill just for the sake of killing. There is almost always a reason, one that seems to the killer a very good reason at the moment.

I would not presume to say that all murders are fundamentally for sex, but most are inspired, in one way or another, by the sex drive. Crimes of violence are often crimes of passion, so sex can never be completely ruled out as a possible motive.

People who get into trouble because their sex problems are more than they can handle make up the vast bulk of our prison population today, as I shall endeavor to show in the pages that follow. If I succeed in contributing a little toward better understanding and more widespread treatment of these problems, it will be well worth the effort.

Rearing of a Sex-Reassigned Normal Male Infant After Traumatic Loss of the Penis

By John Money and Anke A. Ehrhardt

*T*he extreme unusualness of this case of sex-reassignment in infancy lies in the fact that the child was born a normal male and an identical twin, without genital malformation or sexual ambiguity. The idea of sex-reassignment would never have been entertained were it not for a surgical mishap at the age of seven months in which the penis was ablated flush with the abdominal wall. The mishap occurred when a circumcision was being performed by means of electrocautery. The electrical current was too powerful and burned the entire tissue of the penis which necrosed and sloughed off.

The parents were young people of rural background and grade-school education. They were understandably desperate to know what could be done and suffered through a rather long saga of finding no answer. Then a consultant plastic surgeon, familiar with the principles of sex-reassignment, recommended reassignment as a girl. The parents agonized their way to a decision, implementing it with a change of name, clothing and hair style when the baby was seventeen months old. Four months later, the surgical first step of genital reconstruction as a female was undertaken, the second step, vaginoplasty, being delayed until the body is full grown. Pubertal growth and feminization will be regulated by means of hormonal replacement therapy with estrogen.

At the time of surgery, when we saw the parents in person for the first time in the psychohormonal research unit at Johns Hopkins, we gave them advice and counseling on the future prognosis and management of their new daughter, based on experience with similar reassignments in hermaphroditic babies. In particular, they were given confidence that their child can be expected to differentiate a female gender identity, in agreement with her sex of rearing. They were broadly informed about the future medical program for their child and how to integrate it with her sex education as she grows older. They were guided in how to give the child information about herself to the extent that the need arises in the future; and they were helped with what to explain to friends and relatives, including their other child. Eventually, they would inform their daughter that she would become a mother by adoption, one day, when she married and wanted to have a family.

During the follow-up time of nearly six years since surgery, the parents have kept in close contact with us, making visits on an annual basis to get psychological support and guidance. The mother's observations and reports have provided us with an insight into changes in her rearing practices towards the sex-reassigned child, and into the different way that she rears this child as compared with the twin brother.

The first items of change were clothes and hairdo. The mother reported: "I started dressing her not in dresses but, you know, in little pink slacks and frilly blouses . . . and letting her hair grow." A year and six months later, the mother wrote that she had made a special effort at keeping her girl in dresses, almost exclusively, changing any item of clothes into something that was clearly feminine. "I even made all her nightwear into granny gowns and she wears bracelets and hair ribbons." The effects of emphasizing feminine clothing became clearly noticeable in the girl's attitude towards clothes and hairdo another year later, when she was observed to have a clear preference for dresses over slacks and to take pride in her long hair.

Related to being dressed nicely is the sense of neatness. The mother stated that her daughter by four and a half years of age was much neater than her brother, and in contrast with him, disliked to be dirty; "She likes for me to wipe her face. She doesn't like to be dirty, and yet my son is quite different. I can't wash his face for anything . . . She seems to be daintier. Maybe it's because I encourage it." Elsewhere in this same recorded interview, the mother said: "One thing that really amazes me is that she is so feminine. I've never seen a little girl so neat and tidy as she can be when she wants to be . . . She is very proud of herself, when she puts on a new dress, or I set her hair. She just loves to have her hair set; she could sit under the drier all day long to have her hair set. She just loves it."

There is a whole pattern of dimorphism of rearing girls and boys with respect to genitalia, sex and reproduction. Boys and girls learn differently how to urinate—boys to stand up and girls to sit down. This child had not, of course, been able to stand when the penis was ablated at age seven months. When, at the age of two, she tried standing up, as many girls do, her mother made a special point of teaching her how little girls go to the bathroom. In this case it needed perhaps more training than usual, because after surgery the girl's urethral opening was so positioned that the urine sometimes would overshoot the seat of the toilet. At the last follow-up, when the girl was five years and nine months old, her mother reported that she had learned to sit down and, with slight pressure from the fingers, direct the urinary stream downward. Sometimes she still tried copying her brother, usually making "an awful mess," according to her mother.

The family was relatively open in regard to matters of sex and reproduction, so that one can study particularly well the differences in treating a girl and boy regarding sex and their future adult reproductive role. When the twins were four and a half years old, the mother gave a good example of how parents react to boys' versus girls' genital play. Talking about the boy, the mother reported: ". . . in the summer time, one time I caught him—he went out and took a leak in my flower garden in the front yard, you know. He was quite happy with himself. And I just didn't say anything. I just couldn't. I started laughing and I told daddy about it . . ." The corresponding comment about the girl ran thus: "I've never had a problem with her. She did once when she was little, she took off her panties and threw them over the fence. And she didn't have no panties on. But I just gave her a little swat on the rear, and I told her that nice little girls didn't do that and she should keep her pants on . . . And she didn't take them off after that."

Once the children asked what their mother's breasts were for. She explained that when mommies have babies, they give milk. The boy answered that he wanted to be a mommy. His mother explained that he could only be a daddy—"and grow muscles so he could take care of mommy and baby, and just go to work in a car like daddy does. I finally convinced him he might have just as much fun as a mommy does . . . I've explained to each what their function will be as a grown-up, where babies grow, and that a daddy has to have a wife to have a baby and vice versa."

When the girl came across one of her mother's supply of sanitary pads, she was given an appropriate explanation about menstrual care and the fact that it is part of the female's role.

The mother of these two children was particularly good in pointing out the specifics of the female and male adult reproductive roles to her daughter and her son. When an incident happened that could be interpreted as penis envy in the girl and baby or pregnancy envy in the boy, she successfully offered explanations geared to the specific advantage of being a female on the one hand, and a male on the other. The incident happened some time when the children were five years of age. Both children were taking a bath together and the boy was bragging about his penis which was erect. The mother described the situation as follows: ". . . he managed to get a hard on, and he was standing there and saying, look what I got, look what I got, proud as a peacock and she (his sister) got so mad she slapped him—she didn't like it—right on his little penis. I think, she was a little jealous. So then I went and told her you wait and see, women can have babies and boys can't." When the girl had been reassured about the advantage of being female and having babies, the boy was disappointed and jealous. His mother hastened to reassure him that "little boys could have babies too." and she explained that the father was the one who had to provide the sperm or "seed" as she put it.

Of course, girls and boys are not only prepared differently for their future reproductive role as mother and father but also for their other different roles, such as wife and husband or financial supporter of the family and caretaker of children and house. The mother of these two children gave a good example of how her children were copying aspects of the wife and husband role. The parents were quite open in showing affection to each other in the presence of their children. The mother observed how her son would copy some of his father's behavior: "Like he'll bend over and give her a kiss on the cheek or he'll give her a hug . . . and if he (my husband) gives me a swat on the fanny, he'll go and give her a swat on her fanny, too."

The boy was clearly the initiator of affection, copying what he saw in his father's behavior. The girl copied some of her mother's responses—"If she's in an affectionate mood, she'll like it; but very often she'll say, don't do that . . . If he's been playing some place and comes in the house to where she is helping me . . . then she'll give him a little hug like she's glad to see him."

Regarding domestic activities, such as work in the kitchen and house traditionally seen as part of the female's role, the mother reported that her daughter copies her in trying to help her tidying and cleaning up the kitchen, while the boy could not care less about it. She encourages her daughter when she helps her in the housework.

Rehearsal of future roles can also be seen in girls' and boys' toy preferences. The girl in this case wanted and received for Christmas dolls, a doll house, and a doll carriage, clearly related to the maternal aspect of the female adult role, while the boy wanted and obtained a garage with cars and gas pumps and tools, part of the rehearsal of the male role. His father, like many men, was very interested in cars and mechanical activities.

According to today's standards, not only boys, but also girls often pursue a career. Regarding school and future plans, the mother formulated her own hopes, when the children were a year and ten months old, by saying: "Oh well . . . I am leaving it up to them, but I would like for both of them to go to college and university, and have some kind of career. That's what I would like for both of them . . . As long as they get their high school, at least my daughter. My son, it's almost essential, since he will be earning a living for the rest of his life." This standpoint represents the opinion of many parents who encourage education and career plans to a stronger degree for boys than for girls. By the time the twins were five years and nine months of age, they expressed clearly different goals for the future. According to their mother's report:

"I found that my son, he chose very masculine things like a fireman or a policeman or something like that. He wanted to do what daddy does, work where daddy does, and carry a lunch kit, and drive a car. And she didn't want any of those things. I asked her, and she said she wanted to be a doctor or a teacher. And I asked her, well, did she have plans that maybe some day she'd get married, like mommy? She'll get married some day—she wasn't too worried about that. She didn't think about that too much, but she wants to be a doctor. But none of the things that she ever wanted to be were like a policeman or a fireman, and that sort of thing never appealed to her.

So I felt that in a way that's a good sign . . . I think, it's nice if your boy wants to be a policeman or a fireman or something and the girl things like a doctor, or teaching, or something like that, and I've tried to show them that it's very good . . ."

The girl had many tomboyish traits, such as abundant physical energy, a high level of activity, stubbornness, and being often the dominant one in a girls' group. Her mother had tried to modify her tomboyishness: ". . . of course, I've tried to teach her not to be rough . . . she doesn't seem to be as rough as him . . . of course, I discouraged that. I teach her more to be polite and quiet. I always wanted those virtues. I never did manage, but I'm going to try to manage them to —my daughter—to be more quiet and lady-like." From the beginning the girl had been the dominant twin. By the age of three, her dominance over her brother was, as her mother described it, that of a mother hen. The boy in turn took up for his sister, if anyone threatened her.

The examples of different rearing practices towards girls and boys here presented, are by no means a complete sample of the cues and reinforcements parents offer to their children. Most parents give them without conscious effort, routinely. It is unusual to have a mother to be as observant, and as good a reporter as this woman. Her husband, by contrast, was less alert in observing and reporting his own actions and behavior towards his daughter and his son, although he also was reinforcing different behavior in each one of his children. He is more typical than his wife in being relatively inarticulate regarding sex differences in rearing. He was more inclined to stress the idea of lack of favoritism in his responses to both children.

Part Two

THE SOCIO-CULTURAL PERSPECTIVE

When looking at male sexuality and masculinity from a socio-cultural perspective, the role played by social processes in developing and establishing the self-definitions of males is especially important. Rather than search for an underlying sense of maleness, or a sex drive which determines one's relationship to females, authors using this perspective look to society and social interaction processes.

The first two selections in Part Two provide a humorous reflection of social and peer pressures in learning to be masculine. Whereas Lester looks at the interaction dimension in terms of boys learning to act with and towards girls, Cosby recalls the "learning about sex" aspect of growing up. Both provide illustrations of the role played by social and peer pressures in learning to be a man in America.

The final three selections in Part Two deal with the influence of the cultural definition of masculinity upon adult males in American subcultures. The contradictory aspects of the masculine role in a modern, rapidly changing society are examined. Men, having been socialized to achieve in the economic realm, have extended their competitiveness, non-expressiveness, and perceived intellectual superiority into interpersonal relationships.

Being a Boy

By Julius Lester

*A*s boys go, I wasn't much. I mean, I tried to be a boy and spent many childhood hours pummeling my hardly formed ego with failure at cowboys and Indians, baseball, football, lying, and sneaking out of the house. When our neighborhood gang raided a neighbor's pear tree, I was the only one who got sick from the purloined fruit. I also failed at setting fire to our garage, an art at which any five-year-old boy should be adept. I was, however, the neighborhood champion of getting beat up. "That Julius can take it, man," the boys used to say, almost in admiration, after I emerged from another battle, tears brimming in my eyes but refusing to fall.

My efforts at being a boy earned me a pair of scarred knees that are a record of a childhood spent falling from bicycles, trees, the tops of fences, and porch steps; of tripping as I ran (generally from a fight), walked, or simply tried to remain upright on windy days.

I tried to believe my parents when they told me I was a boy, but I could find no objective proof for such an assertion. Each morning during the summer, as I cuddled up in the quiet of a corner with a book, my mother would push me out the back door and into the yard. And throughout the day as my blood was let as if I were a patient of 17th-century medicine, I thought of the girls sitting in the shade of porches, playing with their dolls, toy refrigerators and stoves.

Ms., 2 (July, 1973), pp. 112-113. Copyright © 1973 by *Ms. Magazine.* Reprinted by permission of *Ms.*

There was the life, I thought! No constant pressure to prove oneself. No necessity always to be competing. While I humiliated myself on football and baseball fields, the girls stood on the sidelines laughing at me, because they didn't have to do anything except be girls. The rising of each sun brought me to the starting line of yet another day's Olympic decathlon, with no hope of ever winning even a bronze medal.

Through no fault of my own I reached adolescence. While the pressure to prove myself on the athletic field lessened, the overall situation got worse—because now I had to prove myself with girls. Just how I was supposed to go about doing this was beyond me, especially because, at the age of 14, I was four foot nine and weighed 78 pounds. (I think there may have been one 10-year-old girl in the neighborhood smaller than I.) Nonetheless, duty called, and with my ninth-grade gym-class jockstrap flapping between my legs, off I went.

To get a girlfriend, though, a boy had to have some asset beyond the fact that he was alive. I wasn't handsome like Bill McCord, who had girls after him like a cop-killer has policemen. I wasn't ugly like Romeo Jones, but at least the girls noticed him: "That ol' ugly boy better stay 'way from me!" I was just there, like a vase your grandmother gives you at Christmas that you don't like or dislike, can't get rid of, and don't know what to do with. More than ever I wished I were a girl. Boys were the ones who had to take the initiative and all the responsibility. (I hate responsibility so much that if my heart didn't beat of itself, I would now be a dim memory.)

It was the boy who had to ask the girl for a date, a frightening enough prospect until it occurred to me that she might say No! That meant risking my ego, which was about as substantial as a toilet-paper raincoat in the African rainy season. But I had to thrust that ego forward to be judged, accepted, or rejected by some girl. It wasn't fair! Who was she to sit back like a queen with the power to create joy by her consent or destruction by her denial? It wasn't fair —but that's the way it was.

But if (God forbid!) she should say Yes, then my problem would begin in earnest, because I was the one who said where we would go (and waited in terror for her approval of my choice). I was the one who picked her up at her house where I was inspected by her parents as if I were a possible carrier of syphilis (which I didn't think one could get from masturbating, but then again, Jesus was born of a virgin, so what did I know?). Once we were on our way, it was I who had to pay the bus fare, the price of the movie tickets, and whatever she decided to stuff her stomach with afterward. (And the smallest girls are all stomach.) Finally, the girl was taken home where once again I was inspected (the father looking covertly at my fly and the mother examining the girl's hair). The evening was over and the girl had done nothing except honor me with her presence. All the work had been mine.

Imagining this procedure over and over was more than enough: I was a sophomore in college before I had my first date.

I wasn't a total failure in high school, though, for occasionally I would go to a party, determined to salvage my self-esteem. The parties usually took place in somebody's darkened basement. There was generally a surreptitious wine bottle or two being passed furtively among the boys, and a record player with an insatiable appetite for Johnny Mathis records. Boys gathered on one side of the room and girls on the other. There were always a few boys and girls who'd come to the party for the sole purpose of grinding away their sexual frustrations to Johnny Mathis's falsetto, and they would begin dancing to their own music before the record player was plugged in. It took a little longer for others to get started, but no one matched my talent for standing by the punch bowl. For hours, I would try to make my legs do what they had been doing without effort since I was nine months old, but for some reason they would show all the symptoms of paralysis on those evenings.

After several hours of wondering whether I was going to die ("Julius Lester, a sixteen-year-old, died at a party last night, a half-eaten Ritz cracker in one hand and a potato chip dipped in pimento-cheese spread in the other. Cause of death: failure to be a boy"), I would push my way to the other side of the room where the girls sat like a hanging jury. I would pass by the girl I wanted to dance with. If I was going to be refused, let it be by someone I didn't particularly like. Unfortunately, there weren't many in that category. I had more crushes than I had pimples.

Finally, through what surely could only have been the direct intervention of the Almighty, I would find myself on the dance floor with a girl. And none of my prior agony could compare to the thought of actually dancing. But there I was and I had to dance with her. Social custom decreed that I was supposed to lead, because I was the boy. Why? I'd wonder. Let her lead. Girls were better dancers anyway. It didn't matter. She stood there waiting for me to take charge. She wouldn't have been worse off if she'd waited for me to turn white.

But, reciting "Invictus" to myself, I placed my arms around her, being careful to keep my armpits closed because, somehow, I had managed to overwhelm a half jar of deodorant and a good-size bottle of cologne. With sweaty armpits, "Invictus," and legs afflicted again with polio, I took her in my arms, careful not to hold her so far away that she would think I didn't like her, but equally careful not to hold her so close that she could feel the catastrophe which had befallen me the instant I touched her hand. My penis, totally disobeying the lecture I'd given it before we left home, was as rigid as Governor Wallace's jaw would be if I asked for his daughter's hand in marriage.

God, how I envied girls at that moment. Wherever it was on them, it didn't dangle between their legs like an elephant's trunk. No wonder boys talked about nothing but sex. That thing was always there. Every time we went to the john, there it was, twitching around like a fat little worm on a fishing hook. When we took baths, it floated in the water like a lazy fish and God forbid we should touch it! It sprang to life like lightning leaping from a cloud. I wished I could cut it off, or at least keep it tucked between my legs, as if it were a tail that had been mistakenly attached to the wrong end. But I was helpless. It was there, with a life and mind of its own, having no other function than to embarrass me.

Fortunately, the girls I danced with were discreet and pretended that they felt nothing unusual rubbing against them as we danced. But I was always convinced that the next day they were all calling up all their friends to exclaim: "Guess what, girl, Julius Lester got one! I ain't lyin'!"

Now, of course, I know that it was as difficult being a girl as it was a boy, if not more so. While I stood paralyzed at one end of a dance floor trying to find the courage to ask a girl for a dance, most of the girls waited in terror at the other, afraid that no one, not even I, would ask them. And while I resented having to ask a girl for a date, wasn't it also horrible to be the one who waited for the phone to ring? And how many of those girls who laughed at me making a fool of myself on the baseball diamond would have gladly given up their places on the sidelines for mine on the field?

No, it wasn't easy for any of us, girls and boys, as we forced our beautiful free-flowing child-selves into those narrow, constricting cubicles labeled female and male. I tried, but I wasn't good at being a boy. Now, I'm glad, knowing that a man is nothing but a figment of a penis's imagination, and any man should want to be something more than that.

The Regular Way

By Bill Cosby

*H*er name was Rosemary and she lived in the projects and she was very cute-looking, and guys had gone steady with her, and one day, I'm in, like fifth or sixth grade, I get a note from her. It says, Dear William, I think that you are so cute, and I would like to go with you. So now, I'm in love with her, because I never thought that Rosemary would dig me. I knew that she was going with—and these are real names—Pee Wee. So I write her a note, and I say, Yes, and I love you, but are you still going with Pee Wee? So she writes me back. Yes, I am still going with Pee Wee, but when I get through with him, I would like to go with you. So I say, Yes, you can go with me, but when are you gonna be through with Pee Wee? She says, Whenever Pee Wee doesn't want me anymore, and you should ask Pee Wee. So I go to Pee Wee and I say, Listen, Pee Wee, how long are you gonna be going with Rosemary? So Pee Wee says, Man maybe till next week. So I say, OK, what is that—Friday? He says, About Friday, I guess. So Friday comes, and I look for Pee Wee, and I say, Pee Wee, are you still. . . . He says, I think Monday. So I say, Monday? OK, Monday. So now, I take four baths Sunday night: six times I grease my hair; I brush my hair 982 times—I'm getting these little curls I got down pat; and, like, I wash my face so good—I don't want to get anything that looks halfway like a skin blemish or anything and I clean my toes; everything, man. And I just feel good and crisp; they've never see me coming to school like this before, and Rosemary's not there. She's absent.

So Monday night, I take *eight* baths. Now, Tuesday, she's in school, and I say, Rosemary, are you going with anybody now? She says, No. And I say, Well, can I be your boyfriend? And she says, Yeah. So I say, Well, I'll meet you after school. Man, I was so proud —I do all those things I'd read in the comic books and stuff: I carry her books home, and we get to her home and I say, OK, Rosemary, I gotta go play some football, but I'll see you tomorrow. And my heart is as big as a watermelon.

So I go home and I change my clothes, and I hang them up— things I'd never done before. And I go out, and there's Rufus out there, throwing a football. So I go and we throw the football. Back and forth. And he says, You're goin' with Rosemary, huh? I say, Yeah. He says, Did you get any yet? I say, Get any what? He says, You know man. I say, No, man. I didn't get any . . . get any *what*? He says, Did you get any . . . any p-u-s-s-y? I say, No man. I don't do that kind of thing. He says, What you mean you don't . . . you mean to tell me, if a chick offers you some p-u-s-s-y, you ain't gonna take none? I say, Well . . . I mean, you know, if somebody wanna *give* me some p-u-s-s-y. . . .

Now, the truth is I don't know nothin' about p-u-s-s-y. You walk around the neighborhood, you see signs on the sidewalk, on the walls: PUSSY IS GOOD. And it's somethin' that you just take for granted —you look at it and say, Yeah. But most of the kids who write it never have had any. I used to hear the big guys say, you know, like when they used to talk on the corner. So-and-so man, she's got some gooooooooood p-u-s-s-y. But I never really thought about it; I didn't care, because I wasn't interested in that. I was always interested in the *face*, 'cause I was, like, 11 years old. And another thing I couldn't understand was why guys would look at girls' legs. You know, So-and-so's got some gooooooooood legs. Did you see them . . . man, I'd love to see them legs way up in the air. Hey, why would you wanna see her legs in the air, man? You like to see people fall down, or what?

Anyway, I don't say nothin', and he says, Well, you know Rosemary wanna give you some p-u-s-s-y. So I say, Yeah, I know she wants to give me some p-u-s-s-y, but I'm not gonna take it. He says, How come? I say, Because I'm gonna marry her, and I want her to be a virgin. He says, Well, I think you better go get some of that p-u-s-s-y, because Rosemary ain't nobody's virgin. I say, What you talkin' about? He says, Well you 'bout the *only* cat that hasn't got some of that p-u-s-s-y. He says, *Everybody* got some of *that* p-u-s-s-y:

even ol' weird Harold got some of that p-u-s-s-y underneath the Ninth Street bridge.

Man, I dropped my head *so* low, man, and I looked at the cat, and I said, Man, she ain't never gave *nobody* no p-u-s-s-y. And he said, Don't tell me—I got it in the hallway one time . . . she gave me some gooooooooood p-u-s-s-y.

So I threw the ball down, and I went to her house, man. I was almost ready to cry. And I knocked on her door. I was puffin' mad. She opened the door and she says, Whatcha doin' here? My mother's home. So I said, You been givin' everybody some p-u-s-s-y? She said, What? I said, *Have you been givin' everybody some p-u-s-s-y?* Because Rufus say that you gave him some p-u-s-s-y in the hallway. She said, I didn't give Rufus *nothin'*. I said, Well, did you give some to ol' weird Harold under the Ninth Street bridge? She says, No, I didn't give ol' weird Harold no p-u-s-s-y. I said, Well, who *did* you give p-u-s-s-y to? She said, I didn't give p-u-s-s-y to *nobody*. I said, Well, then, would you give *me* some p-u-s-sy? She said, My *mother's* home. I said, OK, but *when* you gonna give me some? She said, I'll give you some Saturday. I said, Where? She said, Here— my mother goes to work on Saturday.

So, man, Saturday comes, and I've been thinkin' all week about this p-u-s-s-y. You know, and I'm tryin' to ask people questions about how they get some p-u-s-s-y. And I don't want guys to know that I don't know nothin' about gettin' no p-u-s-s-y. But how do you find out how to do it without blowin' the fact that you don't know how to do it? So I come up to a guy, and I say, Say, man, have you ever had any p-u-s-s-y? And the guy says, Yeah. And I say, Well, man, what's your favorite way of gettin' it? He says, Well, you know, just the regular way. And I say, Well, do you do it like I do it? And the cat says, How's that? And I say, Well, hey, I heard that there was different ways of doin' it, man. He says, Well, there's a lotta ways of doin' it, you know, but I think that . . . you know, the *regular* way. . . . I say, *Yeah,* good ol' regular way . . . good ol' regular way of gettin' that p-u-s-s-y.

So now, I'm walkin', and I'm trying to figure out how to do it. And when I get there, the most embarrassing thing is gonna be when I have to take my pants down. See, right away, then, I'm buck naked . . . buck naked in front of this girl. Now, what happens then? Do you . . . do you just . . . I don't even know what to do . . . I'm gonna just stand there and she's gonna say, You don't know how to do it. And I'm gonna say, Yes I do, but I *forgot.* I never thought of her showing me, because I'm a man and I don't want her to show me—I don't want *nobody* to show me, but I wish somebody would kinda slip me a note—if somebody was there. I stopped off at a magazine stand to look and see if there were any sexy magazines about it. I mean if I wasn't going to learn how to do it, I figured there might be some pictures in there of somebody *almost* getting ready to do it. But I don't find nothin'.

So I keep walkin' and the closer I get to the house, the more scared I get. And I get to the house and now I *don't want to do it.* I mean, I DON'T WANT NONE, 'cause it's nasty . . . and it's *dirty* . . . and you will GO TO HELL and she could get pregnant and my mother's gonna cry, and my father's gonna cry, and I'll probably get a beatin' . . . so I really don't want to do it now, I'm not gonna do it to her. But I go and knock on her door. And I'm not shaking or nothin', it's just that I'm knocking on the door and I don't want any. And I'm gonna tell her as soon as she opens the door that I don't want any. Because it is nasty and you could get pregnant from it and all those things. And she opened the door. And she said, Hello, William. And I said, Hello, Rosemary. And then my heart starts thumpin', because I really loved her. So I just kinda stood there. And I really *loved* her, but I knew that I could never marry her or nothin' like that, because she wasn't a virgin.

So I came in, and she closed the door, and I just stood by the door there. She had a sofa and a center table and a big piano. And she just pulled up her dress, and she said, C'mon. Well, had I seen one before, I probably would have just run out the door. But it was interesting and I had never seen one before—not a real one. You know, so I just kinda looked at it. And she kept her dress up while I was lookin' at it. You know, I just kept lookin'. And I said, Well, that's it . . . there. *There* it is . . . that's the thing . . . this is it . . . here it is. And I looked at it . . . and it didn't look like nothing *good*. It just looked like, you know. And I thought, My mother's right, it is nasty, and you *should* get pregnant from playing around with that. Anyway, I came up to her—and we didn't even get on the floor or nothin'—and we were rubbin', doin' the grind, and I pulled her dress down so I wouldn't have to look at it, and we just did some rubbin', just did some rubbin' and grindin' and everything and I kept thinkin' about how you could get pregnant, and about how I would have to come outta school and get a job, and then I would be 13 years old with a lunch pail and some hard boots and coveralls, and I would be goin' to work with these old men and sittin' there, and be talkin' like old people, and then I would have to start smoking, and all those things. So I said, Look, my mother has to see me at twelve o'clock. She said, Well, don't you want to do it? And I said, Yes, I want to do it . . . but when I do it, I got to do it for a long time, see—maybe three, four hours sometimes. She said, For what? I said, That's the way to do it . . . three, four hours. She said, Do you really? I said, Yeah. She said, Mmm, that sound like you could really do it. And I said, Oh, yes, I've been doing it for . . . well, the first time I ever did it was when I was eight years old . . . so I've been doing it for a long time . . . and I got to go . . . And I left . . . and I never came back.

Anyway, I got to the schoolyard and Rufus was throwing the ball. And I walked up to him. And he said, You been over to Rosemary's? And I just pulled up on my belt, you know, and I smiled and I said, Yeah, man, she got some *goooooooood* p-u-s-s-y. He says, Isn't that stuff good? I said, Yeah, man, it was *really* good.

And he says, Well, did you come? I said, What?

He says, Did you come right away? So I said, Yeah, we had a *lotta* fun. He said, Man, did you *come*? So I said, Sure. He said, How was it? I said, Well, she's got some *goooooooooood* p-u-s-s-y. So he said, How did you do it? I said, Uh . . . man . . . if you don't know how to do it, I ain't gonna tell you how to do it, and I got to get home and mop the linoleum, and I walked about half a block away, and I look back and there's Rufus—he still standin' there holdin' the football. And I yell back, Man, we did it the *regular* way!

Executives As Human Beings

By Fernando Bartolome

Since man's only possession is his life, or rather his living, man's most fundamental question is, "How will I do my living?" So the search for a meaningful way of being alive should be a central aspect of man's life.

Man should be free from stereotypes, self-imposed or otherwise, and rigid role definitions that limit his existence. The American business executive is, in my opinion, a man caught in a stereotype. He is limited by a role definition obliging him to be super-masculine, super-tough, super-self-sufficient, and super-strong. It allows him very little freedom to be that mixture of strength and weakness, independence and dependence, toughness and tenderness which a human being is.

When one thinks of the executive's situation, several questions come to mind:

- How does he relate to himself, to others, and to the world?
- Does he conceive of different way of living his life, different ways of relating to himself, to others, and to the world?
- Does he want to live his life differently? Is he tired of being the strong and reliable one, the one who is always on top of things?

The executive, I suspect, has great difficulty conceiving of alternative

Harvard Business Review, November-December, 1972, pp. 62-68.
Copyright © 1972 by the President and Fellows of Harvard
College; all rights reserved. Reprinted by permission.

life styles in realistic terms. But only when he understands and is "tuned in" to these alternatives can he be in a position to choose his own life style.

Not long ago I conducted a study dealing with these questions. At great length I interviewed 40 younger executives and their wives. The executives' average age was 37 and they had been married an average of 13 years. Nearly half (19) were employed by large or medium-sized companies, 7 were entrepreneurs, and 9 were managers of organizations other than business.

I tried to learn how the executive related to himself, to others, and to the world, and I tried to understand why he lives the way he does. In this article I shall discuss what I learned and say what I think it means in terms of alternatives open to the executive.

In the study I tried to discover to what extent executives acknowledge to themselves their own feelings of dependence and tenderness and reveal those feelings at home. And I tried to establish connections between their behavior or "styles" at the office and at home. In general, I tried to discover the factors that influenced the degree to which these executives acknowledged to themselves their own feelings and disclosed or expressed them at home.

Under the label "feelings of dependence" I grouped a complex set of feelings. All of them related to the experiencing of a temporary or permanent inability or insufficient capacity to cope alone with a situation or event, and the feeling (conscious or unconscious) of a need for outside help to deal with this phenomenon. When somebody fills that need—with love, money, cooperation, sympathy, companionship, or whatever—the one in need experiences a feeling of dependence on that person.

By "feelings of tenderness" I mean feelings of caring for, being moved by, loving, taking care of, or being involved with another human being. In other words, I mean all those emotions aroused when a person allows himself to be deeply touched by another person and, being touched, feels warmth toward the other.

Relevance to Executives

A human being should have the courage and the skill to become aware of his feelings, to keep trying to learn how to deal with them, and to become free to choose how and when to express them. It would be good for the executive to increase this awareness, to develop those skills, and to gain that freedom.

Will this sensitivity and this skill improve his performance on the job? The executive's personal growth will improve his functioning in any area of human relations. Moreover, many organizational problems arise from people's inability to cope openly with emotions aroused in performance of their jobs. So, as the executive develops his capacity in private life to relate to his feelings and deal with them constructively, the greater is his capacity to deal with them in performing his executive functions.

If, however, the cultural environment is very rigid in its established behavioral patterns and highly resistant to change, not much individual self-exploration will take place. There are signs that the rigid cultural environment in the United States is breaking down. (More on this later.)

At any rate, the home milieu, because of its small size and private nature, is more flexible than the work milieu. So it is a more suitable place for a man to start exploring himself and trying new behavioral styles.

The failure of methods to improve the executive's performance in the area of relating to others at work is partly due to the erroneous assumption that we should focus our attention on his tasks and behavioral demands at work. In other words, try to improve the executive, not the man. This false dichotomy, executive/man, is the basis for many mistakes. When we do not directly address the man, we fail; and everything that we provide "the executive" so he can manage people better is a gimmick and will not last.

Therefore, I have chosen to relate to the executive as a man and to care about his growth as a human being. This growth will have a positive effect when the person is engaged in his managerial functions.

Expression Of Feeling

In the interviews I conducted, nearly all the men (36) described themselves as seldom experiencing feelings of dependence. While unable to confirm it, I believe they experienced these feelings more often than they acknowledged to themselves. Also, the great majority (32) admitted great reluctance to reveal to their wives their feelings of dependence when they experienced them.

"It's difficult for me to express dependence," said one executive. "Feelings of dependence are identified with weakness or 'untoughness' and our culture doesn't accept these things in men."

With respect to feelings of tenderness, the executives (with one or two exceptions) acknowledged having them often. Nevertheless, they recognized some difficulty in expressing them and great difficulty in fully experiencing and sharing of these feelings.

Most of the men acknowledged that their expressions of tenderness were usually limited to members of their families, especially young children. And even displays of tenderness to their children, particularly boys, were inhibited by fear of "smothering" them or making them too dependent on their parents. "Doing things is more important than people," said one executive during an interview. "I want my children to learn to ski well. In skiing one only needs man and hill; nobody else is needed."

With few exceptions, the women I interviewed shared their husbands' reticence in expressing feelings and desire to encourage children's independence. The wife of the executive I just quoted said, "I'm trying to make my children stand on their own feet. I wouldn't express openly my affection for them because I don't want to smother them. I'm quite cold."

During the course of many hours of interviewing and many purely social occasions, I observed little physical contact between couples and their children, although the parents seemed to love them a lot.

To my surprise, I heard very few complaints on the part of husband or wife about the other's inability to express tenderness, even in those cases where I perceived displays of affection to be rather meager and not very rich in form.

Expression of tenderness to outsiders, including friends—especially a man's display of affection or even regard for a male friend—was very difficult for the men. One of them said, "I consider myself a sentimentalist and I think I am quite able to express my feelings. But the other day my wife described a friend of mine to some people as being my best friend and I felt embarrassed when I heard her say it."

On thinking about what these men and women had told me, I emerged with some ideas about the factors that seem to influence their expression of feelings of dependence and tenderness. They are cultural beliefs, fear of repercussions, and job characteristics. I shall discuss each in turn in the sections that follow.

Cultural Beliefs

All the persons I interviewed mentioned that the Anglo-Saxon culture discourages open and rich expression of emotion—any kind of emotion. Only the four couples of Irish extraction described themselves as experiencing less difficulty in expressing their feelings.

The men interviewed considered character traits such as strength, self-reliance, and "keeping a stiff upper lip" as both masculine and conducive to success. The picture of an executive one gets from one couple's remarks was typical.

Wife: My husband is very self-reliant, secure, self-sufficient. He never expresses his needs.

Husband: At work one gets accustomed not to express dependence and one does the same at home. As a matter of fact, at work I never think in terms of asking for help or expressing my needs but rather in terms of making good use of the available human resources. When I get home, I don't want to talk about any big problem; I just want to rest.

In contrast, the executives considered such characteristics as dependency, a need to be cared for, enjoyment of passive things, and tenderness as unmasculine and leading to failure—except for persons such as artists and "people of that kind." One gets a flavor of this point of view from what one executive said:

"I group my friends in two ways, those who have made it and don't complain and those who haven't made it. And only the latter spend time talking to their wives about their problems and how bad their boss is and all that. The ones who concentrate more on communicating with their wives and families are those who have realized that they aren't going to make it and therefore they have changed their focus of attention.

"The top executive really enjoys himself; he has the company plane and a lot of staff and has it easy. The ones who get the ulcers are those who are trying to get up there."

In some cases the men seemed to agree fully with the cultural beliefs and were intent on inculcating them and developing those culturally desirable characteristics in their children. In other cases, however, I saw indications that these men and women were becoming aware of the relative value of those cultural norms, and I got the impression that they had started to explore the worth of different value systems.

But even in those cases where the process of reevaluation had started on an intellectual level, the executives still appeared to be willing to conform to societal values even if they opposed them. Their conformity influenced what feelings they revealed to their wives and others.

The values of strength and self-reliance remained unquestioned, while the values of toughness and controlled expressiveness were starting to be reconsidered. Often I heard these couples criticize the excessive competitiveness of the American elementary and high school systems, while at the same time they indicated they valued highly the development of the child's strength by facing life without returning to ask for shelter. They wanted to make their children more sensitive but also strong and with equally big needs for high achievement.

With respect to themselves, they were quite conscious of the difficulty of abiding by the values they had adopted. But at the same time they seemed unable to move in another direction. An example of what I mean is their relationship with their friends. Their restraint is typified by one executive's remark: "A very good friend of mine, a school roommate came to visit and grabbed and hugged me. I felt very uncomfortable and awkward."

Many of the men acknowledged that they felt more affection, and with more intensity, than they were able to show, and they would like to express affection more fully. Yet none of them manifested any intention of exploring ways of establishing new and more open forms of relating to their friends and expressing their feelings to them.

Either/Or Proposition

Some of the executives believed strongly that, in the conduct of life, you must be either dependent or independent, expressive or restrained in expression. As one of them put it:

"You can't express dependence when you feel it, because it's a kind of absolute. If you are loyal 90% of the time and disloyal 10%, would you be considered to be loyal? Well, the same happens with dependence: you are either dependent or independent; you can't be both."

They were educated to believe that you cannot develop "contradictory" traits at the same time—you cannot, for example, develop both artistic self-expression and manly self-restraint. This sounds very logical. Furthermore, this dichotomic educational philosophy attaches judgmental labels to character traits, considering some to be "good" and some to be "bad."

Effects Of Fear

Carl R. Rogers describes how "as experiences occur in the life of the individual they are either (a) symbolized, perceived, and organized into some relation to the self, (b) ignored, because there is no perceived relationship to the self-structure, (c) denied symbolization, or given a distorted symbolization, because the experience is inconsistent with the structure of the self."[1]

The desire to avoid or ignore experience which the person unconsciously perceives as damaging to his concept of himself appeared to be quite strong in the group of men I interviewed. They had difficulty in admitting or even thinking about the possibility that "opposing" feelings or characteristics could exist within them at the same time.

The "either/or" value system made it hard to accept as belonging to them those "bad" character traits that the culture condemns. According to Rogers' theory, when the organism encounters information about an experience that threatens the organism's need to view itself as consistent, it automatically sets up defense mechanisms to repress or distort the disturbing information.

Such a reaction could also be construed as a result of a person's natural inclination to adapt to the environment in order to avoid being hurt by it. One executive expressed this reaction in saying, "I know I'm inhibited, but when one has felt dependent many times in his life and has been rebuffed, he finally learns and becomes independent for reasons of security."

This statement implies that the process is conscious, but it actually seldom is. The person fears to acknowledge even to himself the existence of culturally defined negative characteristics that if recognized could trigger punitive action from his social environment.

Personal Relationships

Fear of injury in personal relationships appeared to be a significant factor in inhibiting the executives from fuller and more open expression of their feelings.

Most important was the fear of rejection—that is, if you let your defenses down and let somebody know the depth of your needs, he will not only fail to satisfy your needs but will also lose respect for you. As a consequence, you learn to "play it cool," as evidenced by this executive's remark: "You act out certain games or rituals to provoke the desired reaction in the other and have your needs satisfied without having to ask for anything."

The fear of rejection is closely related to the man's belief that it is his manliness that makes him attractive to his wife and motivates her to give him what he needs. The traits which the culture calls masculine are toughness, strength, self-sufficiency, and ability to succeed. Therefore, a man avoids expressing his needs, disclosing his dependence, or showing tenderness lest his wife think him a weakling and be "turned off" by him.

When a man thinks this way, it becomes easy for him to rationalize his reluctance to "open up" in any way to his wife. "I can try to solve my problems by myself before asking for help," one executive asserted. "Anyway, what's the use of troubling my wife about my job problems when there's nothing she can do about them?"

When the husband expresses dependency, he is for the moment giving up any pretension of superiority or ability to control and determine the relationship. The husband who is engaged in a power struggle with the wife perceives such a temporary abdication as very risky. Here are the comments of one couple.

Husband: If I express tenderness to my wife or let her get away with it in front of my friends, they give me hell. Besides, if you express tenderness and don't get it back, that's also a problem. And it's also a problem because you're always trying to have some authority at home and there is often competition with the wife about who wears the pants and you can't afford to show dependence or tenderness when these other things are going on.

Wife: We compete all the time, for our friends' affection, for the children's affection, for authority at home, for everything!

When such a power struggle is going on, a man's expression of dependence or tenderness to his wife is conditioned on her previous submission to him. She must already have abdicated her power some time ago.

Today women are re-examining the male-female relationship and trying to reclaim equal dignity and equal rights within the relationship. As they do, the issues of power and domination will become central; men, who have previously had the upper hand, will find themselves put increasingly on the defensive. In a defensive position men will tend to disclose less of their feelings of dependence and tenderness than they do now.

Eventually, new ground rules will be established, and, one hopes, women will be less constrained by a definition of what they should be and what their role in the marital relationship should be. In other words, they will gain for themselves the right and the freedom to become more fully themselves.

At the same time, men will be deprived of the unjust privileges that they have enjoyed until today at the expense of women. But they also will be liberated to some extent from the limitations that have been imposed on them by a narrow definition of the masculine role. This deprives them of their freedom to acknowledge their feelings to themselves and to enjoy and express them.

Harming The Child

Still another inhibiting factor for the executives was fear of hurting others, particularly their children. Most of the parents considered themselves free to express physically and in other ways their feelings of tenderness to their children. Only a few recognized having difficulty doing it. However, my impression was that they were far from free in this regard; they seemed quite restrained in showing affection to their children. Their children also seemed to need affection shown to them more openly and frequently and more physically than they were getting it.

The parents' rationale was, as I mentioned earlier, their fear of smothering them, making them overdependent and weak, or violating their right to be independent.

The fear of harming the child by giving him "too much" affection is a wrong interpretation of the basic educational principle of respecting the child as an individual. Giving him love provides him with the confidence and strength to accept his own limitations and the fact of interdependence with other human beings. Acceptance of dependence as well as achievement of self-sufficiency is essential to the development of the mature person.

Job Characteristics

Most of the executives seemed quite satisfied with their work, though they complained that their jobs left too little time for family and other activities. Some of them were indeed putting in a lot of hours.

The consequences can be inhibiting for both husband and wife, as illustrated by the candid remarks of one couple.

Husband: A lot of executives are seduced by their jobs. They become fanatical about their jobs because they like the work and because their companies reward their fanaticism. But as a result they have very little time to be at home and talk about their feelings. When they come back home, there are a thousand things to do or take care of before they have time for themselves.

Wife: When he goes away because of his job, I'm left alone and I have to take care of things. When he comes back, I resent him for abandoning me and it takes some time to unwind, to relax, and be able to feel and express tenderness.

Those who seemed to be most involved in their work described how it took not only most of their time, but nearly all of their energy. So when they returned home, they felt "drained" and able to communicate very little with their wives and children.

The competitive atmosphere, the premium placed on success, and the great value given to self-reliance on the job obviously affect the way an executive feels about himself when he leaves the office for home. And his attitude toward his performance affects his ability, once at home, to "unwind," let his needs be known, and accept affection from his family. As one wife put it:

"When they don't achieve what they think they should, they don't like themselves. And when they don't like themselves, how can they let others know them, how can they believe that others love them?"

Restive Achievers

Most of the men I talked with seemed to have abandoned any romantic views they once had of their marriages. They had seen their marital relationships turn from being in love to loving each other. They had come to realize how marriages change, mature, and lose their original charm and intensity to become partnerships in living. The observation of one man reflected this pragmatic realization:

"It's much riskier to express tenderness and dependence when you're married because you can't interrupt the relationship. Therefore, if your needs are not satisfied or your tenderness is rejected—if the other person doesn't accept what you have to give, or doesn't fulfill your needs, or doesn't understand you and rejects you—there is very little you can do about it. You are rejected and yet you can't abandon the boat you share with the other person."

These men, being very competent and doing interesting work, I felt had learned to examine their jobs for rewards as important as those they received at home—for a sense of work accomplished, objectives achieved, and something built. In their jobs these men sought and often found their creativity, a limited transcendence, and sometimes a way of spending their lives without being aware of too much pain.

Why do they devote so much of their lives to their work and so little, comparatively speaking, to achieving awareness in living and experiencing their feelings? It seems to me there are two reasons:

1. While we train men to become "doers," to succeed in the world of action, we do not train them to explore the world of emotions. As the testimony of executives and their wives in this article has shown, feelings are to be controlled, channeled, repressed, or forced into acceptable molds. Not only are men told how they should express their feelings—big boys don't cry—they are also told what and how to feel.

In the world of business, feelings are considered a nuisance that must be coped with or a possible threat to the effective functioning of the organization. The research of Chris Argyris has amply demonstrated the practice in organizations of denial of feelings and the maneuvers of people in those organizations to avoid situations where emotions might come into play and to smooth over situations where deep emotions have been expressed.[2]

The result is a vicious circle: the less we recognize our feelings and learn to relate to them, the less chance we have of developing skills to deal with them—our own and others'. And the less skillful we are, the more threatening feelings seem, and the more vehemently we deny them or avoid dealing with them.

Men's lack of skill in relating to their feelings exists not only in the business milieu but also in the home environment and in their personal relationships. If you are skeptical of this, stop and think for a moment about the means that you have available to express your tenderness or your needs or your joy to your wife, children, and close friends. Then reflect on your ability to express richly these feelings to people who are close to you.

2. One always falls frustratingly short of gaining complete satisfaction of one's needs. In our personal relationships, we often search, in vain, for somebody who will fulfill us completely, give us all we need.

On the other hand, at work we can complete something—reach our goal. (The goal being usually modest, achieving it may give us a sense of being let down—and perhaps we will feel the shadow of death that is present whenever anything ends.) For an instant we touched our work and it gave us a good feeling because we had created it.

So, men seem to learn to enjoy their achievements as they have learned to give up the search for "everything" in a relationship. Their more or less meaningful world of companionship and work is enough for them.

It should be kept in mind that executives are people with high achievement needs, and one of their characteristics is the desire to measure accurately and unambiguously the extent of their achievement. This is not difficult in the world of action, but indications of achievement in the unstable world of feelings and personal relationships are hard to perceive and measure.

It Begins At Home

As long as the individual perceives the culture as standing ready to condemn him if he acts or feels in a manner counter to its norms and expectations, it is unlikely that he will explore new forms of behavior. So in trying to modify behavior we have to be concerned not only with the "unfreezing" and rearranging of the individual's value system and the development of courage and skills to implement his new values, but also with the unfreezing of his environment.

The environment at home, it seems to me, is already ripe for change. The younger generation insists on the validity of the emotions and wants to become "together" (a great cliché expressing the idea of a better balance of action and feeling, reason and sentiment, objectivity and fantasy). The home is the best place today for a member of the older generation to try exploring the world of feeling actively.

The next time you return home from work and see your son, stop for a second and try to get in touch with what you feel at that moment on seeing him. The feeling may be intense or weak, positive or negative, familiar or unfamiliar, painful or joyful—or to your surprise, you may seem to feel very little. Take it easy and try to stay with your feeling and experience it as fully as you can. Keep exploring your feelings at home and start trying new behavior there.

The executive is a man relating to the world. When he walks into his place of work, he is still himself. He should remain true to himself not only by doing but also by opening up his feelings as he lives.

Tomorrow, when you walk into your office and meet those you work with, take a minute to establish contact with your feelings or lack of feelings toward them. Try to become aware of how alive (or how numb) you are. If you discover that you have strong positive or negative feelings toward the men and women you work with, then ask yourself the simple questions that follow:

- "What am I doing with these feelings?"
- "What do I want to do with them?"
- "How do they affect my living as a man and therefore as a man/executive?"

In suggesting this, I am not talking to you as an executive, a manager, or a businessman. I am talking to you as a man—a man who can become a fuller, more alive human being.

The development of an ability to get in touch with and deal with one's own feelings and those of others, and to express one's feelings as richly as one wishes, is functional for any man and essential to an executive who has constant contact with other individuals.

But being able to get more closely in contact with our own feelings and engaging more deeply in experiencing and expressing them is not something that we can make happen overnight. It requires the development of difficult skills—skills to contact our feelings without being overwhelmed or scared by them, skills to cope with the feelings once we get in touch with them, skills to express our feelings when we want to, and skills to experience and express those feelings richly and confidently.

I have no method to offer for proceeding down this road, but I have found some suggestions of the Gestalt therapists very helpful in the process of owning more of one's self.[3]

The principal purpose of this article is not to offer solutions but to present the landscape of an exciting territory to explore: the land of our own feelings. I could try to incite you to explore this territory by saying that, when you know it better, you will have become a better administrator or a better father and husband. But nobody can guarantee you that.

All I can tell you is that in the process of getting more in touch with our own feelings, we become more fully ourselves and we live more fully the only thing we have, our own lives.

References

1. *Client-Centered Therapy* (Boston, Houghton Mifflin, 1951), p. 503.

2. See, for example, his article, "Interpersonal Barriers to Decision Making," HBR March-April 1966, p. 84.

3. Try the exercises suggested by Frederick Perls, Ralph F. Hefferline, and Paul Goodman in *Gestalt Therapy* (New York, Dell, 1951).

Middle-Aged Working Class Americans at Home: Changing Expectations of Manhood

By Arthur B. Shostak

While our attention in industrial academics remains essentially focused on traditional topics, especially conventional sources of workplace discontent (such as Hertzberg's "factors of hygiene" and "motivators"), we overlook a wide range of highly-personal afterhours issues that might possibly explain much of what is otherwise endlessly bewildering. Clearly the workplace alone, whatever its turbulent agenda of autonomy, pace, pride, and reward grievances, does not entirely explain the volatile temperament, virulent racism, uncertain hawkishness, anti-boss mythology, and political cynicism that corrodes the entire blue-collar way of life. Nor will it suffice to add here such otherwise undeniably helpful explanatory variables as urban anomie, inter-racial jealousy, Vietnam malaise, income redistribution hostilities, and the outside-of-work life.

Rather, to more fully understand the middle-aged Caucasian manual worker we must follow him home, and assess the exceedingly private realities of his after-work private life. We must look into the living room of the Bunkers for revealing clues to Archie's better-known record as a public figure. Indeed, we must go farther and assess his kitchen-table cronnism, his bedroom relationships, and his

Occupational Mental Health, #3 (1972), pp. 2-7. Copyright by the Center for Occupational Mental Health of New York Hospital—Cornell University Medical Center.

inter-generational patterns—if we are to truly enlarge and enrich our grasp of the world that Archie defines for himself.

While the data available here leave much to be desired in scope, currency, and sophistication, they are suggestive—and deeply disturbing—where the contemporary performance of the middle-aged worker as husband, lover, father, and son is concerned: In a mutually-reinforcing fashion the typical blue-collarite appears to do poorly in all four regards. Indeed, the laughter provoked by the stumbling ineptitude of "Archie Bunker" and "Ralph Kramden" probably gives way shortly to grimaces in blue-collar homes once reality replaces the false and placating imagery of TV situation comedy.

As an index of the blue-collar male's performance as a husband, for example, there is disturbing 1967 evidence that suggests blue-collar marriages may fail more often than do those in any other class: The wives of low-income blue-collarites were grimly judged by researchers in 1960 to be "perhaps the most deprived of all women." And a 1962 NORC study of happiness concluded that marital unhappiness was far more characteristic of blue-collar than of any other kind of family.[1]

Middle-aged blue-collar women appear especially aggrieved, and many are not reluctant to make their plight known. Sociologist Mirra Komarovsky's rare 1963 research into the matter found "it was the women who nag, demand, and complain. The husband's action is largely a *reaction* to women's demands, and one which often takes the form of leaving the field of battle."[2] The women conveyed to Komarovsky's interviewers their deep and unmet yearnings for items regularly denied to them in blue-collar marriages, or for reassurance, for loving counsel, for real appreciation, for personal encouragement, and for generous sharing for its own sake. Many of these women lacked confidence that they would soon experience any of this with their inept blue-collar husbands, albeit they laid these expectations daily on them and were daily disappointed in them.

Unsatisfying as husbands many of these blue-collar men may prove little more satisfactory as lovers. To be sure, almost to a man they enjoy putting-on the rest of society with their jovial support of a flattering blue-collar stereotype: As celebrated in barroom lore and in the movie bedroom athletics of Jack Nicholson in "Five Easy Pieces" this identifies them with a hairy-chested, perpetually-horny, foul-mouthed, wolf-whistling, lip-smacking, deep-scratching virile son-of-a-bitch who drives the biggest rig or works the toughest construction job, and hails of course, from Marlboro Country.[3]

Unfortunately the women who ought to know best, not the office birds the hardhats easily intimidate during the downtown lunch hour, but the illusionless hard-nosed middle-aged women back in the neighborhood, are represented by my blue-collar friends as thinking the Marlboro thing is "alotta bull." Where the would-be "Stanley Kowalski" represents himself as virile, sexy, and exciting, certain of his blue-collar women often represent him instead as simple-minded, unimaginative, and sexually bigoted.

Their reputed judgment, and not his, earns support from the only published research known here to me. Indeed, the rare findings in 1965 of sociologist Lee Rainwater give no comfort at all to the self-deceiving "candystore cowboys" from Marlboro Country. For one thing, Rainwater's survey research found that blue-collarites actually engaged in sexual relations no more or less often than any other social class. Second, he found an apparent decline in interest in erotic love as one went down the "social class" scale (not surprising as such love calls on a creative artistry not readily had from a socialization process grounded in adulterated pornography, disinterested whores and a good girl/bad girl perspective). Third, his research found that, as in so many other areas of their lives together, the sex relations of blue-collarites were severely limited. Many of the taboo-ridden men fearfully and rigidly restricted themselves to unimaginative and mechanical bedroom behavior.[4] Given the combination of this bedroom boorishness with the male's tongue-tied inability to speak graciously of desire, love, or lust, it is no wonder that various middle-aged blue-collar women gravitate toward bitchiness, booze, and house-shaking brawls.

The record does not seem any brighter in the matter of parental and filial role performance, albeit data are even scarcer than beforehand.

The point can perhaps best be made by speculating about the impact of the Vietnam War on blue-collar father-son relations, as this impact seems to expose role strains more sharply than anything else at present.

Historically blue-collar fathers were accustomed to sending their sons off to a war they both believed in, were confident could be won, and were quietly certain warranted the highest possible sacrifice. A good number of the fathers felt certain their sons would return still more mature, somewhat more patriotic, and far more manly than ever before. Most recently, from 1966 through 1968, blue-collar fathers struggled to maintain this time-honored posture, as had their fathers before them in 1941-1945, and their grandfathers in 1914-1917. Then, in 1968, the bottom began to fall out. Since that time, according to certain of my Drexel University blue-collar student friends, working-class fathers have been bewildered and painfully confused in this matter. Many of their wives and sons have begun to expect new attitudes and behaviors from them, less hawkish and more dovish than anything the old man or grandpa ever knew in simpler times past.

Today an unknown, but possibly large number of blue-collar sons continue to stream home from 'Nam disillusioned with memories of the old man's backing for a "stinking, lousy war that can't be won, should never have been fought, and wasn't ever worth a single loss of life."[5] Many of their fathers find it hard to argue otherwise, and scratch their heads wondering what their entire role in this rotten mess should have been. To compound the discrediting of the parents, many blue-collar sons are bringing back from 'Nam a souvenir in the form of drug addiction that nobody bargained on before Johnny went off to war. And still other blue-collar fathers are left with the tragedy of a son's death in combat, and a question unknown in comparable working class families in 1914-17 or 1941-45: "How can a man believe that his son's life has been wasted?"[6]

Role expectations of middle-aged blue-collarites as fathers and sons appear confused and unsettled in other areas as well. That the father's authority as a conduct-enforcer may have been eroded almost beyond significance is suggested by the apparent inability of blue-collar fathers to halt the spreading tide of dangerous drug experimentation in once "clean" blue-collar neighborhoods. Far less ominous, but no less revealing is the enormous "generation gap," symbolized in the difference between the expensive mod attire and long-hair of blue-collar youngsters and the Sears Roebuck casuals and short-hair of their fathers. More separates the generations than choice of costume; the "old man" knows he is being asked to "get with it" in more ways than one.

As for the dissatisfaction that blue-collar men know from the contradictory expectations set for them as responsible adults, the literature appears entirely barren on the subject. Provocative, however, is the bitterness that seems to separate the generations in many workplaces: The 35-year olds often show no more sympathy for the pension improvement mania of the 60-year olds than do the dollar-hungry kids among the new 20-year old workforce entrants. Another index of role confusion, with hostility again substituting for empathetic support, may be found in the muted panic of certain 35-year old blue-collar sons who feel helpless to stem the surrender to creeping senility of their retired 66-year old fathers. That this constitutes an ominous forewarning of the fate that may await the blue-collar son himself after his own forced retirement is probably not lost on many wrathful younger men.

No less easy to take are intensified pleas from oldsters for human contact, for daily reminders that someone somewhere still cares. As these pleas appear to be addressed to this generation of 35-year old blue-collar sons in an unprecedented way, you have all the ingredients here necessary for one "hell of a crunch" in role expectations and role performance.

Changing Role Expectations: One Possible Explanation.

Why the considerable discontent that may mark and mar the private lives of middle-aged male blue-collarites? Apparently because many of their blue-collar wives, children, and oldsters have come to ask new things of them they are presently not equal to.

Historically the role expectation of manual workers as husbands, lovers, fathers, and sons was dominated by a *machismo* model of rugged containment, virile braggadocio, authoritarian rule, and proper role-distance. The sons of successive generations of manual worker fathers grew up expecting to be very much like the old man: As husbands, they would "keep 'em in their place." As lovers, they would "get all they could." As fathers, they would damn well "teach them their place." And in later years as adult sons, they would give the

Table 1: Historic Role Analysis: Middle-Age Male Blue-Collarite

Roles	Content	Rule	Expectation	Consequence
Husband	Rugged Containment	"Keep 'em in their place"	Little friendship	"Cold Fish"
Lover	Virile Braggadocio	"Get all you can"	Little ecstasy	Lousy Lover
Father	Authoritarian Rule	"Teach 'em their place"	Little intimacy	Crummy Father
Son	Proper Role-distance	Keep up appearances	Little affect	Callous Son

old 'uns only what they must to keep up appearances in the extended family and the old neighborhood.

From one generation to another role expectations here changed very little. Large numbers of blue-collar men came to expect little friendship in marriage, little ecstasy in (marital) sex relations, little intimacy in fatherhood, and little affect in arms-length dealings with their "old man." Instead they clung to a culturally-induced image of themselves as "real men," not fops or dandies. And, as everyone felt obliged to agree, real men were hard, undemonstrative "sons-of-bitches."

What appears to have been happening unexpectedly over the past 25 years has been the collapse of the agreement—far fewer blue-collar women and children may now believe the middle-aged "real man" is reasonably a cold fish, a lousy lover, a crummy father, and a callous son. Instead, several substantial cultural changes seem to have undermined the old role expectations, and written a new part for the 35-year old blue-collar "walk-on" that he finds even more difficult to play.

An unknown, but possibly significant number of his women, for example, may have been deeply influenced by their unprecedented freedom from "excess fertility" made possible by oral contraceptives. Freed now for the first time from the specter of back-alley abortions and unwanted pregnancies these blue-collar women (albeit self-punishing in their Catholic sense of guilt) are at liberty to expand their expectations regarding the frequency and character of love-making in a way never possible for their vulnerable mothers and birth-weary grandmothers. They are also likely to expect more now of their working-class men as fathers, for this time the decision to conceive, bear, and rear the children can be shared and made with deliberation. As the resultant families appear smaller in every age-cohort it seems reasonable to speculate that pill-using blue-collar women expect more companionship, more emotional support, and more personal attention from their men than was true in earlier colder times. An unknown number are possibly not reluctant as well to use small family size to underwrite their threat to pick up and walk out—if and when their new psychological expectations of their blue-collar men are finally hopelessly disappointed.

As husbands, lovers, and fathers, then, the middle-aged male may be more significantly influenced by the Pill than is often recognized—from outside his household, that is.

Another major source of liberation came 30 years ago when blue-collar women first shook off the shackles and blinders of home and neighborhood for employment in the distant and comparatively cosmopolitan war plant. Remaining ever since in the work force in large (and growing) numbers many seem to have put two very special expectations on their middle-aged men: First, some newly measure them against the engaging, flattering, or sexy "tail-chasing" dudes they meet at work, or that the girl at the next machine never tires of boasting about. Second, an unknown number may newly expect their blue-collar men to contribute to a warmer, more loving home than either working-class spouse may have ever known in their childhood. For especially in this way can such working blue-collar women relieve their considerable anxieties about the cost to their own family of their absence from home; only in this way can they reduce the chill in their bones left by a day spent in the factory or office, the rush-hour restaurant and subway, and the frenzied pre-supper supermarket and liquor store.

Such women may be less class-ethnocentric and far less culturally insulated than at any other time before in recent blue-collar history. The nunnery-like walls of the old blue-collar neighborhood have collapsed, as they explore a dynamic world that their tradition-bound mothers and grandmothers feared, despised, and shunned. What is even more, for the past 20 years the most powerful cultural equalizer we have ever known has been coming into their world: TV afternoon "soap operas," evening situation comedies, late-hour talk shows, and nightly feature movies—along with the "Galloping Gourmet" and Dr. Joyce Brothers—all stir restless, ever-more-liberated, ever-more-animated and independent women to expect more from their blue-collar men.

The situation appears much the same where the worker's children and his own 60-year old parents are involved. The kids often go to more cosmopolitan schools than he did, seem to grow up faster, join a more homogenized teen culture than any he knew, and may learn more from the TV than he ever did from the radio: From popular TV shows like "Bachelor Father," and "My Three Sons," many blue-collar youngsters are regularly exposed to new models of middle-aged parenthood more sensitive, more communicative, and more constructively emotional than what they may be used to in their own households. Captivated by silverscreen shadows, many may look warily to the "old man" for new attitudes and behaviors—and, often a fan of the very same TV shows, the "old man" is probably aware of their new expectations of him.

Still more troublesome may be the situation where the worker's own parents are concerned. Through the end of the Second World War the role expectation here drew mainly on two contradictory sources—animosity between, and residential co-existence of the fathers and sons. Blue-collar oldsters, who, in the 1940's, had sacrificed in order to prepare their children to be better off than themselves, often envied their grown-up 35-year old offspring for fulfilling this very goal, and incidentally leaving the parents behind. In a similarly para- doxical way their persistence in residential co-existence with their envied offspring was based more in the heartless absence of really re- spectable housing alternatives than in happy free choice. Three gen- erations, and sometimes even four, crowded in together in the 1930's and '40's to make the best of a poor possibility; all worked hard at containing both their inconvenience and their thinly veiled mutual animosity.

Never ever satisfactory for either oldsters or their grown-up sons this blue-collar pattern essentially began to collapse with the acute housing shortage of the late 1940's. Indeed, the jerry-built homes that Levitt and others threw up simply excluded the costly addition of rooms earmarked for an entire generation of 60-year old grand- parents—and effectively evicted them. Had the nation at the time— or even since—filled the gap with millions of low cost housing units for the elderly, the grownup sons of the evictees might not have felt their "mean" desertion of their parents so sharply. But the nation did not come through. Instead, many middle-aged blue-collar sons now find themselves saddled both with guilt feelings and related financial assistance bills as large as anything previously known in working-class retirement, and possibly larger yet. As well, many "evicted" oldsters, often left behind in an increasingly unfriendly and decaying urban ethnic slum, now seem to want their blue-collar sons to unhesitatingly provide weekly phone calls, frequent letters, holiday visits, and the feeling that they are welcomed any time in the household of the son as a privileged visitor. In all, this understandably puts a new and try- ing strain on the financially-stripped, emotionally-contained, and "tough-minded" blue-collarite.

To pull this together then, I have been suggesting that certain post-World War II developments may have had a critical and strik- ingly overlooked consequence: This seems to involve a sweeping re- definition of what is reasonably expected of the 35-year old blue-collar male by his loved ones and himself. Where once he was free to be a moody, enigmatic, and male-centric "cowboy," he is now expected to aspire otherwise: He is to strive for expressive, open, and genial affability with most; deep-coursing personal intimacy with some; and erotic artfulness with a very select few. To his dismay this goes *far beyond* his old genial ability to bowl every Thursday with the boys. It entails *more* than a heart-to-heart talk once a year at Thanksgiving with his younger brother in for a weekend from distant St. Louis. And it sails *right past* his proven ability to guiltily sleep with the divorcée in the next building the summer when the "old lady" lingered on unfairly at the vacation seashore boarding house. Expectations here appear much richer than any of this, and seem to go far in explaining the painful transitional situation today of the middle-aged worker caught between his own outmoded role definition and the redefinition put to him in the 1970's.

Closing Thoughts

It is just possible that a special combination of personal needs and cultural dynamics may help large numbers of middle-aged blue-collar men successfully redefine and remake their manhood in the 1970's. Many seem to sense that the 19th century model of the hard-hearted and hard-headed "Old Man" no longer fits. As Komarovsky and Rainwater have demonstrated with their field research, some of the most progressive of the blue-collar families strain to live now as other than muffled human beings, disappointed in life and in one another. They set their faces firmly against the frailties that corrode the working class, against the self-deprecation, the joylessness, and the substitution of dogma and taboo for excitement and engagement with life. These pace-setting modernists promote instead a blue-collar type of renunciation of psychic repression; they urge their Marlboro Country neighbor more by their example than by any direct pressure—to find within himself the courage to seek authentic love and a genuinely bolder life.[7]

So, in many ways we seem poised in the early years of the 1970's for what could prove the most significant and substantial changes in the standard of manhood ever known in the American working class. The not-always amusing gap between traditionalist "Archie Bunker" and his "meathead" of a modern son-in-law may yet be reduced, with "Archie" gaining more than he now cares to admit from the younger man's more daring and emotionally richer model of blue-collar life.

It remains possible, of course, that little of this will finally eventuate. The 19th century *machismo* model that Archie clings to is fed by four hard-to-acknowledge role-related fears that could not course deeper: Archie is wary of finding himself overtly dominated by thoroughly liberated blue-collar women now running wild. He has real doubts about his ability (or that of any man's) to satisfy the sexual appetite of (blue-collar) females if erotically liberated. He fears a cruel abandonment by callous offspring now completely free of filial obligations. And he is reluctant to honestly appraise the costs to himself of filial opportunities he himself let slip by. For these reasons he is prone to resist changes in his unhappy roles as husband, lover, father, and son—and to rely instead on the balm of commercial distractions (media, sports, fringe politics, etc.). Above all, the 35-year old blue-collarite can feel himself in the pain-deflecting mainstream in choosing *not* to ask fundamental questions about his private life, and in declining to attempt fundamental changes in a passive, painful life.

One thing, however, remains certain: As the problems the middle-aged blue-collarite has in redefining his manhood and humanity are clearly *ours* as well the outcome here is hardly a matter of distant academic concern. We share his discontent, not alone in its reverberations in the workplace, neighborhood, and ballot box, but in our private worlds as well—for if the blue-collar class is especially hard-pressed by private life woes no social class in America has escaped this challenge or especially well met it to date. Thanks to the Freudian "trickle-down" in conversational patter, the (uneven) services of all-

Table 2: Explanatory Model

Public Role Linkage	Private Role Discontents	Role Expectations Traditional	Role Expectations Transitional	Source of New Role Definitions
Restlessness	Unhappy marriages	Impersonal Stolidness	Warm Companionship	BC Women as Change-Agents
Envy	Disappointing Sexual Relationships	Marlboro Sexist	Sensitive Co-Explorer	(Workers; "Pill Users"; Cosmopolitans)
Escape-seeking	Dissolution of Paternal Self-Esteem	"Law and Order"	Pal and Modernist	Vietnam
	Exaggeration of Filial Burden	"Hot" Ethnic Fidelity	"Cool" Mass Society Affect	Loss of 3-Generation Households

too-few mental health professionals, and the (comparably superficial) balm of affluence, some of the "have" classes "look better"—but may feel equally as bad. Archie is hardly alone in his confusion about where to turn or what to do—for having swallowed "the whole thing."

Alongside of Archie, then, taking up our ready professional skills and our uneven, still fuzzy humanistic vision, we have a prime obligation and a rare opportunity to assist in the awesome emergence in the 1970's of a new (blue-collar) man.

References

1. The data are footnoted in "Blue-Collar Families," Chapter 8, pp. 139-140, in Shostak, A. *Blue-Collar Life*, Random House, New York 1969. Especially helpful here is Hurvitz, Nathan, "Marital Strain in the Blue-Collar Family," pp. 92-109, in Shostak, A. and Gomberg, W. (Eds.). *Blue-Collar World*, Prentice-Hall, Englewood Cliffs, New Jersey, 1964.

2. Komarovsky, Mirra. *Blue-Collar Marriage*, Random House, New York, 1964, pp. 199, passim.

3. For rare analysis of blue-collar stereotypes, see Haslam, Gerald W. "The Language of the Oil Fields," *Etc.*, June, 1967, pp. 191-197.

4. Rainwater, Lee. *Family Design: Marital Sexuality, Family Size, and Contraception*, Aldine, Chicago, 1965, pp. 68, 100-101. See also Rainwater, Lee, *et al. Workingman's Wife*, Oceana, New York, 1959.

5. See in this connection, "Five Vietnam Veterans," in Boyd, Malcolm. *My Fellow Americans*, Holt, Rinehart, and Winston, New York, 1970, pp. 173-218.

6. Coles, Robert. "The 'Common' Man," *Philadelphia Evening Bulletin*, June 6, 1971, p. 3. See also his new book, *The Middle Americans*, Little, Brown, Boston, 1971. Helpful as well is Boyd, Malcolm. *My Fellow Americans, op. cit.* and Anon. "Returning Heroes Get the Cold Shoulder," *Business Week*, July 31, 1971, pp. 46-48.

7. See here an unpublished paper of mine available on request, "Blue Collar Private Discontents and Pop Culture: Reforms for the Plight of Every Man."

Cultural Contradictions and Sex Roles:
The Masculine Case[1]

By Mirra Komarovsky

*I*n a rapidly changing society, normative malintegration is commonly assumed to lead to an experience of strain. Earlier research (Komarovsky 1946) on cultural contradictions and the feminine sex role showed that women at an eastern college suffered uncertainty and insecurity because the norms for occupational and academic success conflicted with norms for the traditional feminine role. A replication (Wallin 1950) at a western university reported agreement in the questionnaire data, but the interview material led the investigator to conclude that the problem was less important to the women than the earlier study had suggested. However, Wallin pointed out that, in his replication, the respondents were oriented to marriage, while the Komarovsky study had included an appreciable number of women oriented to careers. This finding tended to support the view that women who were satisfied with the traditional female role would show less strain when confronted with contrary expectations than women who hoped to have both a rewarding career and a rewarding marriage.

Men are also confronted with contradictory expectations. For example, the traditional norm of male intellectual superiority conflicts with a newer norm of intellectual companionship between the sexes.

American Journal of Sociology, 78 #4 (January, 1973), pp. 873-884.
Copyright © 1973 by University of Chicago Press. Reprinted by permission of University of Chicago Press and the author.

This research investigated the extent of masculine strain experienced by 62 college males randomly selected from the senior class of an Ivy League male college. The study included a variety of status relationships, but the results reported here deal with intellectual relationships with female friends and attitudes toward working wives.

Methods

Each of the 62 respondents contributed a minimum of three two-hour interviews and also completed a set of five schedules and two psychological tests, the California Personality Inventory and the Gough Adjective Check List. The psychological tests were interpreted by a clinical psychologist. The 13-page interview guide probed for data on actual role performance, ideal role expectations and limits of tolerance, personal preferences, perception of role partner's ideal expectations, and relevant attitudes of significant others. Direct questions on strains came only at the end of this sequence. Extensive use was made of quasi-projective tests in the form of brief episodes. The total response rate of the original sample ($N = 79$) was 78%.

Intellectual Relationships With Female Friends

When fewer women attended college, the norm of male intellectual superiority might have had some validation in experience. But today college women are more rigorously selected than men in terms of high school academic performance (*Princeton Alumni Weekly* 1971). Nevertheless, social norms internalized in early childhood are resistant to change. The first question for this research was, How many men would show insecurity or strain in their intellectual relationships with women when confronted with both bright women and the traditional norm of male superiority?

The Troubled Third

Of the 53 men for whom the data were available (six did not date, three could not be classified reliably), 30% reported that intellectual insecurity or strain with dates was a past or current problem. This number included men who, having experienced stress, sought to avoid it by finding dates who posed no intellectual threat. The following excerpts from interviews illustrate the views of this troubled third:

I enjoy talking to more intelligent girls, but I have no desire for a deep relationship with them. I guess I still believe that the man should be more intelligent.

*   *   *

I may be a little frightened of a man who is superior to me in some field of knowledge, but if a girl knows more than I do, I resent her.

*   *   *

Once I was seeing a philosophy major, and we got along quite well. We shared a similar outlook on life, and while we had some divergent opinions, I seemed better able to document my position. One day, by chance, I heard her discussing with another girl an aspect of Kant that just the night before she described to me as obscure and confusing. But now she was explaining it to a girl so clearly and matter-of-factly that I felt sort of hurt and foolish. Perhaps it was immature of me to react this way.

The mode of strain exemplified by these men might be termed "a socially structured scarcity of resources for role fulfillment." Apart from the ever-present problem of lack of time and energy, some social roles are intrinsically more difficult to fulfill, given the state of technical skills, the inherent risks, or other scarcities of facilities. The strain of a doctor called upon to treat a disease for which modern medicine has no cure is another case in point.

Selective dating and avoidance of superior women solved the problem for some troubled youths, but this offered no solution for six respondents who yearned for intellectual companionship with women but dreaded the risk of invidious comparisons. The newly emerging norm of intellectual companionship with women creates a mode of strain akin to one Merton and Barber (1963) termed "sociological ambivalence." Universalistic values tend to replace sex-linked desiderata among some male undergraduates who now value originality and intelligence in female as well as in male associates. The conflict arises when, at the same time, the norm of masculine intellectual superiority has not been relinquished, as exemplified in the following case: "I am beginning to feel," remarked one senior about his current girl friend, "that she is not bright enough. She never says anything that would make me sit up and say, 'Ah, that's interesting!' I want a girl who has some defined crystal of her own personality and does not merely echo my thoughts." He recently met a girl who fascinated him with her quick and perceptive intelligence but this new girl made him feel "nervous and humble."

The problem of this youth is to seek the rewards of valued attributes in a woman without arousing in himself feelings of inferiority. It may be argued that in a competitive society this conflict tends to characterize encounters with males as well. Nonetheless, if similar problems exist between two males, the utility curve is shaped distinctively by the norm of male intellectual superiority because mere equality with a woman may be defined as a defeat or a violation of a role prescription.

The Adjusted Majority

The 37 students who said that intellectual relationships with dates were not a problem represented a variety of types. Eleven men felt superior to their female friends. In two or three cases, the relationships were judged equalitarian with strong emphasis on the rewards of intellectual companionship. In contrast, several men—and their dates—had little interest in intellectual concerns. In a few instances the severity of other problems overwhelmed this one. Finally, some eight men were happily adjusted despite the acknowledged intellectual superiority of their women friends. What makes for accommodation to this still deviant pattern?

In seven of the eight cases, the female friend had some weakness which offset her intellectual competence, such as emotional dependence, instability, or a plain appearance, giving the man a compensating advantage. A bright, studious, but relatively unattractive girl may be acceptable to a man who is not as certain of his ability to win a sexually desirable female as he is of his mental ability. In only one of the eight cases the respondent admitted that his steady girl was "more independent and less emotional, actually a little smarter than I. But she doesn't make me feel like a dunce." Her superiority was tolerable because she provided a supportive relationship which he needed and could accept with only mild, if any, emotional discomfort.

Another factor which may account for the finding that 70% of the sample reported no strain is the fact that intellectual qualities are no longer considered unfeminine and that the imperative of male superiority is giving way to the ideal of companionship between equals. This interpretation is supported by responses to two standard questions and by the qualitative materials of the interviews. A schedule testing beliefs on 16 psychological sex differences asked whether the reasoning ability of men is greater than that of women.

Only 34% of the respondents "agreed" or "agreed somewhat," while 20% were "uncertain"; almost half "disagreed" or "disagreed somewhat."

Another question was put to all 62 respondents: what are for you personally the three or four most desirable characteristics in a woman (man) who is to be close to you? Of all the traits men desired in a woman, 33% were in the "intellectual" cluster, in contrast with 44% of such traits if the friend were male. The fact that the sex difference was not larger seems significant. The major difference in traits desired in male and female intimates (apart from sexual attractiveness and love) was the relative importance of "social amenities and appearance" for women.

The qualitative data amply document the fact that the majority of the respondents ideally hoped to share their intellectual interests with their female as well as their male friends. To be sure, what men occasionally meant by intellectual rapport with women was having an appreciative listener: "I wouldn't go out," declared one senior, "with any girl who wasn't sharp and perceptive enough to catch an intellectual subtlety." But for the majority a "meaningful relationship" with a woman included also a true intellectual interchange and sharing. As one senior put it, "A guy leaving a movie with his date expects her to make a stimulating comment of her own and not merely echo his ideas." Another man wanted a date with whom he could "discuss things that guys talk about," and still a third man exclaimed: "What I love about this girl is that she is on my level, that I can never speak over her head."

It is this ideal of intellectual companionship with women, we suggest, that may explain the relative adjustment of the men in this sphere. As long as the expectation of male superiority persisted, anything near equality on the part of the woman carried the threatening message to the men: "I am not the intellectually *superior* male I am expected to be." But when the ideal of intellectual companionship between equals replaces the expectation of male superiority, the pressure upon the man eases and changes. Now he need only reassure himself that he is not inferior to his date, rather than that he is markedly superior to her. Once the expectation of clear superiority is relinquished, varieties of relationships may be accommodated. Given a generally similar intellectual level, comparative evaluations are blurred by different interests, by complementary strengths and weaknesses, and occasionally by rationalizations ("she studies harder") and other devices.

One final explanation remains to be considered. May the intellectual self-confidence of the majority be attributed in part to women's readiness to play down their intellectual abilities? That such behavior occurs is attested by a number of studies (Komarovsky 1946; Wallin 1950).

When respondents were asked to comment upon a projective story about a girl "playing dumb" on dates, the great majority expressed indignation at such "dishonest," "condescending" behavior. But some three or four found the behavior praiseworthy. As one senior put it, "Her intentions were good; she wanted to make the guy feel important."

Although we did not interview the female friends of our respondents, a few studies indicate that such playing down of intellectual ability by women is less common today than in the 1940s. Questionnaires filled out in 1970 and 1971 by 87 members of two undergraduate classes in sociology at an eastern women's college duplicated earlier studies by Wallin (1950) and Komarovsky (1946). The 1970 class was a course on the family, and the 1971 class probably recruited a relatively high proportion of feminists. Table 1 indicates that the occasional muting of intellectual competence by women

Table 1: Readiness of Women to Play Down Intellectual Abilities (%)

	Wallin 1950 (N = 163)	Sociology Class 1970* (N = 33)	Advanced Sociology Class 1971* (N = 55)
When on dates how often have you pretended to be intellectually inferior to the man?			
Very often, often, or several times.	32	21	15
Once or twice.	26	36	30
Never.	42	43	55
In general, do you have any hesitation about revealing your equality or superiority to men in intellectual competence?			
Have considerable or some hesitation.	35	21	13
Very little hesitation.	39	33	32
None at all.	26	46	55

* Mirra Komarovsky, unpublished study.

may have played some role in the adjustment of the men, but it would appear to be a minor and decreasing role.

The hypothesis that the emerging ideal of intellectual companionship serves as a buffer against male strain needs a test which includes (as our study did not) some index of intellectual ability as well as indices of norms and of strain. Of the 27 men who disagreed with the proposition that the reasoning ability of men is greater than that of women, only five reported intellectual insecurity with women, whereas of the 34 men who believed in masculine superiority or were uncertain, nine experienced strain. Most troubled were the 12 men who were "uncertain"; four of them were insecure with women. Case analyses suggest that the interplay between a man's experience, personality, and beliefs is complex. For example, one traditional man, having confessed feelings of intellectual insecurity on dates, clung all the more tenaciously to the belief in superior male reasoning ability.

Some men took the "liberal" position on sex differences as a matter of principle. Of the nine black students, eight rejected the belief in male superiority, perhaps because they opposed group comparisons in intelligence. Again, in some cases, the direction of the causal relation was the reverse of the one we posited: men who felt in fact intellectually superior were hospitable to the "liberal" ideology. In view of these complexities, our suggestive results as to the positive association between egalitarian norms and the absence of strain remain to be tested in larger samples.

Attitudes Toward Future Wives' Occupational Roles

The ethos on the campus of this study clearly demanded that men pay at least lip service to liberal attitudes toward working wives. If the initial responses to structured questions were accepted as final, the majority would have been described as quite feminist in ideology. But further probing revealed qualifications which occasionally almost negated the original response. For example, an affirmative answer to a proposition, "It is appropriate for a mother of a preschool child to take a fulltime job," was, upon further questioning, conditioned by such restrictions as "provided, of course, that the home was run smoothly, the children did not suffer, and the wife's job did not interfere with her husband's career." The interview provided an opportunity to get an assessment of normative expectations, ideal and operative, as well as of actual preferences. The classification of attitudes to be presented in this report is based on the total interview. Preferences reported here assume that a wife's paycheck will not be an economic necessity. The overwhelming majority were confident that their own earnings would be adequate to support the family. Throughout the discussion of working, only two or three men mentioned the temptation of a second paycheck.

Four types of response to the question of wives' working may be identified. The "traditionalists," 24% of the men, said outright that they intended to marry women who would find sufficient fulfillment in domestic, civic, and cultural pursuits without ever seeking outside jobs. "Pseudofeminists," 16% of the men, favored having their wives work, at least when the question was at a high level of abstraction, but their approval was hedged with qualifications that no woman could meet.

The third and dominant response included almost half (48%) of the respondents. These men took a "modified traditionalist" position which favored a sequential pattern: work, withdrawal from work for child rearing, and eventual return to work. They varied as to the timing of these stages and as to the aid they were prepared to give their wives with domestic and child-rearing functions. The majority saw no substitute for the mother during her child's preschool years. Even the mother of school-age children, were she to work, should preferably be at home when the children return from school. Though they were willing to aid their wives in varying degrees, they frequently excluded specific tasks, for instance, "not the laundry," "not the cleaning," "not the diapers," and so on. Many hoped that they would be "able to assist" their wives by hiring maids. The greater the importance of the wife's work, the more willing they were to help her. (One senior, however, would help only if his wife's work were "peripheral," that is, not as important to her as her home.)

The last, the "feminist" type, was the smallest, only 7% of the total. These men were willing to modify their own roles significantly to facilitate their future wives' careers. Some recommended a symmetrical allocation of tasks—"as long as it is not a complete reversal of roles." In the remaining 5% of the cases, marriage was so remote that the respondents were reluctant to venture any views on this matter.

The foregoing summary of types of male attitudes toward working wives fails to reveal the tangled web of contradictory values and

sentiments associated with these attitudes. We shall presently illustrate a variety of inconsistencies. But underlying them is one basic
problem. The ideological support for the belief in sharp sex role
differentiation in marriage has weakened, but the belief itself has
not been relinquished. Increasing skepticism about the innate character of psychological sex differences and some convergence in the
ideas of masculinity and femininity (see McKee and Sherriffs 1957,
1959) have created a strain toward consistency. The more similar the
perceptions of male and female personalities (see Kammeyer 1964),
the more universalistic must be the principles of evaluation applied
to both sexes. "If you could make three changes in the personality of
the girl friend who is currently closest to you, what would they be?"
we asked the seniors. Universalistic values were reflected in the following, as in many other responses: "I would like her to be able to set
a goal for herself and strive to achieve it. I don't like to see people
slacking off." Earlier cross-sex association in childhood and early
adolescence (see Udry 1966) has raised male expectation of enjoying
an emotional and intellectual companionship with women. These
expectations, however, coexist with the deeply rooted norm that the
husband should be the superior achiever in the occupational world
and the wife, the primary child rearer. One manifestation of this
basic dilemma is the familiar conflict between a value and a preference. "It is only fair," declared one senior, "to let a woman do her
own thing, if she wants a career. Personally, though, I would want
my wife at home."

More interesting are the ambivalent attitudes manifested toward
both the full-time homemaker and the career wife. The image of
each contained both attractive and repellent traits. Deprecating remarks about housewifery were not uncommon, even among men with
traditional views of women's roles. A conservative senior declared,
"A woman who works is more interesting than a housewife." "If I
were a woman," remarked another senior, "I would want a career.
It must be boring sitting around the house doing the same thing day
in, day out. I don't have much respect for the type of woman whom I
see doing the detergent commercials on TV."

But the low esteem attached by some of the men to full-time
homemaking coexisted with other sentiments and convictions which
required just such a pattern for one's wife. For example, asked about
the disadvantages of being a woman, one senior replied, "Life ends
at 40. The woman raised her children and all that remains is garden
clubs and that sort of thing—unless, of course, she has a profession."

In another part of the interview, this young man explained that he enjoyed shyness in a girl and detested aggressive and ambitious women. He could never be attracted to a career woman. It is no exaggeration to conclude that this man could not countenance in a woman who was to be his wife the qualities that he himself felt were necessary for a fulfilling middle age.

A similar mode of contradiction, incidentally, was also disclosed by some seniors with regard to women's majors in college. "There are no 'unfeminine' majors," declared one senior: "I admire a girl who is premed or prelaw." But the universalistic yardstick which led this senior to sanction and admire professional goals for women did not extend to the means for their attainment, as he unwittingly revealed in another part of the interview. Questioned about examples of "unfeminine" behavior, this senior answered: "Excessive grade consciousness." If a premed man, anxious about admission to a good medical school, should go to see a professor about a C in chemistry, this senior would understand although he would disapprove of such preoccupation with grades. But in a woman premed he would find such behavior "positively obnoxious."

If the image of the full-time homemaker contained some alienating features, the main threat of a career wife was that of occupational rivalry, as illustrated in the following excerpt from the interviews. A senior speaks:

> I believe that it is good for mothers to return to fulltime work when the children are grown, provided the work is important and worthwhile. Otherwise, housewives get hung up with tranquilizers, because they have no outlet for their abilities. . . . Of course, it may be difficult if a wife becomes successful in her own right. A woman should want her husband's success more than she should want hers. Her work shouldn't interfere with or hurt his career in any way. He should not sacrifice his career to hers. For example, if he is transferred, his wife should follow—and not vice versa.

In sum, work for married women with grown children is approved by this young man, provided that the occupation is of some importance. But such an occupation is precisely one which carries a threat to the husband's pride.

The expectation that the husband should be the superior achiever appears still to be deeply rooted. Even equality in achievement of husband and wife is interpreted as a defeat for the man. The prospect of occupational rivalry with one's wife seems intolerable to contemplate. "My girl friend often beats me in tennis," explained one senior.

"Now, losing the game doesn't worry me. It in no way reduces my manhood. But being in a lower position than a woman in a job would hurt my self-esteem."

Another student, having declared his full support for equal opportunities for women in the occupational world, added a qualification: "A woman should not be in a position of firing an employee. It is an unpleasant thing to do. Besides, it is unfair to the man who is to be fired. He may be a very poor employee, but he is still a human being and it may be just compounding his unhappiness to be fired by a woman."

In sum, the right of an able woman to a career of her choice, the admiration for women who measure up in terms of the dominant values of our society, the lure but also the threat that such women present, the low status attached to housewifery but the conviction that there is no substitute for the mother's care of young children, the deeply internalized norm of male occupational superiority pitted against the principle of equal opportunity irrespective of sex—these are some of the revealed inconsistencies.

Such ambivalences on the part of college men are bound to exacerbate role conflicts in women. The latter must sense that even the men who pay lip service to the creativity of child rearing and domesticity reserve their admiration (if occasionally tinged with ambivalence) for women achievers who measure up in terms of the dominant values of our society. It is becoming increasingly difficult to maintain a system of values for women only (Komarovsky 1953).

Nevertheless, to infer from this account of male inconsistencies that this is an area of great stress for them would be a mistake. It is not. By and large, the respondents assumed that the women's "career and marriage" issue was solved by the sequential pattern of withdrawal and return to work. If this doomed women to second-class citizenship in the occupational world, the outcome was consistent with the conviction that the husband should be the superior achiever.

Men who momentarily worried about the fate of able women found moral anchorage in their conviction that today no satisfactory alternative to the mother's care of young children can be found. Many respondents expressed their willingness to help with child care and household duties. Similarly, many hoped to spend more time with their own children than their fathers had spent with them. But such domestic participation was defined as assistance to the wife who was to carry the major responsibility. Only two or three of the men approved a symmetrical, rather than a complementary, allocation of domestic and occupational roles. An articulate senior sums up the dominant view:

> I would not want to marry a woman whose only goal is to become a housewife. This type of women would not have enough bounce and zest in her. I don't think a girl has much imagination if she just wants to settle down and raise a family from the very beginning. Moreover, I want an independent girl, one who has her own interests and does not always have to depend on me for stimulation and diversion. However, when we both agree to have children, my wife must be the one to raise them. She'll have to forfeit her freedom for the children. I believe that, when a woman wants a child, she must also accept the full responsibility of child care.

When he was asked why it was necessarily the woman who had to be fully responsible for the children, he replied:

> Biology makes equality impossible. Besides, the person I'll marry will want the child and will want to care for the child. Ideally, I would hope I'm not forcing her to assume responsibility for raising the children. I would hope that this is her desire and that it is the happiest thing she can do. After we have children, it will be her career that will end, while mine will support us. I believe that women should have equal opportunities in business and the professions, but I still insist that a woman who is a mother should devote herself entirely to her children.

The low emotional salience of the issue of working wives may also be attributed to another factor. The female partners of our respondents, at this particular stage of life, did not, with a few exceptions, force the men to confront their inconsistencies. Apparently enough women will freely make the traditional-for-women adjustments—whether scaling down their own ambitions or in other ways acknowledging the prior claims of the man's career. This judgment is supported by the results of two studies of female undergraduates done on the same campus in 1943 and 1971 (table 2). The big shift in postcollege preferences since 1943 was in the decline of women undergraduates who opted for full-time homemaking and volunteer activities. In 1971, the majority chose the sequential pattern, involving withdrawal from employment for child rearing. The proportion of committed career women who hope to return to work soon after childbirth has remained constant among freshmen and sophomores.

If women's attitudes have not changed more radically in the past 30 years, it is no doubt because society has failed to provide effective supports for the woman who wishes to integrate family life, parenthood, and work on much the same terms as men. Such an option will

not become available as long as the care of young children is regarded as the responsibility solely of the mother. In the absence of
adequate child care centers, an acceptance of a symmetrical division
of domestic and work responsibilities, or other facilitating social arrangements, the attitudes of the majority of undergraduates reflect
their decision to make some kind of workable adjustment to the status
quo, if not a heroic struggle to change it.

Summary

Role conflicts in women have been amply documented in numerous studies. The problem underlying this study was to ascertain
whether recent social changes and consequent malintegration with
regard to sex roles have created stressful repercussions for men as
well as for women. In a randomly selected sample of 62 male seniors
in an eastern Ivy League college, nearly one-third experienced some
anxiety over their perceived failure to live up to the norm of masculine intellectual superiority. This stressful minority suffered from
two modes of role strain: scarcity of resources for role performance
and ambivalence. The absence of strain in the majority may be ex-

Table 2: College Women's Attitudes toward Work and Family Patterns (%)

	Random Sample of Sophomore Class at Women's Liberal Arts College 1943 (N = 78)	Class in Introductory Sociology, Same College 1971 (N = 44)
Assume that you will marry and that your husband will make enough money so that you will not have to work unless you want to. Under these circumstances, would you prefer:		
1. Not to work at all, or stop after childbirth and decide later whether to go back.	50	18
2. To quit working after the birth of a child but definitely to go back to work.	30	62
3. To continue working with a minimum of interruption for childbearing.	20	20

Source.—Mirra Komarovsky, unpublished studies.

plained by a changed role definition. Specifically, the normative expectation of male intellectual superiority appears to be giving way on the campus of our study to the ideal of intellectual companionship between equals. Attitudes toward working wives abounded in ambivalences and inconsistencies. The ideological supports for the traditional sex role differentiation in marriage are weakening, but the emotional allegiance to the modified traditional pattern is still strong. These inconsistencies did not generate a high degree of stress, partly, no doubt, because future roles do not require an immediate realistic confrontation. In addition, there is no gainsaying the conclusion that human beings can tolerate a high degree of inconsistency as long as it does not conflict with their self-interest.

References

1. This research is supported by NIMH grant MH 14618. Associated with the author in the interviewing were Mr. Wesley Fisher, Mrs. Susanne Riveles, and Dr. Edith Sanders. Mrs. Ana Silbert analyzed the scored psychological tests and prepared the 62 psychological profiles. The field work was done in 1969-70.

Kammeyer, Kenneth. 1964 "The Feminine Role: Analysis of Attitude Consistency." *Journal of Marriage and the Family* 26 (August): 295-305.
Komarovsky, Mirra. 1946 "Cultural Contradictions and Sex Roles." *American Journal of Sociology* 52 (November): 182-89.
_____. 1953 *Women in the Modern World, Their Education and Their Dilemmas.* Boston: Little, Brown.
McKee, John P., and Alex C. Sherriffs. 1957 "The Differential Evaluation of Males and Females." *Journal of Personality* 25 (March): 356-63.
_____. 1959 "Men's and Women's Beliefs, Ideals, and Self-Concepts." *American Journal of Sociology* 64 (4): 356-63.
Merton, Robert K., and Elinor Barber. 1963 "Sociological Ambivalence." In *Sociological Theory, Values and Socio-cultural Change,* edited by E. A. Tiryakian. Glencoe, Ill.: Free Press.
Princeton Alumni Weekly, February 23, 1971, p. 7.
Udry, J. Richard. 1966 *The Social Context of Marriage.* Philadelphia: Lippincott.
Wallin, Paul. 1950 "Cultural Contradictions and Sex Roles: A Repeat Study." *American Sociological Review* 15 (April): 288-93.

Part Three

MASCULINITY / FEMININITY

*A*s should be evident at this point in the book, it is impossible
to discuss the concept of masculinity without reference to femininity.
For in the social construction of these definitions, the assumed
characteristics of one have been derived as reactions to the assumed
characteristics of the other. Thus, "being feminine" means not
"being masculine," and "being a man" is defined in response to
perceived female inadequacies.

Joffe discusses social processes operating in the nursery school
which help to reinforce the cultural definitions of masculinity and
femininity. Balswick and Peek look, in detail, at one of the major
defining characteristics of the masculine/feminine dichotomy, i.e., the
absence of emotional expressiveness in males.

Gordon and Shankweiler demonstrate the ways in which the male's
culturally defined power over females, as a part of the definition of
masculinity, extends itself into the realm of sexual performance, and
the manner in which this power distribution is supported by the
authors' marriage manuals. The marriage bed is seen as the male's
"home court," whereas women are seen more as reluctant participants,
needing the male's assertiveness to spark their innate lack of
sexual response.

Both Mailer and Korda discuss dimensions of the male ego and its
importance in learning to establish a personal sense of masculinity.
Mailer, perhaps America's best known chauvinist, defines relationships
between the sexes in terms of a combination of the biological
(the child-bearing potential of women) and the social (the male right
to dominate). Korda, on the other hand, attempts to show how
male chauvinism, that necessary ingredient in the traditional concept
of masculinity, is a way of insuring the perpetuation of male
dominance—not only in the social world, but also in our minds.

Sex Role Socialization and the Nursery School: As the Twig Is Bent

By Carole Joffe

A problem within the field of socialization that has recently been raised with new urgency is that of sex roles. This renewed attention is coming about in large part as a result of issues currently being raised in the women's movement; a central theme of the analysis emanating from this movement is that American society demands the socialization of both men and women into fixed sex roles, at great cost to the individual needs of members of both sexes.[1] This socialization is said to be omnipresent, literally starting at birth with the proverbial blue or pink blanket that is given to the newborn infant. But although the women's movement has caused a new focus of attention on this phenomenon of early socialization into sex roles, certain social scientists have long given attention to the same topic. Kagan, for example, has noted the significance of the differential treatment ac corded male and female infants and the effects this has for the child's subsequent sexual identity (Kagan, 1964). But although it is generally agreed—both by those who adopt a critical stance and those who seemingly are interested only in description—that sex role socialization is everywhere, certain institutions are of course more crucial in the cultural transmission of these expectations than others. Two of the most centrally involved agencies in the sex role socialization of the young (and hence two that are currently undergoing severe

Journal of Marriage and the Family, August, 1971, pp. 467-475.
Copyright © 1971 by the National Council on Family Relations.

criticism) are the family and the schools. In this paper, I will discuss experiences of children with respect to socialization in one of these institutions, the nursery school. For many children, it must be remembered, their attendance at nursery school marks their first institutional contact outside of the home and thus this kind of school can justifiably be seen as performing critical socialization functions. In my analysis, I will attempt to demonstrate both what the school seemed to be demanding from the children in terms of sex-appropriate behavior and how the children themselves conceived of their sex role obligations. It is hoped that a close look at the quality of sex role socialization received by persons in their first institutional setting will not only enlighten us further as to the meaning of sex roles in American society, but also, for those of us committed to some form of change in the institutions "serving" our children, such a study might suggest some policy implications.

Before proceeding to my own findings, I will briefly comment on work done to date on nursery schools and socialization into sex roles. Although no major work appears to have been done specifically on nursery schools as *facilitators* of sex roles,[2] there has recently been some attention paid to other educational institutions as they relate to sex roles. Several writers have noted the significance of the fact that at the elementary school level most teachers are women and the effects this has on children of both sexes in terms of classroom behavior (Clausen, 1968; Sexton, 1969; and Silberman, 1970:153). Because elementary schools are geared, in Silberman's terms, toward "docility," this reinforces cultural messages about appropriate behavior little girls are already receiving elsewhere; in the case of little boys, this sets up a conflict in view of their masculine-oriented socialization, with the result being that some claim the only boys who do well academically at the elementary level are those who become "feminized" (Sexton, 1969). But other than noting these two quite important facts—that most primary school teachers are female and that the school situation puts forth an ideal of docility among students—there does not yet seem to be accounts of the *specific* ways in which schools foster socialization into sex roles. Certainly there remains a gap in studies of the nursery school in this respect. In this paper I will attempt to pinpoint various structural and ideological features of the preschool and discuss their relationship to this kind of socialization.

A final digression before I begin will be to make clear my own bias about the issues under discussion, "sex roles." The treatment of sex roles in this paper will be substantially different from that it receives in much of the socialization literature. A common feature of the huge number of studies of pre-school children and sex roles is that, for the most part, what constitutes appropriate "sex roles" is not made problematic (Oetzel, 1966). The researchers had a preconceived idea of what the content was of proper masculine and feminine roles and tested the children to see how well they conformed to these already existing measures.[3] Thus, for the majority of the researchers in this field there is a seeming acceptance of prevailing ideas about maleness and femaleness: children who don't comply with these concepts become listed as deviants. I will be taking the position that the idea of sex roles, particularly for children of preschool age,[4] is a very problematic matter and should be approached with great skepticism. The reader should understand that what I will be discussing is how the school fosters contemporary *notions* of sex roles and what use of these notions the children make; I will not be speaking to the issue of what the "real" differences between the sexes are and therefore what would constitute legitimate sex role socialization. An additional bias that will occur is that in spite of the lack of discussion about what sex role socialization *should* be, I nevertheless will take a position against what I feel are the most blatantly damaging forms of sex role socialization that are the norm now, e.g. channeling members of each sex into restrictive roles that limit the life options and behavioral choices of each. Accordingly, in this paper the "good" school will be one in which these attempts at imposing such damaging sex roles are minimized while the "bad" school is one that encourages them.

A Case Study of One School

In this section I will report on two separate periods of participant observation at a nursery school. Although at the time of the observations, I was also concerned with other factors, I will deal here exclusively with the findings on sex role socialization and how the children themselves conceived sex roles. I will first briefly describe the research situation.

The first series of observations were made over a period of two months in the spring of 1970 at a parent-nursery school in the California Bay area. (A parent-nursery is one in which in addition to two full-time teachers, each of the participating parents takes a weekly shift at the school). The school I observed was affiliated with the Bay

Area Unified School District, although some of the parents paid tuition. There were regular teacher-parent meetings and parents were encouraged to help formulate school policy.

The children observed in the first series consisted of 22 students, 9 male and 13 female, ranging in age from three and one half to four and one half. The school was racially mixed, consisting of about an equal number of children of white professionals and graduate students, and black children from lower-income families. The second set of observations, carried out in January-February 1971, were of the afternoon session of the same parent-nursery and thus a certain proportion of children who had been seen in 1970 were seen again almost a year later. Twelve of the children observed during the afternoon session had initially been seen earlier and nine had not been seen before. In this second group, there were fourteen females and 9 males, with the percentage of black children being somewhat higher than it had been in the previous group. The age of the children in this group covered a span from four and one half to five.

Each of the classes had two full-time female teachers (one black and one white in each case) and each day from three to five mothers would also work. (The school claimed to be eager to have fathers of the children participate as well, but except on a very sporadic basis e.g., emergencies, fathers did not participate during the periods of my observation). As an observer, I essentially took the role of a participating mother (*albeit* without a child), e.g. watching children in the yard, reading stories, etc. Additionally I attended parent-teacher meetings and had opportunities for extended conversations with both teachers and parents.

I will start my discussion by offering in broadest terms an analysis of the school's overall "attitude" toward sex roles and the type of behavior that seemed to be expected from the children in this respect. In each of the sessions I observed, there was an extremely positive (in terms of the value bias mentioned earlier) orientation toward sex roles: there was no active move to impose any notion of correct sex-typed behavior and most impressive, there was a very relaxed response towards those children who violated normal expectations about members of their sex group. Clearly then, the school I happened to study represents a negative case in terms of any attempt to show dramatically how damaging socialization takes place in nursery schools. I do believe, however, that such a school is useful to us in spite of its atypical quality. First, in examining such a "good" school, it is possible to draw out policy implications for other less liberated institutions; second, as we shall see, even in a school committed to avoiding imposition of these notions of sex stereotypes, inadvertent sex role socialization does take place.

Starting a discussion of sexism in the schools in reverse, therefore, I will list the features of this particular school that are indicative of its policy of not stressing sex roles. Most generally, there was no structural indication of two separate categories of persons: bathrooms, for example, were not segregated and often children of both sexes would use them together; all activities in the school program were officially open to both sexes and the participation of all children in some of the more traditionally sex-typed activities, e.g., cooking, washing dishes, was consistently sought. Most striking, as I already indicated, was the tolerance shown those children whose behavior showed varying degrees of sex identity "confusion," e.g., those children who with regularity would dress as members of the opposite sex and assume the "wrong" sexual identity in games of "house." The school's most notable example of what elsewhere might be termed as "deviation" is K., a Polynesian male who frequently dresses in women's clothes, occasionally wears his hair in "feminine" fashion, and in games with the other children, often assumes female identities, e.g., "sister." As I will discuss later, there is a certain variation among the children as to how K's behavior is received. In terms of his teachers, however, I was struck by the firm commitment on their part to non-interference. Both felt it would be unnecessarily upsetting, both to K. and to the other children, to in any way make an issue out of this behavior. Rather, in discussion with the observer, one of the teachers stressed she viewed such behavior as very creative and emotionally beneficial—"it's good for him to have all kinds of experiences." Both of the teachers referred to K.'s foreign background as a factor which although not entirely understood by them, might conceivably explain some of his actions, particularly his mode of dancing. In sum, then, the vocabulary of motive which seemed to be in operation among the teachers with regard to sex identity "switching" was that it was common to many children; it was in many aspects a "creative" exercise; it would only be to all the children's detriment to have such action questioned by adults.

What I have described above is the school's official position towards socialization into sex roles; I believe that this represents a type of institution, on an imaginary continuum of "bad" to "good" schools, that is in ideological terms, impressively free from sexism. However special attention must be paid to the variety of ways in which inadvertently sex-typing nonetheless does take place in this school. The first point to make is that while it is easy to gain a sense of the teachers' policies, one cannot as readily presume to summarize all the parents' attitudes. As mentioned, this school is one in which parents work a weekly shift, and thus each child was exposed regularly to approximately 18-20 different women. To understand all the subtle influences playing on the children, ideally one would have to determine systematically each of these women's own attitudes about sex roles. While observations suggest that most of the mothers shared the teachers' assumptions in this regard,[5] there nevertheless occurred a series of small events in the interactions between children and mothers (and teachers to a certain degree as well) that in a cumulative sense, could well serve to convey to the children messages about sex role expectations. One of these seemingly trivial events, which occurred fairly often, was the acknowledgment of the girls' clothing:

> M. walks in wearing a dress she has not worn before. One of the mothers says to her, "M., what a pretty little lady you are today."

One might argue of course that admiring a child is not the same thing as sex-typing her. Nor will I suggest that admiring a child is "wrong" and should not be done. I have to point out however, that in some cases this unavoidably has consequences for the child's self-conception in terms of gender identity. Not surprisingly, the pattern I noted of compliment giving was that girls were more frequently admired than boys, and moreover, girls received more compliments on days they wore dresses rather than pants. It is outside the context of this paper to consider how ultimately damaging it is for little girls to be responded to in this way. I use this example simply as an illustration of one of the variety of subtle ways in which girls (and boys) get cues as to differing social images of femininity and masculinity. An event which I observed far less frequently and which conceivably served the same function of transmitting cues as to appropriate sex-linked behavior was the occasional positive reinforcement a boy would get when he ably defended himself against a physical attack, as in the following:

> L. and N. have been arguing over the use of a spade. N. pushes L. and L. responds by delivering a solid punch to N.'s chest. A mother who has witnessed the scene says to the observer (within hearing of L.), "Did you see the punch L. gave N.? He really can take care of himself like a man."

Because there is such strong prohibition against fighting in the school, in fact incidents like the above do not occur very often, i.e., the fights occur, but most mothers would not give this kind of approval; but whether in this context or in others, e.g., physical strength contests in games, there no doubt occurs a differential amount of reinforcement accorded to boys' physical exploits than to girls, with the obvious implications for self-concept of each sex.

A far more clear-cut example of damaging sex roles socialization offered to the children can be found in the quality of the media in use at the nursery school. There is clearly a lag—perhaps somewhat unavoidable—between the school's own attitudes toward sex-typing and quality of materials in use at the school. The storybooks read to the children, the songs taught them at music time, the traditional children's games they play[6]—all contain to a great extent vestiges of dominant social attitudes towards sex roles. For example, a mother leading the children in singing, sings a form of the typical children's song in which each character performs a different task:

And the daddy went spank-spank, and the mommy went "shh-shhh" (The song concerned a child who had made noise on a bus).

The lag, as I stated, is at least in part unavoidable. There simply do not yet exist adequate nursery school materials, especially story books, that are free from sex-typing.[7] An accommodation made by some who work in the nursery school is simply to alter the stories as they read them to the children (Denzin, 1970:20). But until the same serious effort is made to prepare materials that are free from sexism that recently appears to have at least been started in the preparation of non-racist material the quality of children's objects in the school (here I am including both literature and toys) will remain a major source of traditional sex roles.

Another factor in the school that I see as inadvertently contributing to an unfortunate notion of sex specialization is the fact of all the adults working there are female. Again, this is something that the school itself does not prefer, but rather it is a reflection both of the structure of the individual families participating in the school program and the job arrangements that presumably most of the children's fathers have. We can speculate about several possible consequences the all-female population of the school might have on the children's conceptions of sex roles. I would suspect that for these children the main consequence of this situation is the realization that in our society child care is exclusively a female function. For these children, their school life is essentially a continuation of their family life, in that they predominately spend time with their mothers (and other females) and rarely see adult males. In a situation such as this, one can readily understand the source of the pattern noted by many—that children make clear distinctions between expectations from father and mother (Henry, 1963:127-146).[8] For those working toward a future in which there is meaningful sharing of childcare responsibilities between parents, the lack of men at institutions such as these makes the attainment of such a goal more difficult. We can see how the unfortunate cycle of American family life as it now exists is maintained in these and similar situations: fathers due both to their own lifelong socialization which has stressed extensive interest in nurturant functions as "unmasculine" and to their actual job situations, don't participate in this type of school; mothers even with cooperative schools such as these, don't have careers and spend far more time with the child than the father does. The father takes on a somewhat formal role, seen largely as the final authority in disciplinary matters (Henry, 1963)—thus it ultimately becomes somewhat a bizarre deal to all concerned (father, mother, child) to have men take an active role in childcare.

Awareness of Sex Roles among Children

In this section I will discuss how the children seemed to respond to the school's efforts to minimize sex role imperatives and to the inadvertent socialization that nonetheless took place. The reader should bear in mind that how children perceived sex roles is of course not simply a function of what transpired in the school; their own families as well as numerous other influences in their lives (e.g., television)[9] also contributed to this awareness.

On the basis of my observations, I conclude that while all the children in the school had correct knowledge about their gender identity[10], there did not exist among these children any patterned recognition of appropriate sex roles; the children as a group did not perceive certain activities or modes of behavior as being the exclusive property of one sex. Although there were no systematic efforts to articulate the rights of males and females, on a more sporadic basis the simple fact of sex difference itself would occasionally be invoked as an attempt at behavior control. Under the appropriate conditions, e.g., an encounter between persons of both sexes, one of the parties would sometimes point to the fact of sex difference as an attempt to justify his actions. The following is an example of this use of sex categories as an "ideology of control."

C. and two other girls are playing on top of a large structure in the yard. A. (male) comes over and C. screams, "girls only!" to which A. screams back, "No, boys only!"

I think the above example is especially useful because it emphasizes the reciprocal (and thus in a sense, meaningless) character of these exchanges. "Girls only" is immediately countered with "boys only" and thus one can reasonably conclude that to neither of the contestants is there any serious belief in an essential "male" or "female" aspect of the structure under dispute. Rather, sex differences are called forth as a seeming last-ditch effort to impose one's will when the other means of behavior control typically in use have not been effective.

Further evidence that this use of sex categories is quite unrelated to the child's actual perception of sex-appropriate behavior can be found in the behavior of K., the boy who was mentioned earlier as often assuming the identity of a female. K., who elsewhere tampered with quite fundamental assumptions about proper "male" conduct, nonetheless used sex categories in the same way as mentioned in the previous case.

S. (female) is playing the guitar. K. comes over and asks her to let him play it. When she refuses, K. says, "that's for boys, not girls."

In general then the pattern is that the children will make reference to sex categories when there is a reason to do so (which usually means when a piece of property is under dispute). It should also be pointed out that this ideology was consistently quite unsuccessful; I never in fact saw a child yield to his or her opponent, simply because sex categories were cited, although other ideologies, e.g., the value of sharing, in similar situations sometimes do work. In sum, we might look at the use of sex as an ideology of control in childhood as a revealing caricature of the adult world and its usage of sex categories. Like these children, adults also invoke sex as a means of behavior control; the crucial differences are that among adults, the two categories are utilized in a patterned way (some would call it male supremacy) and both male and female adults—unlike these children—actually behave in accordance with this ideology.

The only other regular mention of sexual categories that I observed on the part of the children came in the reactions of some to the sex identity "switching" of K. and several others (in addition to K., I noted about five others—one male and four females—who also periodically assumed roles of the opposite sex[11]). For example, upon seeing K. dressed in feminine apparel, a typical comment would be, "Hey, that's for *girls*." However, neither K.'s nor any of the other children's violations of behavioral expectations in this matter ever became a major issue in the school for the remainder of the children (in large part, I believe, because of the low-keyed reaction of the adults in the school). Thus, for example, although in games of "house," the clear majority of the children chose identities consistent with their sex, there was minimal or no questioning of the fact that some of their playmates acted in the opposite way. So it might be concluded, therefore, that on a daily basis, a conscious awareness of different sexual categories were not a dominant theme in the life of this nursery school—although comparative studies suggest that the situation can be very different in other preschools (Greenwald, 1970).

Male and Female Subcultures

Although the children themselves did not articulate sex categories as a major factor in their school lives, I, as an observer, did nonetheless see very intriguing patterns of "sex differences" in terms of friendship networks and play preferences. A small percentage of the school population (4-5 girls and 3-4 boys) assumed on a fairly consistent basis elements of what might be called traditional sex roles. The boys in question established a form of "maculine subculture," playing mainly with each other out of doors, and while the girls I refer to did not establish as exclusive a social grouping, they did spend a great deal of time in an all-female society, and for the purposes of discussion, we can analyze their activities in terms of a female subculture. In this section, I will further describe each of these so-called subcultures, explore the possible relationships to male and female groupings found later in the life cycle, and finally ask what these subcultures reveal about the school itself as a facilitator of sex roles.

The group I have designated as the "male subculture" consisted of a friendship circle of three boys, L., P., and G., all black with the occasional participation of W., also black (the four made up the entire black male population of the school; thus, as will be discussed later, race is obviously a central factor here also). It is on the following grounds that I have chosen to see this group in this particular light: they, of all the other individuals or informal groups in the school, spend the greatest amount of time outdoors, mainly playing at very active games, e.g., racing tricycles; they are the most "aggressive" persons in the school, judged simply on the number of physical fights they have with one another and with outsiders; their speech, finally, contains frequent use of phrases of "toughness" that one does not as often hear from the other children, e.g., "don't mess with me," "I'm gonna take care of you," *etc.*

This group neither exclusively plays with each other nor only plays at active outdoor games. It is interesting to note though that in their intersections both with other children and with other activities, they typically bring their "masculine" mode of behaving to the new situation. In other words, when they play with other children, they immediately attempt to assert dominance; when at cooking sessions, they will demand to be first, take the other children's materials as they are needed, etc. Finally, perhaps most interesting—although least susceptible to generalization—is the quality of the friendship I noted between one member of this group, L., and a black female, V. I noted that on those occasions that L. breaks away from his friends and plays separately with V., they both refer to themselves as the "L. Brothers." In other words, this seems to suggest that V. is accepted as long as she literally becomes one of the boys. In general, then, I am arguing that both in terms of the large amount of time this group chooses to spend solely with each other and in view of their prevailing interpersonal style, it is useful for us to consider them as a masculine subculture within this school. (It should be stressed this decision is partially reached by comparing them with the other males in the school who show a far greater range of behavior).

The group I consider as the female subculture participated to a far greater extent in a variety of activities and associated with persons of both sexes outside of their immediate circle than did the males mentioned above. The reason I am treating them in this light is because of the very definite group identity that existed among them, and more particularly, because of the daily recurring rituals that took place within the group. These rituals included, for each member, the scheduling of individual actions in relation to the group and also the constant location of oneself in the group's very powerful social hierarchy. Although they often made forays to persons and events outside of the group, members seemed to return periodically to a "quorum" (e.g. at least two out of the five) both to report on themselves and to reaffirm their group ties. In the following example, we can see a case of the most simple function performed by this group, e.g., members' use of one another to orient themselves to school life:

M. arrives at school and immediately goes up to J. and H. (both also part of this circle) and says, "Hi, J., I'm playing with you today, right?" J. answers, "No, I'm playing with H. now."

It should thus be noted that although the group is looked to as a primary source of companionship, it is also the constant source of rejections, as persons trying to maintain places in the social hierarchy of the group drop low-status friends for higher ones. In the next example, there is a more dramatic case of a group member rejecting her companion of the moment (who actually is only a marginal member of the group), but then attempting some accommodation:

H. and A. (marginal member) are playing together in the yard. J. and a group of others call out to H. to join them at the swing. Although A. hasn't been invited, she goes along also and hangs around on the fringes of the group. H. looks at A. sheepishly and then says to the observer standing nearby, "Carole, would you play with A. for a while?"

The reader might very well question at this point my labeling as "female" this tendency toward exclusion and social ranking. As I have reported elsewhere (Joffe, 1970), in fact, nearly all the children engaged in it on occasion; the point is that it appeared to be only within this group that this behavior was so regularly tied to the same persons and hence had meaning in a *social group*.

Our next task is to see the resemblances that exist between the male and female subcultures I have described and those that occur elsewhere in the life cycle. In fact there does seem to be a quite uncanny resemblance between the behavior noted in the nursery school and that observed by Henry in his study of adolescent culture in a high school. Speaking of the differing nature of male and female friendship groups, Henry said:

Boys flock; girls seldom get together in groups above four . . . Boys are dependent on masculine solidarity . . . the emphasis is on masculine unity; in girls' cliques the purpose is to shut out other girls (Henry, 1963: 150).

In the behavior of these nursery school children we appear, then, to have a case of what might be seen as anticipatory socialization; the male and female subcultures noted in the nursery can almost be considered embryonic forms of those that occur in adolescence. What do these recurring patterns tell us about the "nature" of males and females, and more specifically, about the role of the varying institutions providing behavior settings for the children and the adolescents? The first point to be stressed is that for Henry, the difference in male and female culture he saw were directly traceable to the different social circumstances of each of the groups. The tendency of the boys to "flock" was attributable to the fact that the most significant activity in their lives was team sports; the girls' competitive behavior was basically due to a variety of circumstances which all converged to make the chief task of their lives an overwhelming necessity to be "popular," i.e., compete for boyfriends and other affirmations of their "femininity." Obviously in such a developed form, these same circumstances do not have meaning at the nursery school level: the boys do not play team sports and the girls are not involved with courtship. To understand why therefore such similar patterns were observed at the nursery, we have to first consider the possible salience of some factors not directly related to sex itself, but mainly we have to take fresh account of the strength of the sex role socialization that has already imposed itself by the age of five.

In explaining the particular cases of male and female subcultures that were observed in this school, we have also to consider the relevance of race as a contributing factor in the former and conceivably "idiosyncrasy" in the case of the latter. As mentioned, all participants in the male subculture were black, and counting the fourth occasional member, this group included the entire black male population of the school. While the question of the situation of black children in a nursery school such as this one deserves far more extended consideration, initial observations suggest that it is very likely that the group in question, in its impetus to establish a separate identity, was at the very least attempting to assert a mixture of both maleness *and* blackness. As for the idiosyncratic nature of the female subculture, it should be remembered that in a nursery school of a fairly small and stable population, one child can establish a tone that is picked up by others and becomes a part of school ritual. In the case of the exclusionary behavior that I mentioned as being a central aspect of the female society, I noted in the first set of observations that it appeared to be J., a member of this group, who initially introduced the particular vocabulary of exclusionary categories to the entire school. Thus, in its particular forms in this school, it might be reasonably said that this behavior was partially due to one or two children.

To the extent that the behavior I noted goes beyond the limits imposed by race and idiosyncrasy (and certainly in the case of the girls, I am convinced it does), and can be validly related to sex, I think that what we have is eloquent testimony not to the "differences" between the sexes, but to the degree to which these children have somehow picked up notions of how their society both expects and encourages separate cultures of male and female. Going beyond this initial fact of separateness, the differing characters of each of the societies suggests evidence of the very early age at which at least some children perceive the existence of differing assumptions of correct male and female behavior. Somehow, the little boys I observed "knew" that a comfortable[12] sense of self, in relation to masculine identity, was achieved by at least partial isolation from female things and by disproportionate aggressive behavior. Similarly the notion had somehow been conveyed to the little girls in question that one defines oneself by one's friends and if necessary, betrays one's friends. Seen in a certain way, the lack of female solidarity—which has both been put forward as a central theme of the analysis of many in Women's Liberation and which also has started to yield as a result of the exposure of many women to the Movement—can be seen to have taken root among some females at an astonishingly early age.

To end the discussion with an attempt to link these arguments to the nursery school, specifically to determine the extent to which the school itself is accountable for this situation—on the surface, the findings are puzzling. I have shown a "good" school—one that in no way appeared to consciously foster notions of sex stereotypes—and yet some of the children acted in traditional ways. This leads to two quite obvious conclusions: The first is that the nursery school does not exist in a vacuum; teachers, parents, and children all bring to the school experiences from outside settings, e.g., the family, which often have drastically different conceptions about sex roles. The second conclusion is simply that this study has actually learned very little about the *mechanisms* by which sex role expectations are transmitted. We have seen very clear-cut policies adopted in this school to minimize children's awareness of sexual differentiation, but we have seen their limitations. In terms of research strategy, it would seem that to understand completely how sex role socialization takes place, especially in such a good setting, participant observation is only the first of several necessary lines of action. A final comment pertinent to further research is to reiterate that the present paper represents a task only half-completed. It is imperative next to study a "bad" traditional school and examine its structural and ideological aspects as well as its students' responses. It is only by such a comparative approach that we will be able to gain a fuller sense of the role actually played by the school itself in the transmission of sexual stereotypes.

References

1. For example, Millett's statement: "Because of our social circumstances, male and female are really two cultures and their life experiences are utterly different . . . Implicit in all the gender identity development which takes place through childhood is the sum total of the parents', the peers', and the culture's notions of what is appropriate to each gender by way of temperament, character, interests, status, worth, gesture, and expression. Every moment of the child's life is a clue as to how he or she must think and behave to attain or satisfy the demands which gender places upon one." Millett, p. 31.

2. Although there has of course been a huge amount of work done on nursery school-age children in the area of "sex differences."

3. A pleasant exception to this genre is the work of Hartley (esp. 1959) who tested *conceptions* of sex roles among children, and found, among other things, that children of working mothers sex-typed fewer items than those of non-working mothers.

4. Even for those who take the fact of physiological differences between the sexes as a legitimate basis for the establishment of fixed sex roles, it is generally agreed that the physiological differences that exist between children of pre-school age are of minimal significance. See Hamburg, 1966.

5. One teacher told me of having at one point had some difficulty persuading some parents to accept the idea of non-segregated bathrooms.

6. To gain a sense of the extent to which sex-typing occurs in traditional children's games, see Iona and Peter Opie, *The Lore and Language of Children*, Oxford, Clarendon Press, 1959.

7. One might argue though that the situation is better in nursery schools than in elementary schools because so much of nursery school literature is concerned with animals and fantastic adventures, etc. It is in the elementary school textbooks that the worst offenses take place, with the very stereotyped notions of sex roles presented in the family scenes. A movement is currently starting in California to take legislative action against these textbooks.

8. One of Henry's most revealing findings was that although children made these sharp differentiations between role of mother and father, they in fact were very unhappy about them! "But many expressions of traditional masculinity and femininity are now felt by children to be intolerable." Henry, p. 137.

9. With regard to television, it must be mentioned that the favorite program of nearly all the children in the school I studied, "Sesame Street" although in other respects excellent—does very little, if anything, to challenge traditional conceptions of sex roles.

10. It is generally believed that children gain a sense of gender at approximately eighteen months. See Hamburg, 1966.

11. An additional tribute to the strength of sex role socialization in our society can be seen in the fact that in a non-threatening environment such as this, only 5-6 children regularly experimented with assuming opposite sexual roles.

12. I use this word "comfortable" of course in a very tentative way. I am trying to convey the idea that acting in such ways as they did clearly fulfilled some notion they had of "what made sense."

Clausen, John. 1968 *Socialization and Society*. Boston: Little, Brown.

Denzin, Norman K. 1970 "Children and their caretakers." Paper prepared for Social Science Research Council, Self-Concept Work Group of the "Learning and the Educational Process Subcommittee on Compensatory Education."

Greenwald, Susan. 1970 "A study of sex identity, self-imposed sex segregation and the peer group in pre-school children." Unpublished paper.

Hamburg, David and Donald T. Lunde. 1966 "Sex hormones in the development of sex differences in human behavior." In Eleanor Maccoby (ed.), *The Development of Sex Differences*. Stanford: Stanford University Press.

Hartley, Ruty. 1959 "Sex role concepts among elementary school age girls." *Marriage and Family Living*, 21:59-64.

Henry, Jules. 1963 *Culture Against Man*. New York: Vintage.

Joffe, Carole. 1970 "Taking young children seriously." Paper presented to the 1970 American Sociological Association meeting.

Kagan, Jerome. 1964 "The acquisition and significance of sex-typing." In M. Hoffman (ed.), *Review of Child Development Research*. New York: Russell Sage.

Millett, Kate. 1970 *Sexual Politics*. New York: Doubleday.

Oetzel, Roberta. 1966 "Annotated bibliography of research on sex differences." In Eleanor Maccoby (ed.), *Development of Sex Differences*. Stanford: Stanford University Press.

Seward, George and Robert E. Williamson. 1970 *Sex Roles in Changing Society*. New York: Random House.

Sexton, Patricia. 1969 *The Feminized Male*. New York: Vintage.

Silberman, Charles. 1970 *Crisis in the Classroom*. New York: Random House.

The Inexpressive Male:
A Tragedy of American Society

By Jack O. Balswick and Charles W. Peek

*T*he problem of what it means to be "male" and "female" is a problem which is faced and dealt with in its own way in every society. Through cross-cultural research one now surmises that culture rather than "nature" is the major influence in determining the temperamental differences between the sexes. It may be no accident that a woman, Margaret Mead, did the classic study demonstrating that temperamental differences between the sexes are explained very little in terms of innateness, but rather in terms of culture. In her book, *Sex and Temperament,* Mead reported on the differences in sex roles for three New Guinea societies. Using ethnocentric western standards in defining sex roles, she found that the ideal sex role for both the male and female was essentially "feminine" among the Arapesh, "masculine" among the Mundugumor, and "feminine" for the male and "masculine" for the female among the Tchambuli. Tchambuli represents a society that defines sex roles in a complete reversal of the traditional distinctions made between masculine and feminine roles in the United States.

It is the purpose of this paper to consider a particular temperament trait that often characterizes the male in American society. As sex role distinctions have developed in America, the male sex role, as compared to the female sex role, carries with it prescriptions which

The Family Coordinator, October, 1971, pp. 363-368.
Copyright © 1971 by the National Council on Family Relations.

encourage inexpressiveness. In some of its extreme contemporary forms, the inexpressive male has even come to be glorified as the epitome of a real man. This will be discussed later in the paper when two types of inexpressixe male are examined.

The Creation of the Inexpressive Male

Children, from the time they are born, both explicitly and implicitly are taught how to be a man or how to be a woman. While the girl is taught to act "feminine" and to desire "feminine" objects, the boy is taught how to be a man. In learning to be a man, the boy in American society comes to value expressions of masculinity and devalue expressions of femininity. Masculinity is expressed largely through physical courage, toughness, competitiveness, and aggressiveness, whereas femininity is, in contrast, expressed through gentleness, expressiveness, and responsiveness. When a young boy begins to express his emotions through crying, his parents are quick to assert, "You're a big boy and big boys don't cry." Parents often use the term, "he's all boy," in reference to their son, and by this term usually refer to behavior which is an expression of aggressiveness, getting into mischief, getting dirty, etc., but never use the term to denote behavior which is an expression of affection, tenderness, or emotion. What parents are really telling their son is that a real man does not show his emotions and if he is a real man he will not allow his emotions to be expressed. These outward expressions of emotion are viewed as a sign of femininity, and undesirable for a male.

Is it any wonder, then, that during the most emotional peak of a play or movie, when many in the audience have lumps in their throats and tears in their eyes, that the adolescent boy guffaws loudly or quickly suppresses any tears which may be threatening to emerge, thus demonstrating to the world that he is above such emotional feeling?

The Inexpressive Male as Single Man

At least two basic types of inexpressive male seem to result from this socialization process: the cowboy and the playboy. Manville (1969) has referred to the *cowboy type* in terms of a "John Wayne

Neurosis" which stresses the strong, silent, and two-fisted male as the 100 percent American he-man. For present purposes, it is especially in his relationship with women that the John Wayne neurosis is particularly significant in representing many American males. As portrayed by Wayne in any one of his many type-cast roles, the mark of a real man is that he does not show any tenderness or affection toward girls because his culturally-acquired male image dictates that such a show of emotions would be distinctly unmanly. If he does have anything to do with girls, it is on a "man-to-man" basis: the girl is treated roughly (but not sadistically), with little hint of gentleness or affection. As Manville puts it:

> The on-screen John Wayne doesn't feel comfortable around women. He does like them sometimes—God knows he's not *queer*. But at the right time and in the right place—which he chooses. And always with his car/ horse parked directly outside, in/on which he will ride away to his more important business back in Marlboro country. (1969, 111)

Alfred Auerback, a psychiatrist, has commented more directly (1970) on the cowboy type. He describes the American male's inexpressiveness with women as part of the "cowboy syndrome." He quite rightly states that "the cowboy in moving pictures has conveyed the image of the rugged 'he-man,' strong, resilient, resourceful, capable of coping with overwhelming odds. His attitude toward women is courteous but reserved." As the cowboy equally loved his girlfriend and his horse, so the present day American male loves his car or motorcycle and his girlfriend. Basic to both these descriptions is the notion that the cowboy does have feelings toward women but does not express them, since ironically such expression would conflict with his image of what a male is.

The *playboy* type has recently been epitomized in *Playboy* magazine and by James Bond. As with the cowboy type, he is resourceful and shrewd, and interacts with his girlfriend with a certain detachment which is expressed as "playing it cool." While Bond's relationship with women is more in terms of a Don Juan, he still treats women with an air of emotional detachment and independence similar to that of the cowboy. The playboy departs from the cowboy, however, in that he is also "non-feeling." Bond and the playboy he caricatures are in a sense "dead" inside. They have no emotional feelings toward women, while Wayne, although unwilling and perhaps unable to express them does have such feelings. Bond rejects women as women, treating them as consumer commodities; Wayne puts women on a pedestal. The playboy's relationship with women represents the culmination of Fromm's description of a marketing-oriented personality in which a person comes to see both himself and others as persons to be manipulated and exploited. Sexuality is reduced to a packageable consumption item which the playboy can handle because it demands no responsibility. The woman in the process becomes reduced to a playboy accessory. A successful "love affair" is one in which the bed was shared, but the playboy emerges having avoided personal involvement or a shared relationship with the woman.

The playboy, then, in part is the old cowboy in modern dress. Instead of the crude mannerisms of John Wayne, the playboy is a skilled manipulator of women, knowing when to turn the lights down, what music to play on the stereo, which drinks to serve, and what topics of conversation to pursue. The playboy, however, is not a perfect likeness; for, unlike the cowboy, he does not seem to care for the women from whom he withholds his emotions. Thus, the inexpressive male as a single man comes in two types: the inexpressive feeling man (the cowboy) and the inexpressive non-feeling man (the playboy).

The Inexpressive Male as a Married Man

When the inexpressive male marries, his inexpressiveness can become highly dysfunctional to his marital relationship *if* he continues to apply it across-the-board to all women, his wife included. The modern American family places a greater demand upon the marriage relationship than did the family of the past. In the typical marriage of 100 or even 50 years ago, the roles of both the husband and the wife were clearly defined as demanding, task-oriented functions. If the husband successfully performed the role of provider and protector of his wife and family and if the wife performed the role of homemaker and mother to her children, chances were the marriage was defined as successful, both from a personal and a societal point of view. The traditional task functions which in the past were performed by the husband and wife are today often taken care of by individuals and organizations outside the home. Concomitant with the decline of the task functions in marriage has been the increase in the importance of the companionship and affectionate function in marriage. As Blood and Wolfe (1960, 172) concluded in their study of the modern American marriage, "companionship has emerged as the most valued aspect of marriage today."

As American society has become increasingly mechanized and depersonalized, the family remains as one of the few social groups where what sociologists call the primary relationship has still managed to survive. As such, a greater and greater demand has been placed upon the modern family and especially the modern marriage to provide for affection and companionship. Indeed, it is highly plausible to explain the increased rate of divorce during the last 70 years, not in terms of a breakdown in marriage relationships, but instead, as resulting from the increased load which marriage has been asked to carry. When the husband and wife no longer find affection and companionship from their marriage relationship, they most likely question the wisdom of attempting to continue in their conjugal relationship. When affection is gone, the main reason for the marriage relationship disappears.

Thus, within the newly defined affectively-oriented marriage relationship male inexpressiveness toward *all* women, wife included, would be dysfunctional. But what may happen for many males is that through progressively more serious involvements with women (such as going steady, being pinned, engagement, and the honeymoon period of marriage), they begin to make some exceptions. That is, they may learn to be *situationally rather than totally inexpressive,* inexpressive toward women in most situations but not in all. As the child who learns a rule and then, through further experience, begins to understand the exceptions to it, many American males may pick up the principle of inexpressiveness toward women, discovering its exceptions as they become more and more experienced in the full range of man-woman relationships. Consequently, they may become more expressive toward their wives while remaining essentially inexpressive toward other women; they learn that the conjugal relationship is one situation that is an exception to the cultural requirement of male inexpressiveness. Thus, what was once a double *sexual* standard, where men had one standard of sexual conduct toward their fiancee or wife and another toward other women, may now be primarily a double *emotional* standard, where men learn to be expressive toward their fiancee or wife but remain inexpressive toward women in general.

To the extent that such situational inexpressiveness exists among males, it should be functional to the maintenance of the marriage relationship. Continued inexpressiveness by married males toward women other than their wives would seem to prohibit their forming meaningful relationships with these women. Such a situation would seem to be advantageous to preserving their marital relationships, since "promiscuous" expressiveness toward other women could easily threaten the stability of these companionship-oriented marital relationships. In short, the authors' suggestion is that situational inexpressiveness, in which male expressiveness is essentially limited to the marital relationship, may be one of the basic timbers shoring up many American marriages, especially if indications of increasing extramarital sexual relations are correct. In a sense, then, the consequences of situational inexpressiveness for marital relationships do not seem very different from those of prostitution down through the centuries, where prostitution provided for extramarital sex under circumstances which discouraged personal affection toward the female partner strong enough to undermine the marital relationship. In the case of the situationally inexpressive husband, his inexpressiveness in relations with women other than his wife may serve as a line of defense against the possible negative consequences of such involvement toward marital stability. By acting as the cowboy or playboy, therefore, the married male may effectively rob extramarital relationships of their expressiveness and thus preserve his marital relationship.

The inexpressiveness which the American male early acquires may be bothersome in that he has to partially unlearn it in order to effectively relate to his wife. However, if he is successful in partially unlearning it (or learning a few exceptions to it), then it can be highly functional to maintaining the conjugal relationship.

But what if the husband does not partially unlearn his inexpressiveness? Within the newly defined expressive function of the marriage relationship, he is likely to be found inadequate. The possibility of an affectionate and companionship conjugal relationship carries with it the assumption that both the husband and wife are bringing into marriage the expressive capabilities to make such a relationship work. This being the case, American society is ironically short changing males in terms of their ability to fulfill this role expectation. Thus, society inconsistently teaches the male that to be masculine is to be inexpressive, while at the same time, expectations in the marital role are defined in terms of sharing affection and companionship which involves the ability to communicate and express feelings. What exists, apparently, is another example of a discontinuity in cultural conditioning of which Benedict (1938) spoke more than 30 years ago.

Conclusion and Summary

It has been suggested that many American males are incapable of expressing themselves emotionally to a woman, and that this inexpressiveness is a result of the way society socialized males into their sex role. However, there is an alternative explanation which should be explored, namely, that the learning by the male of his sex role may not actually result in his inability to be expressive, but rather only in his thinking that he is not supposed to be expressive. Granted, according to the first explanation, the male cannot express himself precisely because he was taught that he was not supposed to be expressive, but in this second explanation inexpressiveness is a result of present perceived expectations and not a psychological condition which resulted from past socialization. The male perceives cultural expectations as saying, "don't express yourself to women," and although the male may be capable of such expressiveness, he "fits" into cultural expectations. In the case of the married male, where familial norms do call for expressiveness to one's wife, it may be that the expectations for the expression of emotions to his wife are not communicated to him.

There has been a trickle of evidence which would lend support to the first explanation, which stresses the male's incapacity to be expressive. Several studies (Balswick, 1970; Hurvitz, 1964; Komarovsky, 1962; Rainwater, 1965) have suggested that especially among the lowly educated, it is the wife playing the feminine role who is often disappointed in the lack of emotional concern shown by her husband. The husband, on the other hand, cannot understand the relatively greater expressiveness which his wife desires, since he does not usually feel this need himself. As a result of her research, Komarovsky (1962, 156) has suggested that "the ideal of masculinity into which . . . (men are) . . . socialized inhibits expressiveness both directly, with its emphasis on reserve, and indirectly, by identifying personal interchange with the feminine role." Balswick (1970) found that males are less capable than females of expressing or receiving companionship support from their spouses. His research also supports the view that inadequacy of expressiveness is greatest for the less educated males. Although inexpressiveness may be found among males at all socioeconomic levels, it is especially among the lower class male that expressiveness is seen as being inconsistent with his defined masculine role.

There may be some signs that conditions which have contributed toward the creation of the inexpressive male are in the process of decline. The deemphasis in distinctiveness in dress and fashions between the sexes, as exemplified in the "hippy" movement can be seen as a reaction against the rigidly defined distinctions between the sexes which have characterized American society. The sexless look, as presently being advanced in high fashion, is the logical end reaction to a society which has superficially created strong distinctions between the sexes. Along with the blurring of sexual distinctions in the world of fashion may very well be the shattering of the strong, silent male as a glorified type. There is already evidence of sharp criticisms of the inexpressive male and exposure of him as constituting a "hangup." Marriage counselors, sensitivity group leaders, "hippies," and certainly youth in general, are critical of inexpressiveness, and seek candid honesty in interpersonal relations. Should these views permeate American society, the inexpressive male may well come to be regarded as a pathetic tragedy instead of the epitome of masculinity and fade from the American scene. Not all may applaud his departure, however. While those interested in more satisfactory male-female relationships, marital and otherwise, will probably gladly see him off, those concerned with more stable marital relationships may greet his departure less enthusiastically. Although it should remove an important barrier to satisfaction in all male-female relationships via an increase in the male's capacity for emotional response toward females, by the same token it also may remove a barrier against emotional entanglement in relations with females outside marital relationships and thus threaten the stability of marriages. If one finds the inexpressive male no longer present one of these days, then, it will be interesting to observe whether any gains in the stability of marriage due to increased male expressiveness *within* this relationship will be enough to offset losses in stability emanating from increasing displays of male expressiveness *outside* it.

References

Auerback, Alfred. 1970 The Cowboy Syndrome. Summary of research contained in a personal letter from the author.

Balswick, Jack O. 1970 The Effect of Spouse Companionship Support on Employment Success. *Journal of Marriage and the Family*, 32, 212-215.

Benedict, Ruth. 1938 Continuities and Discontinuities in Cultural Conditioning. *Psychiatry*, 1, 161-167.

Blood, Robert and Donald Wolfe. 1960 *Husbands and Wives: The Dynamic of Married Living.* Glencoe, Illinois: The Free Press.

Cox, Harvey. 1966 Playboy's Doctrine of Male. In Wayne H. Cowan (Ed.), *Witness to a Generation: Significant Writings from Christianity and Crisis (1941-1966).* New York: Bobbs-Merrill Company.

Hurvitz, Nathan. 1964 Marital Strain in the Blue Collar Family. In Arthur Shostak and William Gomberg (Eds.), *Blue-Collar World.* Englewood Cliffs, New Jersey: Prentice-Hall.

Komarovsky, M. 1962 *Blue-Collar Marriage.* New York: Random House.

Mead, Margaret. 1935 *Sex and Temperament in Three Primitive Societies.* New York: William Morrow and Company.

Manville, W. H. 1969 The Locker Room Boys. *Cosmopolitan,* 166 (11), 110-115.

Popplestone, John. 1966 The Horseless Cowboys. *Transaction,* 3, 25-27.

Rainwater, Lee. 1965 *Family Design: Marital Sexuality, Family Size, and Contraception.* Chicago: Aldine Publishing Company.

Different Equals Less:
Female Sexuality in Recent
Marriage Manuals

By Michael Gordon and Penelope J. Shankweiler

Coitus can scarcely be said to take place in a vacuum; although of itself it appears a biological and physical activity it is so deeply within the larger context of human affairs that it serves as a charged microcosm of the variety of attitudes and values to which the culture subscribes. (Millett, 1970:23)

*T*his quotation from Kate Millett's *Sexual Politics* reveals the theme of the present paper. We are in agreement with her thesis that what takes place between men and women in the bedroom has something to tell us about the relationship that prevails between them in the world at large. While Millett draws primarily upon the work of three major novelists to document this thesis we will use non-fictional sources, more specifically marriage manuals published in the last two decades.[1] This form of literature was chosen because we feel it contains the currently regnant views on human sexuality, and also because it receives reasonably wide circulation (e.g., David Reuben's *Everything You Always Wanted to Know About Sex* has already sold over a million copies in the hard-bound edition alone).[2] Furthermore, the experts, often self-proclaimed, who write these manuals influence the views of those who provide sexual counseling in our society. Whether these books influence behavior in any important sense is

Journal of Marriage and the Family, August, 1971, pp. 459-466.
Copyright © 1971 by the National Council on Family Relations.

moot, but at the very least they do help create the sexual expectations of those directly or indirectly exposed to them.

We see this as a study in sexual ideology. As traditionally defined, ideology refers to the body of beliefs and values which legitimate the status quo, an important aspect of which may be a dominant group's position vis-à-vis other groups in a society. If women are conceived of as a "minority" group it then becomes important to explore the ideology which perpetuates this status. It is our contention that a significant dimension of this ideology is the manner in which women have had their sexuality *defined* for them. Women have had specific boundaries imposed on the expression of their sexuality. To be sure, the same is true of men, but the constraints have been looser and fewer. Moreover, these boundaries are the creations, for the most part, of male "experts," whose opinions and advice have reflected the interests of a patriarchal society. We will begin by examining the manner in which female sexuality has been depicted in the manuals published in the period between 1830 and 1950.[3]

Female Sexuality, 1830-1950

Stereotypes do on occasion reflect a considerable degree of the reality they generally simplify and distort. The popular image of nineteenth century, middle-class society being one in which the professed values placed sex in the category of an unfortunate procreative necessity is for the most part substantiated by the contents of the marriage manuals published during this period. Such books generally advocate a policy of sex for reproduction only, as is attested to by continence being the most frequently recommended form of contraception. Women are granted any form of sexual desire so begrudingly that for almost all intents and purposes it is nonexistent.

As a general rule, a modest woman seldom desires any sexual gratification for herself. She submits to her husband, but only to please him; and, but for the desire of maternity, would far rather be relieved from his attentions. The married woman has no wish to be treated on the footing of a mistress (Hayes, 1869:227).

However, as the century draws to a close one can see the *beginnings* of an acceptance of non-procreative marital sexuality, as well as female sexual desire, in some of the manuals.

In the early years of the twentieth century what was hinted earlier becomes the prevailing view, *viz.*, sex in the context of marriage is not only right and proper, but an important aspect of married life as well. As one might expect, this point of view is tied to a reorientation toward female sexuality. Its existence is now recognized, but in a form which distinctly sets it apart from male sexuality:

> It is the complexity of woman's sex nature you have not understood. A wife needs the affection of attention, interest. With her it is not merely a craving for carnal pleasures; it is something deeper, something of a spiritual nature which sweetly blended with her physiological demands (Howard, 1912:22).
>
> To a great percentage of men a strictly monogamous life is either irksome, painful, disagreeable or an utter impossibility. While the number of women who are not satisfied with one mate is exceedingly small (Robinson, 1917:325).

These two excerpts, which are typical of the period, are related to one another in an important fashion. One might say that the ideas contained in one almost logically flow from the other. Women are presented with a definition of their sexuality that conveniently excludes the possibility of engaging in the kind of non-marital sexual behavior men are granted. Here, then, we have one rationale for the "double-standard" that has been with us so long, and that is only now beginning to break down.

Another important dimension of the conception of female sexuality that arose at the beginning of the century is its alleged dormancy. That is to say, in contrast to the male who from puberty on is confronted by imperious sexual impulses females supposedly do not experience strong desire until sex is initiated—in the marriage bed, of course.

> No doubt women differ greatly, but in every woman who truly loves there lies dormant the capacity to become vibrantly alive in response to her lover, and to meet him as a willing and active participant in the sacrament of marriage (Gray, 1922:145).

What is of significance here is that female sexuality becomes a male creation, without his intercession it remains incipient at best, and non-existent at worse.

Once a woman's sexual desire has been "awakened" by her husband, its satisfaction, not surprisingly, falls on his shoulders, and in a specific way, *viz.*, coitus culminating, ideally, in simultaneous climax. Writing in 1926 Margaret Sanger had the following to say on this matter:

Experience will teach the husband to watch for and recognize in his be-
loved the approach of the culminating ecstasy. Not until this point is at-
tained may he release his own emotions from control so that both together
at the same moment may yield themselves for the final ecstatic flight (Sanger,
1926:142).

Such statements are encountered as early as 1900; by the 1930s
their number has reached such proportions that it has been described
as "a cult of mutual orgasm" (Gordon, in press). This emphasis on a
particular form of orgasmic ordering is noteworthy because it defines
the appropriate mode for sexual satisfaction in terms of the male's
orgasmic potential.[4]

Thus, while the very recognition of female sexuality at the beginning of the century was in itself revolutionary, it was presented
in invidious terms: not only was it different and less clamorous than
that of the male, but essentially dependent upon him for its arousal
and satisfaction. We hope to show that new evidence and knowledge
is beginning to lead to a reappraisal of female sexual potential, but
that the idea of male domination continues to be as firmly entrenched
in the sexual sphere as it is in male-female relationships in the society
as a whole.

The Manuals

The eighteen manuals on which this study is based were for the
most part the best-sellers of the 1950-70 period.[5] This is not to say
that all of them were first published during these two decades. Some
appeared earlier in the century, e.g., Chesser's *Love Without Fear*
(1947), but continued to sell in large number through the sixties.[6]
We have adopted this selection procedure rather than sampling systematically from the manuals published in this two decade interval
because we were not concerned with the views that were most representative of this type of literature, but rather with the views the
greater number of people were being exposed to, and which thus
could be viewed as being the most influential. In discussing this material we shall first explore what we see as indications of a broad
changing sexual ethic and then focus on the treatment of female
sexuality in this context.

Findings

The New Sexual Ethic

One of the most notable shifts in the recent manuals is the growing acceptance, often implicit, of nonmarital sex for women. As we have already noted, men in the past have been granted more sexual license than women and it was expected that they would engage in a certain amount of pre- or extramarital sex. This view holds through the 1950s with most writers appearing to direct their books to couples entering marriage with the wife a virgin and the husband furtively experienced. In the 1960s we notice not only a less critical attitude toward premarital sex for women but the appearance of books which provide instruction for its successful pursuit as well. Among the earliest of these, and certainly the most widely read was Helen Gurley Brown's *Sex and the Single Girl* (1962).[7]

> Nice, single girls *do* have affairs, and they do not necessarily die of them! They suffer sometimes, occasionally a great deal. However, quite a few "nice" girls have affairs and do not suffer at all! (Brown, 1962:225)

The cheering can stop. While Helen Gurley Brown did openly and approvingly discuss nonmarital sex she was committed to the status quo insofar as male-female relationships are concerned. The same holds true of *The Sensuous Woman*, a recent best seller that graphically explores the frontiers of sexual behavior while clinging to conventional notions of broader relationships between the sexes. This book might have been appropriately subtitled, *How to Get to a Man's Heart Through His Genitals*.

It should be stressed that the acceptance of premarital experience in the majority of the manuals is much less explicit than in the books discussed above. For the most part, even throughout the sixties, sex is assumed to take place within the social context of love and marriage, the latter being "the most precious and deeply satisfying relationship we know" (Calderone, 1960:13). Even those writers most deeply committed to sensuality still subscribe to the idealized view of sex as a sacrament, a means of communicating love for another person and ideally in a marital setting.

In view of such a sentiment it is not surprising to find that extramarital affairs are almost overwhelmingly rejected in the books included in the study, and concomitantly, a major concern is with improving marital sex so as to avert this eventuality. Some authors assume that the basic recipes have been mastered and "a couple who will not be content with a static love, even if it is a satisfying love, will have to keep up a constant search for ways of introducing a freshness into their sexual experience" (Chartham, 1970: 27). Moreover, it is expected that the approach of old age will not mark the end of the couple's sexual life. Increasingly we are finding books containing sections on what we might call gerontological sex. Masters and Johnson's (1966) finding on the abilities of the elderly, when in good health, to function adequately sexually has lent support to this position.

Part of the concern with reinvigorating marital sex is manifested in the growing interest in what we might call "gourmet" sex as indicated by the titles of books such as *Sex for Advanced Lovers* (1970) and *Sophisticated Sex Techniques* (1967). These books are usually less programmatic than earlier ones such as, for example, Van de Velde's *Ideal Marriage* (1930). While the latter, as did similar books in the 1930s and 1940s, presented a demanding sexual regimen involving the specification of appropriate behavior at all stages of the sex act, more recent books in general seem to place more emphasis on spontaneity and the willingness to experiment. Alternative forms of sexual expression such as oral-genital and anal-genital, while previously either ignored, or relegated to foreplay, are now beginning to be elevated to ends in their own right, and represent part of a generally freer orientation toward recreative sex. The boundaries of human sexuality are slowly being expanded. Hedonism within the context of marriage is the new norm.

An important illustration of the rejection of the stress on technique and rationality in sex and the new hedonism, as well, is the reappraisal of simultaneous climax in the past two decades. In the first half of the century and particularly since the 1930s, "mutual orgasm" had been presented as the ultimate in sexual bliss. Recently some voices have been raised in opposition to this view. On the one hand there are those who feel it has created standards that most couples find difficult to meet:

> In many books of sexual enlightenment, simultaneous orgasm or almost simultaneous orgasm is put forth as being the normal, common and desirable thing. It is, however, a lie that has caused much damage in the course of time because it has resulted in many couples feeling abnormal or 'no good' without reason (Hegeler and Hegeler, 1963:196).

Others criticize it on what we may call aesthetic grounds:

Although there is certainly no denying that mutual simultaneous orgasm is very enjoyable, there is also something to be said for consecutive orgasm. Since the precise moment of orgasm usually brings on a lapse of consciousness, neither man nor woman is able to enjoy the orgasm of their partner (Reuben, 1969:56).

Still others raise questions which relate to female sexuality:

This pursuit of a fanciful notion will operate to maintain a woman at a single-orgasm level, a loss of completion far more to be deplored than that resulting from separate orgasm (Street, 1959:67).

The last excerpt was written in the year that Masters and Johnson began their research. Ironically enough, in the years since their research has been published we have not seen similar critiques.

The Nature of Female Sexuality

In the context of a growing emphasis on pleasure and spontaneity there is occurring a gradual change in ideas about female sexuality. In the books published between 1950-1965 men are perceived as having greater sexual needs than women, whereas in those appearing in the 1965-70 period the predominant idea is that men and women are equal in sexual desire but the nature of their sexuality is, in a variety of ways, different. The latter is witnessed by statements such as the following: "men can enjoy sex, in an animal sort of way, without love. Women can't, so remind her of your love often, in some way or another" (Hall, 1965:12). Female sexuality is still seen as more emotional and idealized than its male counterpart, something which grows out of love rather than physical desire.

What is important here is the persistence of a restrictive definition of female sexuality. If one is continually told that one has to care for, if not love, a man in order to sleep with him, then it can act as a self-fulfilling prophecy, and lo and behold many women find truth in David Reuben's words ". . . before a woman can have sexual intercourse with a man she must have social intercourse with him" (Reuben, 1969:103).

Furthermore, women are portrayed as likely to be negative about sex. In discussions of sexual maladjustment and experimentation it is generally the woman who is seen as the problematic partner. While socialization is frequently viewed as the source of female inhibitions, other differences are seemingly attributed to biological factors. Thus, Greenblat maintains:

... in many women, as a result of physical development and social training, the desire for actual sexual intercourse as distinct from kissing and petting may develop somewhat later than in young men. However, it is also true that the greater complexity of a woman's sexual organs makes possible a much deeper and more lasting physical emotional [sic] response. This response is not easy to sum up in a few words and not easy to achieve or to satisfy in the few seconds or minutes of sexual activity that would satisfy most males (Greenblat, 1956:8).

Here we see the persistence of the belief in the dormancy and slow development of female sexuality. In fact, women are believed to reach sexual "maturity" 10 to 12 years later than men, who are at the peak of their desire and performance at eighteen, a point to which we will return later in the paper.

In general, men are presented as simple creatures sexually whose desire is as easily satisfied as it is aroused. They are supposedly capable of responding to what they think, imagine or see, while women are thought to be "touch" creatures who have to be slowly stimulated by gentle kisses and caresses. One author expresses concern that men should not base their idea of what "normal" women are like sexually on their experiences with women who:

because of their unusually high sexual endowments are prone to have many voluntary and non-prostitutional premarital affairs. Such females are frequently so easily aroused and satisfied sexually that their male partners receive the erroneous impression that all normal females are, or should be, the way the minority of females behave (Ellis, 1966:19).

Reservations such as these notwithstanding, the prevailing view is that once a woman is aroused her desire is as strong as a man's—some books even mention the female capacity for multiple orgasm, but almost all fail to discuss its implications.

It is important to assess the extent to which such views of female sexuality are based on ideology. The findings of Masters and Johnson (1966) lend support to the position that while there are differences in the sexual response cycles of men and women, with the exception of orgasmic capacity, they resemble each other more than they differ. That is to say, the excitement, plateau, orgasmic and resolution phases are essentially similar. One does, of course, have to consider the degree to which cultural overlay masks some of these similarities. For example, a recent study carried out by the Institute for Sex Research at the University of Hamburg found that when exposed to erotic photographs women tend to judge them to be less arousing than do men but "the women showed almost the same degree of sexual-physiological reactions and activation of sexual behavior as the men" (Sigusch *et al.*, 1970:23). The importance of the Hamburg findings is that they indicate the extent to which women are responding to cues that define socially appropriate and inappropriate situations calling for a sexual response, rather than their own bodies.

The Masters and Johnson (1966) study has been iconoclastic in a number of ways. Not only have their findings raised serious doubts about the differences between male and female response cycles, but, as is well known, they have also toppled the oft-proclaimed distinction between vaginal and clitoral orgasms, and with this have prepared the ground for the emergence of a new view of female sexuality.[8]

The impact of their work has not been strongly felt in the marriage manuals. A number of recent manuals do discuss the findings on the clitoris and gerontological sex, but they generally fail to explore the implications of the findings on the multi-orgasmic capacities of women not only for sexual technique, but for the broader relations between men and women as well. Only one book even broaches the latter topic. In commenting on Masters and Johnson's findings on multiple orgasm Robert Chartham notes:

If multiple-orgasm becomes a widespread experience however, the whole sexual relationship with regard to the sensual content of swiving [coitus] is likely to go reverse. Whereas in the past men have taken it for granted that theirs was the superior experience, since they could never bring an episode of swiving to its natural ultimate conclusion without coming off, now though they will still have this advantage, their responses are bound to be inferior to the multiple-orgasm partner (Chartham, 1970:85).

Others have carried such ideas much further, most notably Mary Jane Sherfey in her masterful essay on female sexuality.

Dr. Sherfey reviews the findings of Masters and Johnson and concludes that:

. . . the more orgasms a woman has, the stronger they become; the more orgasms she has, the more she *can* have. To all intents and purposes, *the human female is sexually insatiable in the presence of the highest degrees of sexual satiation* (Sherfey, 1966:99).

Moreover, she views monogamous marriage as something which men have never fully accepted and women have been coerced into accepting: "... women's inordinate orgasmic capacity did not evolve for monogamous, sedentary cultures" (Sherfey, 1966:118).

Another point raised by Sherfey that is important for our understanding of prevailing views of female sexuality is that of the differential sexual "maturation" rate of males and females. That is to say, men and women reach the height of their responsiveness at different times. The source of this view is the Kinsey study:

We have pointed out that the male's capacity to be stimulated sexually shows a marked increase with the approach of adolescence, and that the incidences of responding males and the frequency of response to the point of orgasm, reach their peak within three or four years after the onset of adolescence. . . . On the other hand, we have pointed out that the maximum incidences of sexually responding females are not approached until some time in the late twenties and in the thirties. . . . (Kinsey *et al.*, 1953:714-715).

This has been frequently commented upon in the marriage manuals and plays an important role in defining current notions of women's sexual uniqueness. In the words of Maxine Davis woman "is an early-leafing but late-flowering plant" (Davis, 1963:88). Sherfey explores what others had hinted at: The roots of this difference may be more social than biological.

Less than one hundred years ago, and in many places today, women regularly had their third or fourth child by the time they were eighteen or nineteen, and the life span was no more than thirty-five to forty years. It could well be that the natural synchronization of the peak periods for sexual expression in men and women have been destroyed only in recent years (Sherfey, 1966:118-119).

One would have to interpret this to mean that with the postponed age of marriage in industrial societies and the differential sexual license granted men and women, natural synchronization has broken down. Or, to put it differently the reason women are "maturing" more slowly than men is they have less opportunity to engage in heterosexual relations and perhaps more importantly they are socialized in such a way as to suppress rather than encourage the expression of their sexuality early in adolescence in autoerotic forms.

What makes all of this especially interesting is the new data that is becoming available on changes in rates of premarital intercourse for college students. The studies of Bell and Chaskes (1970) and Christensen and Gregg (1970) found that between 1958 and 1968 there was an increase in female premarital sex. Bell and Chaskes also found that the context in which sexual intercourse had first occurred had changed with the dating and going steady settings increasingly replacing engagement. Moreover, there is in general a growing convergence of the rates for men and women with this being especially notable in Denmark where Christensen and Gregg report 95 percent of the men and 97 percent of the women having had premarital coitus. Findings such as these suggest that as the differences between male and female premarital experience rates begin to decrease, we may also see a growing convergence in sexual "maturation" rates.

Male and Female Sexual Roles

Even the growing number of authors who are advocating an "equal but different" image of female sexuality still subscribe, for the most part, to a belief in the importance of male leadership and initiative. Brissett and Lewis in their study of sex manuals note that "between three and four times as many prescriptions for behavior are directed to the male as to the female" (1970:42). Nevertheless, a common theme is the encouragement of female initiative as means of improving the couple's sex life. "The bride should overcome her modesty and let him know which caresses are most desirable and the manner of their performance" (Levine, 1950:5). What this and similar authors are trying to do is have women overcome the passivity they feel impedes sexual pleasure, but the focus is always on the man:

> In lovemaking your body is your instrument. You shouldn't settle for less than the best. An Arthur Rubenstein or Van Cliburn is not going to select a clunky, unresponsive, out-of-tune piano on which to perform his artistry ("J", 1969:28).

The metaphor here is a rather revealing one.

For a number of authors the importance of male control takes on the character of an imperative for general domestic as well as sexual adjustment:

> Manly self-assertion can be *tempered* with gentleness and consideration, but both your sex life and your marriage suffer if you allow it to be smothered or overrestrained by such qualities. Emotionally and physically, your wife needs the assertiveness of a masculine figure to make a good marital adjustment. The highest form of considerateness in the long run is to become such a figure in her eyes (Eichenlaub, 1968:82).

So we see that while the trend toward what we have earlier called "gourmet" sex may have contributed to the emergence of a more active conception of the woman's role, it has not altered more fundamental sexual behavior. There is nothing irreconcilable between the feminine mystique and a woman who plays a more active role in bed, as long as control resides with the man.

Conclusion

We trust that our discussion of the manner in which female sexuality has been depicted in the marriage manuals of the past two decades has revealed the ideological overtones of such literature. Women in this century have been granted the right to experience sexual desire and have this desire satisfied, but always with the man calling the tune. This we have suggested is a manifestation of the minority group status of women. Given their primary roles of wives and mothers their sexuality is something which has been subject to masculine definitions of its purity, spoilage, ruination and so on. Women have been given the sop of sexual spirituality in return for the sexual freedom they have been denied. In short, they have been offered a conception of their sexuality that has not allowed it to follow its underlying physiology.

We see this as an ideology reflecting the prevailing social relations between the sexes. As James Coleman notes:

... when [a woman's] status and ultimate position do not depend greatly on her husband she need not be so cautious. Her sexual activity may now be a pleasure to be enjoyed more nearly for its own sake, without regard for its loss in value through promiscuity and loss of 'reputation.' Her sexual activity is not so much a commodity by which she establishes her ultimate social position, and she need no longer withhold it for exchange purposes. She becomes more like the male in this regard, having less reason to maintain her sexual activity as a scarce good in a market, more reason to consume it for its direct enjoyment (Coleman, 1966:217).

Since women are not independent in this regard, it is not surprising that the changes that have occurred in recent sex manuals do not represent a dramatic reorientation toward female sexual roles. The new findings on female sexuality appear to be poured into the old bottles of male-female relationships. If women have been encouraged to take more initiative it is in order that they might give more pleasure to their husbands rather than achieve more autonomy in the sexual realm.

References

1. We use the term marriage and sex manuals interchangeably in this paper, though a good argument can be made for the point that the term sex manuals is best left reserved for those books which focus almost exclusively on sex education, in contrast to marriage manuals which focus on a broader spectrum of domestic life. By this definition books used in this study are sex manuals.

2. In order to understand just how impressive this figure is, one must realize that Van de Velde's *Ideal Marriage* (1930) has not in the American edition sold as many copies in the forty years it has been in print, and it is one of the most popular marriage manuals ever published.

3. For a more complete discussion of the literature of this period the reader is referred to Gordon (in press) and Gordon and Bernstein (1970).

4. Some people have seen Freudian influence in the development of "the cult of mutual orgasm." As we have indicated, there were writers advocating this well before Freud had written on any topic bearing on this subject. However, in the 1920s and 1930s his conception of "mature" female sexuality being vaginal sexuality probably was a factor accounting for the growth of those recommending this form of orgasmic ordering, and, of course, was the source of what Koedt has called "the myth of vaginal orgasm."

5. In the first author's earlier studies the manuals were selected differently. Because of their small numbers an attempt was made to locate the total universe of nineteenth century manuals, and 63 were ultimately found to be useable. Twentieth century manuals were selected by means of representative sample of manuals published in each decade of the century.

6. Furthermore, several of the books included in this study have gone through innumerable printings and several editions and revisions. The year given for a book is usually that of its most recent revision, where it was possible to establish this date.

7. This book is not a sex or marriage manual and is thus not included in the enumeration of manuals in this study. Its discussion is felt to be warranted because of the radical character of its theme.

8. It should be pointed out that Kinsey and his associates in *Sexual Behavior in the Human Female* (1953:582-583) discussed evidence that seriously if not irrefutably questioned the possibility of a "vaginal orgasm." Interestingly enough this was virtually ignored while other sections of the book such as the differential sexual "maturation" rate of the sexes was frequently commented upon by authors of marriage manuals. This would seem to be a case of facts being widely disseminated which can be reconciled with prevailing beliefs and those which cannot, dismissed or ignored.

Bell, Robert R. and Jay B. Chaskes. 1970 "Premarital sexual experience among coeds, 1958 and 1968." *Journal of Marriage and the Family,* 32 (February): 30-35.

Brissett, Dennis and Lionel Lewis. 1970 "Guidelines for marital sex: An analysis of fifteen popular marriage manuals." *The Family Coordinator,* 19 (January): 41-48.

Brown, Helen Gurley. 1962 *Sex and the Single Girl.* New York: Bernard Geis.

Butterfield, Oliver M. 1967 *Sexual Harmony in Marriage.* New York: Emerson Books.

Calderone, Mary S. 1960 *Release from Sexual Tensions.* New York: Random House.

Chartham, Robert. 1970 *Sex for Advanced Lovers.* New York: New American Library.

Chesser, Eustace. 1947 *Love Without Fear.* New York: Roy Publishers.

Chesser, Eustace. 1970 *Love and the Married Woman.* New York: New American Library.

Christensen, Harold T. and Christina Gregg. 1970 "Changing sex norms in America and Scandinavia." *Journal of Marriage and the Family,* 32 (November): 616-627.

Coleman, James S. 1966 Letter to the editor. *American Journal of Sociology,* 72 (September): 217.

Davis, Maxine. 1963 *Sexual Responsibility in Marriage.* New York: Dial Press.

Eichenlaub, John E. 1961 *The Marriage Art.* New York: Dell.

Eichenlaub, John E. 1968 *New Approaches to Sex in Marriage.* New York: Dell.

Ellis, Albert. 1966 *The Art and Science of Love.* New York: Bantam Books.

Gordon, Michael. In press "From an unfortunate necessity of a cult of mutual orgasm: Sex in American domestic education literature, 1830-1940." In James Henslin (ed.), *The Sociology of Sex.* New York: Appleton-Century-Crofts.

Gordon, Michael and M. Charles Bernstein. 1970 "Mate choice and domestic life in the nineteenth-century marriage manual." *Journal of Marriage and the Family,* 32 (November): 665-674.

Gray, A. H. 1922 *Men, Women and God.* New York: Association Press.

Greenblat, Bernard R. 1956 *A Doctor's Marital Guide for Patients.* Chicago: Budlong Press Company.

Hall, Robert E. 1965 *Sex and Marriage.* New York: Planned Parenthood.

Hayes, A. 1869 *Sexual Physiology of Woman.* Boston: Peabody Medical Institute.

Hegeler, Inge and Sten. 1963 *An ABZ of Love.* New York: Medical Press of New York.

Howard, William Lee. 1912 *Facts for the Married.* New York: Edward J. Clode.

"J". 1969 *The Sensuous Woman.* New York: Lyle Stuart.

Kinsey, Alfred, *et al.* 1953 *Sexual Behavior in the Human Female.* Philadelphia: Saunders.

Levine, Lena. 1950 *The Doctor Talks with the Bride and Groom.* New York: Planned Parenthood.

Masters, William H. and Virginia E. Johnson. 1966 *Human Sexual Response*. Boston: Little, Brown.

Millett, Kate. 1970 *Sexual Politics*. New York: Doubleday.

Reuben, David. 1969 *Everything You Always Wanted to Know About Sex ...* New York: David McKay.

Robinson, William J. 1917 *Woman, Her Sex and Love Life*. New York: Eugenics Publishing Company.

Sanger, Margaret. 1926 *Happiness in Marriage*. New York: Blue Ribbon Books.

Sherfey, Mary Jane. 1966 "The evolution and nature of female sexuality in relation to psychoanalytic theory." *Journal of the American Psychoanalytic Association*, 14 (January): 28-127.

Sigusch, Volkmar, *et al*. 1970 "Psychosexual stimulation: Sex differences." *Journal of Sex Research*, 6 (February): 10-24.

Stone, Hannah and Abraham. 1953 *A Marriage Manual*. New York: Simon and Schuster.

Street, Robert. 1959 *Modern Sex Techniques*. New York: Lancer Books.

Van de Velde, Th. H. 1930 *Ideal Marriage*. New York: Random House.

Woodward, L. T. 1967 *Sophisticated Sex Techniques in Marriage*. New York: Lancer Books.

Prisoner of Sex

By Norman Mailer

S till he had not answered the question with which he began. Who finally would do the dishes? And passed in his reading through an Agreement drawn between husband and wife where every piece of housework was divided, and duty-shifts to baby-sit were divided, and weekends where the man worked to compensate the wife for chores of weekday transportation. Shopping was balanced, cooking was split, so was the transportation of children. It was a crystal of a contract bound to serve as model for many another, and began on this high and fundamental premise:

We reject the notion that the work which brings in more money is more valuable. The ability to earn more money is already a privilege which must not be compounded by enabling the larger earner to buy out his/her duties and put the burden on the one who earns less, or on someone hired from outside.

We believe that each member of the family has an equal right to his/her own time, work, value, choices. As long as all duties are performed, each person may use his/her extra time any way he/she chooses. If he/she wants to use it making money, fine. If he/she wants to spend it with spouse, fine, If not, fine.

As parents we believe we must share all responsibility for taking care of our children and home—not only the work, but the responsibility. At least during the first year of this agreement, sharing responsibility shall mean:

1. Dividing the jobs (see "Job Breakdown" below):
and

2. Dividing the time (see "Schedule" below) for which each parent is responsible.

There were details which stung:

10. Cleaning: Husband does all the house-cleaning, in exchange for wife's extra childcare (3:00 to 6:30 daily) and sick care.

11. Laundry: Wife does most home laundry. Husband does all dry cleaning delivery and pick up. Wife strips beds, husband remakes them.

No, he would not be married to such a woman. If he were obliged to have a roommate, he would pick a man. The question had been answered. He could love a woman and she might even sprain her back before a hundred sinks of dishes in a month, but he would not be happy to help her if his work should suffer, no, not unless her work was as valuable as his own. But he was complacent with the importance of respecting his work—what an agony for a man if work were meaningless: then all such rights were lost before a woman. So it was another corollary of Liberation that as technique reduced labor to activities which were often absurd, like the housework of women take on magnitude, for their work was directed at least to a basic end. And thinking of that Marriage Agreement which was nearly the equal of a legal code, he was reminded of his old campaign for mayor when Breslin and himself had called for New York City to become the fifty-first state and had preached Power to the Neighborhoods and offered the idea that a modern man would do well to live in a small society of his own choosing, in a legally constituted village within the city, or a corporate zone, in a traditional religious park or a revolutionary commune—the value would be to discover which of one's social ideas were able to work. For nothing was more difficult to learn in the modern world. Of course, it had been a scheme with all the profound naivete of assuming that people voted as an expression of their desire when he had yet to learn the electorate obtained satisfaction by venting their hate. Still he wondered if it was not likely that the politics of government and property would yet begin to alter into the politics of sex. Perhaps he had been living with the subject too closely, but he saw no major reason why one could not await a world—assuming there would be a world—where people would found their politics on the fundamental demands they would make of sex. So might there yet be towns within the city which were homosexual, and whole blocks legally organized for married couples who thought the orgy was ground for the progressive action of the day. And there would be mournful areas of the city deserted on Sunday, all suitable for the mood of masturbators who liked the open air and the street, perhaps even psuedo-Victorian quarters where brothels could again be found. There could be city turfs steaming with the nuances of bisexuals living on top of bisexuals, and funky tracts for old-fashioned lovers where the man was the rock of the home; there would always be horizons blocked by housing projects vast as the legislation which had gone into the division of household duties between women and men. There would be every kind of world in the city, but their laws would be founded on sex. It was, he supposed, the rationalized end of that violence which had once existed between men and women as the crossed potential of their love, violence which was part perhaps of the force to achieve and the force to scourge, it had been that violence which entered into all the irrationality of love, "the rooting out of the old bodily shame" of which Lawrence had spoke, and the rooting out of the fear in women that they were more violent than their men, and would betray them, or destroy them in the transcendence of sex; yes, the play of violence had been the drama of love between a man and a woman, for too little, and they were friends never to be gripped by any attraction which could send them far; too much, and they were ruined, or love was ruined, or they must degenerate to bully and victim, become no better than a transmission belt to bring in the violence and injustice of the world outside, bring it in to poison the cowardice of their home. But the violence of lovers was on its way to disappear in all the other deaths of the primitive which one could anticipate as the human became the human unit—human violence would go to some place outside (like the smog) where it could return to kill them by slow degree—and equally. But he had made his determination on beginning his piece that he would not write of sex and violence too long, for that would oblige him to end in the unnatural position of explaining what he had attempted in other work. So he would step aside by remarking that a look at sex and violence was the proper ground of a novel and he would rather try it there. And content himself now with one last look at his remark that "the prime responsibility of a woman probably is to be on earth long enough to find the best mate for herself, and conceive children who will improve the species." Was it too late now to suggest that in the search for the best mate was concealed the bravery of a woman, for to find the best mate (whatever ugly or brutal or tyrannical or unbalanced or heart-searing

son of misery he might appear) was no easy matter but indeed a profound and artistic search for that mysterious fellow of concealed
values who would eventually present himself in those twenty-three
most special chromosomes able to cut through fashion, tradition,
and class.

But now he could comprehend why woman bridled at the thought
she must "find the best mate for herself and . . . improve the species."
How full of death was the idea if one looked at any scheme which
brought people who were fundamentally unattracted to each other
down marriage aisles, their qualifications superb, their qualities neuter. So he was grateful to a writer who wrote a book, *The Lady*, published in 1910, Emily James Putnam, first dean of Barnard. She was a
writer with a whip of the loveliest wit. He would give the last quotation to her for she had given the hint of a way.

Apart from the crude economic question, the things that most women
mean when they speak of "happiness," that is, love and children and the
little republic of the home, depend upon the favour of men, and the qualities that win this favour are not in general those that are most useful for
other purposes. A girl should not be too intelligent or too good or too
lightly differentiated in any direction. Like a ready-made garment she should
be designed to fit the average man. She should have "just about as much
religion as my William likes." The age-long operation of this rule, by which
the least strongly individualised women are the most likely to have a chance
to transmit their qualities, has given it the air of a natural law.[1]

It was finally obvious. Women must have their rights to a life
which would allow them to look for a mate. And there would be no
free search until they were liberated. So let woman be what she would,
and what she could. Let her cohabit on elephants if she had to, and
fuck with Borzoi hounds, let her bed with eight pricks and a whistle,
yes, give her freedom and let her burn it, or blow it, or build it to
triumph or collapse. Let her conceive her children, and kill them in
the womb if she thought they did not have it, let her travel to the
moon, write the great American novel, and allow her husband to send
her off to work with her lunch pail and a cigar; she could kiss the
cooze of forty-one Rockettes in Macy's store window; she could
legislate, incarcerate, and wear a uniform; she could die of every male
disease, and years of burden was the first, for she might learn that
women worked at onerous duties and men worked for egos which
were worse than onerous and often insane. So women could have the
right to die of men's diseases, yes, and might try to live with men's

egos in their own skull case and he would cheer them on their way—
would he? Yes, he thought that perhaps they may as well do what they
desired if the anger of the centuries was having its say. Finally, he
would agree with everything they asked but to quit the womb, for
finally a day had to come when women shattered the pearl of their
love for pristine and feminine will and found the man, yes that man
in the million who could become the point of the seed which would
give an egg back to nature, and let the woman return with a babe
who came from the root of God's desire to go all the way, wherever
was that way. And who was there to know that God was not the
greatest lover of them all? The idiocy was to assume the oyster and the
clam knew more than the trees and the grass. (Unless dear God was
black and half-Jewish and a woman, and small and mean as mother-
wit. We will never know until we take the trip. And so saying realized
he had been able to end a portentous piece in the soft sweet flesh
of parentheses.)

References

1. Emily James Putnam, *The Lady* (Chicago: University of Chicago
Press, 1970), p. 70.

The Domestic Chauvinist

By Michael Korda

*B*ehind the male chauvinist's supercilious and patronizing attitude toward "all the little girls getting together" lies real fear, the fear that we may no longer be able to impose upon women our vision of ourselves as men. Most men do not control their wives, cannot, possibly don't even want to. Oh yes, they exert as a rule a kind of spurious financial control, but despite the arguments of the radical feminists woman's domestic role gives her far more opportunities for exerting control over domestic decisions than a man, and while it is certainly true that it is the man who goes out and earns the money in the average American marriage, it is notorious that women play the decisive role in determining how that money will be spent. What men want in marriage is not power so much as "face," in the Oriental sense. A woman may dominate a man in any number of ways, provided she allows him to play the dominant role in public, and the surest way for a man to lose prestige among his peers still remains losing an argument with his wife in public.

The price of male chauvinism is terrible confusion; the male chauvinist is trying to combine in one person so many contradictory attitudes toward women that he can only end by fearing and hating them. A powerful and successful speculator I know is a good example of these contradictions. When he appears in public with his wife, he makes it quite clear that he is the boss, and in private conversations he emphasizes that his is an "old-fashioned" marriage. "I make the money, and I don't put up with any nonsense. Somebody has to make decisions, and it's my job to make them." One visit to his home is enough to convince any observer that this is a facade; it is quite obvious that he treads cautiously, stumbling around his house as if he didn't really live there, as if everything in it, furniture, pictures, kitchen appliances, children even, were extensions of his wife's personality, to be treated with extreme care and delicacy. Though inclined to make fun of his wife when he's with other men ("She can't balance a checkbook to save her life, all she needs to make her happy is a charge account, she's terrific with children, but you know, women are a lot more like children than men are, they understand them better, they have more patience"), he can switch instantly to her defense, and even use her as his reason for doing something ("If I told my wife I'd said yes to a deal like this she'd laugh her head off, she'd say, What kind of a man are you anyway?"). He grimaces and winks at his young secretary while speaking to his wife on the telephone (I'm not taking any of this seriously, he is implying, it's just my wife talking, gab, gab, gab, that's the way wives are), then sends her out into the streets on a hot July afternoon to pick up theater tickets for the very same woman he's just been making fun of. A man I know has a wife who paints; he makes ritual fun of her efforts when he's with his friends and colleagues (for no man is supposed to take a woman's occupations seriously), but when she has an exhibition, he dragoons every passing acquaintance into going to the exhibit, and stands by the same paintings he has made fun of, saying, "Aren't they great? Isn't she great?"

What is wrong with us that we are willing to settle for such a mass of contradictory attitudes in the one area of life where we should expect consistency? And how can men be expected to have a consistent attitude toward woman—her needs, her role, her ambitions—when their feelings about women are both inconsistent and self-serving? Most men do not see women as fellow human beings at all; they merely have a set of responses toward the idea of women in various roles, from which they can pick and choose the one that seems most appropriate in any given circumstance: domination, submission, sexual passion, patience, fatherly advice, fear, contempt, sentimental adulation. The same man can, within twenty-four hours, shout at his secretary, make a show of negotiating a contract with a woman lawyer on equal terms, make fun of the same women to his colleagues, appear at a party with his wife on his arm, looking strong and protective, and return home listening to her criticize him for behaving like an idiot at the party. Since all these responses, attitudes and postures are constantly getting crossed—fatherly interest serving as a cover-up for lust, a public attitude of domination concealing a private posture of submission, rage at one's secretary compensating for surrender to one's wife—men are inclined to live in a morass of conflicting impulses when it comes to women, however clear-minded they may be about politics, business or technology. "Women," wrote Virginia Woolf, "have served all these centuries as looking glasses possessing the power of reflecting the figure of man at twice its natural size." Yes, men use women as mirrors, but the worst of this is not just that it has reduced women to "looking glasses," it has reduced men to creatures who can only define themselves by means of women. And unfortunately for men the mirror is like the ones in an amusement park that distort and split up the image, showing us to ourselves as a giant with a dwarf's head, or as a pygmy with a gorilla's torso.

Marriage at least serves one purpose: it gives men the chance to come to terms with at least one women. In marriage a man senses the possibility of reducing an infinite problem to finite proportions, of isolating at least one member of this capricious and mysterious species in the hope that this controlled laboratory experiment will either answer his questions or provide a good reason for not asking them. Yet obstinately, women remain as unfathomable as they were for Sigmund Freud ("The great question that has never been answered, and which I have not yet been able to answer despite my thirty years of research into the feminine soul, is: What does a woman want?"). Isolate a woman, reduce her contacts with the outside world, sleep with her on an exclusive basis, share in the business of living, of procreating, and perhaps we will discover what it is that woman wants, more to the point what she is. But no answers are forthcoming so long as we continue to assume that she is radically different and mysterious, so long as we cling to the notion that her biology makes her mind, her "soul" (to use Freud's somewhat ambiguous word) somehow different from our own. If it is different, after all, it must either be inferior or superior, and a large part of what passes for social custom and business convention in our world is in fact a defense set up to convince man that it is he who is superior and she who is limited. The notion that "her" limits are our own is seldom considered. And if we can't find the answer to Sigmund Freud's question, we can always take refuge in the question itself, in the notion that women are after all possessed of some separate sensibility, that there isn't any possibility of "understanding" them in the first place, that by definition they represent a kind of monstrous puzzle that God has created for men to wrestle with hopelessly. We can even be proud of not understanding them, for the failure to understand women is the ultimate proof of our masculinity. It is not surprising that Ira Levin, the author of *Rosemary's Baby,* should have chosen as his new horror story the theme of male chauvinism, rightly perceiving that it is a form of modern witchcraft and superstition. In *The Stepford Wives,* Levin shows us a suburban community that seems emptily familiar and unexceptional. A young couple moves there; she is a talented photographer, mildly "liberated," he is a quiet, "reasonable" man. She soon finds that the women around her are remarkably submissive, addicted to housework, unwilling to express an opinion about anything. When Joanna invites her next-door neighbor, Carol, over for a cup of coffee, she refuses, saying "Thanks, I'd like to, but I have to wax the family room tonight . . . I've put it off too long as it is. It's all over scuff marks . . . There's always something or other that has to be done. You know how it is. I have to finish the kitchen now."

Gradually, Joanna thinks she has discovered that the men of the community have perfected a way of turning their wives into robots, that there is a conspiracy to make each woman into a perfect replica of the male chauvinist husband's ideal. As Joanna says, complimenting the owner of the local drugstore, "You have a lovely wife. Pretty, helpful, submissive to her lord and master; you're a lucky man." "I know," he replies.

In the end Joanna comes to realize that her husband is part of the conspiracy, that whatever is being done is going to be done to her too, and though she fights it, she is caught. When a friend asks her, in the supermarket, how her work is coming along, Joanna replies, "I don't do much photography any more . . . I wasn't especially talented, and I was wasting a lot of time I really have better uses for . . . Housework's enough for me. I used to feel I had to have other interests, but I'm more at ease with myself now. I'm much happier too, and so is my family. That's what counts, isn't it?" She has been turned into a robot too.

There is more significance in this than would at first appear, for both Ira Levin's successes represent a kind of horror-myth portrayal of male chauvinism. In *Rosemary's Baby,* a husband sells his wife to the Devil to further his career as an actor, in *The Stepford Wives,* the ultimate fantasy of male chauvinism is enacted, the recognition that the domestic world men created to enclose women is so important to them as a symbol of power that it need no longer be shared or en-joyed—it is sufficient that it continue to exist!

As a psychoanalyst told me, "I have to spend hours breaking through my [male] patients' defenses. They tell me about their jobs, their houses, the money they make, everything they've done for their families. I have to tell them, 'Look, I'm not interested in any of this, I don't care how much your house cost, or about the trip to Europe you took your wife on, you wouldn't be here if you hadn't discovered that your wife doesn't give a damn about any of that, and you have to learn that you don't give a damn either. I don't care how important you are, to me you're a man whose wife thinks he's no good in bed, and it's no good clinging to the $150,000 house as if that were the answer to everything, because if you don't learn to treat her as a per-son, she will walk out that $150,000 front door, get in her Mercury Cougar convertible, and go off to someone who's alive.' The first step in analysis, for me, is teaching men humility, making them under-stand that it doesn't matter how well they function as businessmen, they have to function as bodies, as people, as lovers. Success in one area doesn't compensate for deficiency in another. I've seen successful men, with male chauvinist attitudes, sit here and weep because their wives are threatening to leave, and most of them say *How could she do this to me?* Well, she did it to him because he isn't a *person* any more, because he's afraid of feeling, living. All he wants is security. And when women begin to think about themselves, the first thing they realize is what we all know: in an existential world there isn't any security, and there isn't any way a woman can provide security for someone else. As one woman said to me, 'I can't be a liberated woman and his mother and purpose in life at the same time. I refuse to be a living proof that his life makes sense. Maybe nobody's does.' "

Men cling to their hope that somebody else will make sense of their lives, trusting in Theodor Reik's dictum that "Women in general want to be loved for what they are and men for what they accom-plish." Accomplish enough and we will be loved, hence the propensity of the domestic male chauvinist to accomplish a great deal, to pour into his work a disproportionate amount of psychic energy. Anything is better than admitting that life is a question of feeling, that nobody can guarantee us anything, that we cannot demand of another human being that she cut herself off from life to prove to us that we have the capacity, like small gods, to impose order and security in one small corner of the universe.

Meanwhile, a recent survey revealed that the majority of women
don't object to moving to further their husband's careers "even if it
causes them some pain," and pointed out that in such corporate moves
the responsibility for moving is usually the wife's—she is "the key
person in establishing the home and making the move successful."[1]
A group of executives' wives—whose attitude might best be described
as "loyalist," as opposed to "liberated"—were quoted recently on the
benefits of being a housewife. "As an executive wife, you don't pursue
your own personal life as much as a career woman would," said Mrs.
Graham J. Morgan (wife of the chairman of the board of the U.S.
Gypsum Company). "You gear yourself to your husband's life." Another wife of a successful corporation executive, who has to be "a ray
of sunshine" at breakfast because her husband "gets a corporate look
on his face at dawn" reported that her husband expects her to be
"useful, punctual, efficient, pleasant, alert and healthy. He has no
patience with the opposites of any of these. He wants me to be
feminine, to have a sense of humor without being witty and not be
emphatic."[1]

There is a slightly hallucinating quality to this litany, which is
not to deny its sincerity. It sounds like something that the husbands
of *The Stepford Wives* might have invented as a credo. "Useful" implies that the husband defines his wife's use, that she's a functional
object at his service. "Alert" is a word that is usually applied to guard
dogs and horses, rather than the woman one supposedly loves.
"Healthy"? Well, of course we want those we love to be healthy, but
the marriage sacrament itself, outdated as it may be in some respects,
is quite explicit about "sickness and health," and it seems a bit extreme to demand health of one's wife—though presumably this kind
of nonhuman freedom from sickness could be programmed into the
female robots of Ira Levin's imagination. "A sense of humor without
being witty" perfectly expresses the male chauvinist attitude that
women can be amusing, if they're capable of amusing us, but must
never be witty or clever, which might be uncomfortable or ego-
destroying to men. ("If I'd wanted to marry a Dorothy Parker, I'd
have married one," a friend of mine told his wife, a former Benning-
ton girl with a quick wit and a sharp tongue, who sensibly took her
wit and her child to San Francisco, from whence she wrote, "Despite
my reputation for being the serpent's tooth of Riverdale, I'm really a
perfectly loving person. It takes a real background of romanticism
and masochism to make a good cynic, but men automatically assume
a cynical wife is a disaffected one. When I told him that a girl can

have enough of bed and bored, and he got angry instead of laughing, I thought to myself, I am *not* a monster, and got out.")

On the other hand, Mrs. Lee Allen Muench, the wife of the technical director of the General Motors Technical Center, commented, during a conference of a hundred thirty wives whose husbands earn more than $25,000 a year (in most cases much more): "I just feel appreciated by my husband. That's what enables me to function as a person. Oh, I'm taken for granted like most wives. But once in a while he says and does something that makes me feel important. I get my satisfaction from looking good in his eyes and not anyone else's." Clearly the extreme measures taken by Ira Levin's husbands are not by any means always necessary, particularly since the hundred thirty ladies were given a lecture by the manager of mining at the Ford Motor Company, who told them—a *deus ex machina* in more ways than one—that if an executive wife wanted outside interests "she should take painting, music, go to school but under no circumstances take a job." He added that an executive wife should "watch her figure and don't nag."[1]

One would like to feel that there is some misunderstanding here, that this doesn't really represent a serious view of life, but it does. A woman publishing executive whose success is considerable, remarks that her husband never lets her go out at night. "What do you mean," he asked, "I never let you go anywhere? I let you go to work, don't I?" (Needless to say, male chauvinism at the office does not disturb her unduly—she expects it, hardly even notices it. His work is important, meaningful, a part of the universe; hers is an aberration, a whim to be humored, like eating pickles during pregnancy.)

The authors of *Open Marriage,* George and Nena O'Neill, point out that "both persons have to put something (into a marriage)." They recommend "undependent living," individual freedom, flexible roles, mutual trust, "the combined, cooperative action of two people working in concert, where, as one person grows, he benefits and also gives the other partner an assist in her growth and vice versa."[2] But this is precisely what the male chauvinist cannot accept. He refuses to grow, refuses to see life as a fluid and changing state, he wants to have one toehold chiseled for him in the rock face of eternity. As one male participant in a discussion of women's liberation said, "Nancy has an idea she thinks is fantastic. She keeps bringing it up every few months: Let's have one month where you do all my jobs and I do all your jobs. Now on the face of it, that sounds like a terrific Women's Lib kind of thing. To me it represents hell because I can tell you what would happen in that month. Nancy, who is an expert cook, would be giving way to me and I would be serving things like Swanson's TV dinners at night, heating up a lot of macaroni, so we'd be eating—. I take, I think, rather splendid care of our bills and bill-paying. Nancy is generally overdrawn at the bank and thinks that I think it is cute. I don't. But she thinks I think so and I certainly can't change her. So if she took over the bills we'd be in bad shape. We'd lose all our credit. But my balking makes me a male chauvinist pig, right?"

Alas, right! Why can't he learn to cook decently, and if he can't what is wrong with eating macaroni, or alternating the cooking by days so that one good dinner is followed by a TV dinner? And what's so important about food anyway, in comparison to finding a new and more interesting way to live together? As to the bills, surely a little confusion is a small price to pay for an experiment that might, after all, convince Nancy that it isn't "cute" to be overdrawn at the bank? Poor Nancy. When it comes to her sexual fantasies, her loving husband says, "Nancy claims that she has not told anyone the full fantasy—and her only sex fantasy since the age of eleven—and principally the broad outlines are that she is . . . people rip her clothes off . . . I think it's a fairly universal woman's fantasy to be raped, to be used as a sexual object, and so on."[3]

There you have it: they see themselves as "sex objects," their fantasy is rape, and if that's the way they see themselves, what's the point of trying to treat them differently? Men are still desperately looking for the small concessions that will allow them to preserve their greater illusions, unable to face a life that has to be lived, ultimately, among equals, in which the possession of a penis does not serve as a substitute for brains, charm or originality, in which no status attaches to it by divine right, in which money and material objects can no longer be used as weapons to guard a false view of the world, to protect us against the demons. One young woman who has recently gone back to work after marriage told me, "You have to feel what it's like to make your own money and not have to depend on someone, even if it's someone you love. It's the root of women's liberation. I think I'm badly treated at the office, yes, because I'm attractive and young, and I get a lot of fatherly protection that I don't really need and that I have to fight to prevent myself accepting, because it's easier to accept. And at home, we have this system in which we split up all the bills, and each of us writes out a check for one half of whatever it is, and that works, but still my husband thinks of things as being his, even when I've paid for my half of whatever it is. We bought a camera, and when I wanted to take it to the beach, he said, 'Listen, don't do that, you might lose it.' A year ago I'd have accepted that, but not any more. It's ours, if I lose it, I'm responsible, and why would I be any more likely to lose it than he is? He thinks women's liberation is Ti-Grace Atkinson, or Jill Johnston, a whole big sexual thing, total change right now, but it isn't. It's what we're doing, and we're making it work. I'm not all that 'liberated' myself. I have sexual inhibitions, I'm attracted to other men, and I don't have the courage to do anything about it, and maybe it's just as well, I don't know. And I'm not involved in politics. But I do know that right here, in this life, right now, I'm going to be equal in the relationship I've chosen, I won't accept anything less. And once I've made that work, I'm going to go to work on this office, because if my husband can learn that I'm a person and not an extension of what he wants to do, then the men here can learn the same thing about me and my work, even if they're still treating their wives like second-class citizens. I took the first step yesterday, when I told a senior executive, very politely, 'It's my decision. I made it. I'm sticking to it.' He said, 'I never figured you for a women's libber.' And I told him, 'I'm not one. Try not thinking of me as a woman at all, try thinking of me as somebody who knows how to do this job.' And he said, 'To me you'll always be a woman.' And do you know what? He meant it as a compliment! That's male chauvinism!"

References

1. *The New York Times,* June 4, 1972.
2. George O'Neill, as quoted in *The New York Times.*
3. *The New York Times,* June 18, 1972.

Part Four

MALE LIBERATION AND THE NEW MASCULINITY

*A*s with others of the current works on masculinity, the articles
contained in Part Four have been written, for the most part, in
response to a sense of dissatisfaction with the traditional concept of
masculinity and the strictures which such a definition has placed
upon males. They range from highly personal experiences, such as
that described by Silverstein, to analyses of changing definitions
and the power structure, e.g., the articles by Olstad and Polatnick.

These selections are indicative of the reevaluation process which
progressively increased with the rise of the women's movement.
While still in the beginning stages, this process represents, for males,
an examination of themselves and the anchor which has been
traditionally provided for their self concept by a taken-for-granted
view of masculinity. More and more, approaches to masculinity
and males, in opposition to earlier works, are pointing out the
disadvantages for personal fulfillment embodied in the traditional
masculine role and self concept. Furthermore, the new masculinity
is being derived not as a response and reaction to the assumed
characteristics of females, but from a view towards "correcting the
wrongs" of the current masculine concept relative to women.

Brave New Men:
A Basis for Discussion

By Keith Olstad

Maccoby Davis and Jill Melby plan to practice medicine together someday. Maccoby wants a big family, but Jill is leery of having children. "I don't understand it," says Maccoby, "I could easily support her while the kids are young."

Jim Wilson and Paul Meyer have been inseparable all three years they have roomed together at college. Recently Paul has been spending most of his time with a woman, and Jim thinks he soon will request a room change; they are not able to talk productively with each other about what is happening to them.

Larry Rimmer has been in two men's consciousness groups, and agrees with Kay Olson that they are equally responsible for preventing another unwanted pregnancy. But he does not enjoy a condom and worries about the possible irreversibility of a vasectomy.

Dan Rawls is committed to sharing the care of his children with his future wife, and is doing his senior honors work on child development. He spent this last summer working in a small nursery school, and feels that not only was he the least effective teacher (the rest were women), but he simply did not find spending several hours daily with young children the least bit rewarding.

This article first appeared in the *Oberlin Alumni Magazine*, September-October, 1973, and was written by Mr. Olstad when he was a Danforth Religious Intern at Oberlin College. The article has been revised by the author for inclusion in this anthology.

In order to find out how common these situations are at Oberlin, Greg Best, '75, and I developed a questionnaire survey last spring. We designed this survey to identify contradictions or ambiguities within male students' value structures, and also between specific values and behaviors. We assumed that if most men expected women with whom they planned to live to pursue professional careers, but also expected them to do all the housework and provide sole care for children, considerable anxiety and stress would result. We expected that in the confluence of values expressed in the women's movement, the emerging men's movement, and traditional middle class life styles, we might identify among Oberlin men a number of specific contradictions and ambiguities regarding friendship, male emotionality and decisiveness, rights and responsibilities in marriage and family life, contraception and abortion, and male-female and male-male sexuality. Our hope was that, by identifying several of these tensions, we could stimulate further study of these issues at Oberlin and more conversation among men and women to the end of resolving these tensions.

Because of limitations involved in any questionnaire survey, because of theoretical ambiguities in our hypotheses, and because we lack experience in designing and analyzing such a survey, we intended our survery to provide a basis for a tentative discussion of issues involved. We doubt that any of the data presented here constitutes adequate evidence to support broad or definitive conclusions. Rather the data *suggest* tensions which need more research and study. What is discussed here is important; the strength of our methods and the data itself demand attention. But only much more conversation and study will bring the understanding needed for adequate response.

We distributed our questionnaire by mail to a random sample of 300 male students, 75 from each class. Of these, 211 or 71% returned completed questionnaires.[1] Though our return was not equal by class, it was close: 27% freshmen, 25% sophomores, 22% juniors, 25% seniors and 1% others.

In our return sample, 92% said they were white, 5% said they were black and 3% listed another race. We were interested in this because we wanted to get a tentative reading on whether black males differed as a group from white males in their responses to our questions. Assuming that our random sampling procedures gave us approximately the same proportion of black males in our sample as the proportion of black males on campus, we received a very low return rate from black men. We have no reliable way to account for this discrepancy.

Our return sample consisted of 27% men with primary religious training in Judaism, 43% with training in a Protestant religion, 15% in Roman Catholicism, and 15% with either religious training in a different religion or no religious training. The vast majority of the respondents identified either suburbia or a large metropolitan city as their primary childhood residence: 53% said that during most of childhood they lived in a suburb in a metropolitan area and another 19% said they lived in a large metropolitan city, 14% said they lived in a small city in a rural area, 11% came from towns in rural areas, and only 3% came from rural areas. Thus our sample return was highly urban.

Only 29% of the respondents said that since their births, their mothers had not been employed outside the home. Another 62% reported their mothers had worked more than a year; almost half of these for more than six years. Of the mothers who worked, 64% worked part time and 35% worked full time. Among the mothers who worked, 26% began or resumed work before the respondents were six years old, and another 43% when the respondents were seven to 15 years old. Virtually all the respondents reported primary care by either their mothers or both parents; none primarily from fathers.

Table 1: Friendship patterns with male best friends

		First male best friend	Second male best friend	Third male best friend	Fourth male best friend
I tell this friend	Disagree	6%	11%	11%	19%
very personal	Uncertain	20%	42%	50%	50%
concerns.	Agree	74%	47%	39%	31%
This friend tells me	Disagree	6%	11%	11%	15%
very personal	Uncertain	26%	41%	52%	55%
concerns.	Agree	68%	48%	37%	30%
I have consulted this	Disagree	12%	11%	16%	Missing
friend concerning	Uncertain	24%	47%	51%	Data
an important decision	Agree	64%	42%	33%	
I had to make.					
When we are in the same	Less than				
vicinity, we are	one hour	4%	3%	6%	9%
together each week:	1 - 2 hours	6%	9%	12%	13%
	2 - 5 hours	19%	26%	26%	30%
	5 - 10 hours	25%	26%	26%	26%
	more than				
	10 hours	46%	36%	30%	22%

Tables One and Two: Friendship Patterns

In order to get information about male and female friendship patterns, we first asked respondents how many of their best friends were males and how many were females. The response indicated that the majority of Oberlin males have more male best friends than female best friends. In fact, a large percentage have only one or two females among their best friends.

We asked three kinds of questions about the nature of relationships to best friends. Concerning a respondent's willingness to trust confidential information with a friend, we asked whether he told very personal concerns to each friend, and conversely whether each friend told him very personal concerns. Concerning a respondent's willingness to trust the judgment of his friends, we asked whether he consulted each friend regarding important decisions he had to make. Concerning a respondent's contact with his best friends, we asked how many hours each week he spent with each friend.

According to our data, Oberlin male students tended to place greater confidence in their first best female friends than in any of their male best friends. The same pattern held for consultation and

Table 2: Friendship patterns with female best friends

		First female best friend	Second female best friend	Third female best friend	Fourth female best friend
I tell this friend	Disagree	3%	6%	3%	17%
very personal	Uncertain	15%	47%	58%	56%
concerns.	Agree	82%	47%	39%	27%
This friend tells me	Disagree	2%	6%	8%	10%
very personal	Uncertain	15%	45%	51%	56%
concerns.	Agree	83%	49%	41%	34%
I have consulted this	Disagree	6%	15%	18%	39%
friend concerning	Uncertain	20%	47%	49%	46%
an important decision	Agree	74%	38%	33%	15%
I had to make.					
When we are in the same	Less than				
vicinity, we are	one hour	3%	2%	6%	15%
together each week:	1 - 2 hours	8%	15%	15%	13%
	2 - 5 hours	12%	28%	42%	21%
	5 - 10 hours	22%	32%	25%	33%
	more than				
	10 hours	55%	23%	12%	18%

the amount of time spent with each friend. However, the second greatest level of confidence, consultation and contact fell on first best male friends, not on other female friends. Once the relationships with first best male friends and first best female friends were taken out of the picture, the only significant cross-sex differences between the remaining male and female friendships were that the respondents tended to spend slightly more time with their male friends.

Table Three: Impulsiveness And Emotionality

One of the dimensions of self-image that concerned us most was the relationship between the value males place on impulses and emotions, and secondly their ability and willingness to express or withhold them. Traditionally, men have been expected to be calculating and rational, rarely impulsive or emotional. These expectations more recently have been attributed to sex roles cultivated for and by middle-class men in Western cultures. These culturally-induced expectations have been challenged both by humanistic education and the feminist movement. Joseph Pleck has suggested that

men are reacting to . . . *decreased female willingness to exclusively serve male emotional needs.* In traditional sex role relationships, men depend on women to facilitate their emotional expression, if not experience their emotions for them. . . . For many men, it takes some effort to learn to express themselves emotionally without a facilitative woman. Women becoming more emotionally independent can be quite threatening for this reason.[2]

Presumably if a male depends heavily on women to facilitate his emotional expression, he frequently is able to avoid responsibility for his own emotions. In such a case, does the emotion expressed belong to the woman who expresses or helps express it, or to the male who may feel anxious but is unwilling or unable to vent actual emotion? I think of the husband whose only resolution to his anger is making his wife cry, and of the many families where the father stands proudly silent while the mother praises their child's achievements with sobs and tears.

Avoiding ownership of expressed emotion may be a central reason so many of our respondents answered "uncertain" to the four statements that dealt with expressing impulses or emotions. The percentage of "uncertain" responses ranged from 41% for "I trust my impulses" and "I am generally indecisive" to 32% for "I cry easily" and

33% for "I would rather be an emotional person than an unemotional person."

In our sample, 57% of the male students agreed that they would rather be emotional persons than unemotional persons, and only 10% disagreed. The large uncertainty category constituted 33%.

With cross-tabulation, the data showed that, in general, men who wanted to be emotional were less judgmental of the effectiveness of impulsive people. This may suggest that men who value their emotions are clearer about the connection between impulses and emotions. Only further study can give a more thorough explanation of this phenomenon.

Response to preferring to be an emotional person predicted response to ease of crying: of those who would rather be emotional, somewhat more said they cry easily than in the whole sample, but the number is still small. With those wanting to be emotional, it was not difficult to hurt their feelings. However, response to whether one would rather be emotional did not predict response to whether a man expressing deep sorrow and hurt is apt to undermine others' confidence in him.

Though whether or not respondents preferred being emotional did not predict the number of their male best friends, it did marginally predict the number of their female best friends: men who preferred being emotional were more likely to have three or more female best friends. Only further study can bear out whether a male who is less emotionally expressive tends to have just one close friend on

Table 3: Impulsiveness and Emotionality

	Disagree	Uncertain	Agree
IMPULSIVENESS:			
I generally trust my impulses.	10%	41%	49%
I am generally indecisive.	46%	41%	14%
Impulsive people are generally less effective in getting things done.	44%	45%	12%
EMOTIONALITY:			
I would rather be an emotional person than an unemotional person.	10%	33%	57%
I cry easily	57%	32%	11%
It is generally difficult to hurt my feelings.	53%	32%	15%
A man expressing deep sorrow and hurt is apt to undermine others' confidence in him.	56%	26%	18%

whom he depends for facilitating his emotional expression. Or conversely whether males who prefer being emotional tend to have more female best friends because they have less need to find one person on whom they can rely for help in emotional release. Our data suggested that Oberlin male students who place less value on being emotional are somewhat more likely to find just one female best friend.

Intellectual Relationships

Mirra Komarovsky has noted that regarding sex roles, "men are ... confronted with contradictory expectations. For example, the traditional norm of male intellectual superiority conflicts with a newer norm of intellectual companionship between the sexes."[3] In her study of 62 males from the senior class of an Ivy League male college, she found evidence that for 30% of her sample "intellectual insecurity or strain with dates was a past or current problem."[4]

In our survey, we asked two kinds of questions regarding intellectual insecurity with women and we got two different kinds of responses. When we blatantly stated, "Women generally do not enjoy intellectual conversation," 88% of our respondents disagreed and only 10% felt uncertain. But when we asked questions about whether our respondents preferred intellectual conversations with members of one sex more than with members of the other, uncertainty skyrocketed. In response to "I am usually more comfortable having an intellectual conversation with a man than with a woman," 13% agreed, 29% were uncertain and 58% disagreed, meaning the latter might be equally comfortable with either a man or a woman or that they would be more comfortable with a woman. A similar statement but about men generally, "A man is more likely to enjoy an intellectual conversation with another man than with a woman," received 10% agreement, 40% uncertainty and 50% disagreement. And when we suggested, "I am more comfortable talking with an intellectually superior woman than talking with an intellectually superior man," only 7% agreed, 44% were uncertain and 49% disagreed, meaning they might be equally comfortable with either or more comfortable with a man. It would be specious to draw conclusions from these ambiguous statistics, except to note that the very high level of uncertainty for the latter statements—higher than virtually any other aspect of the survey—is suspicious and demands further study. If Oberlin is dedicated to cultivating the intellectual capacities of its women students, but this occurs in an environment of great uncertainty among male students concerning the desirability of intellectual discourse with women, the inevitable result will be confusion, frustration and stress.

When we stated rather strongly, "If men feel emasculated by a female authority figure, she should not be given authority over them," almost 60% of the respondents disagreed; only 12% agreed. But when we stated, "Qualified women who seek positions of authority ought to be given such positions before equally qualified men," almost three-quarters of the respondents disagreed; only 9% agreed. Apparently the prevailing feeling among Oberlin men is that women in positions of authority should not be limited by men who are uncomfortable with a female authority figure. But generally Oberlin men do not endorse the notion that among equally qualified candidates, women should be given preference for positions of authority in order to compensate for the present male dominance of authority positions.

Table Four: Family and Career Roles

Komarovsky's study of males on an Ivy League campus showed men there paying lip service to liberal attitudes toward working wives. She classified four types of response to questions about working wives. About a quarter of her respondents were "traditionalists," men who intended to marry women content with domestic, civic and cultural pursuits without ever seeking outside jobs. "Pseudo-feminists," 16% of the men, approved of the idea of their wives working, "but their approval was hedged with qualifications that no woman could meet." Almost half of Komarovsky's interviewees were "modified traditionalists," favoring a sequential pattern: work, withdrawal from work for child-rearing, and eventual return to work. And "feminists," men willing to modify their roles significantly to facilitate their wives' careers, comprised 7% of her sample.

Our survey of Oberlin men was not conducted in a manner which would identify these specific populations. It did suggest, however, that many of the tensions which led to Komarovsky's classifications do indeed exist among Oberlin men.

According to our data, Oberlin men subscribe heavily to egalitarianism as the ideal in family life. Fully 84% of our respondents agreed that "Ideally, a father and mother should spend an equal amount of time with their young children." Over 90% agreed that

"In my household, I want all major decisions to be made mutually." And, though with a higher level of uncertainty (25%), 58% agreed that "As a matter of principle, a man and woman living together should do an equal amount of housework."

In response to more specific questions about roles relating to housework, the men in our sample were usually consistent. Among those who subscribe to the egalitarian ideal, 80% disagreed that the father should make the major decisions concerning finances and 76% disagreed that the mother should make the major decisions concerning child care. Aside from child care, cooking was the most distasteful housework, but only one per 20 respondents said they would refuse to cook. Three-fourths of those holding egalitarian ideals disagreed with, "I do not want the woman with whom I live to work if it means the household is run less smoothly." In Komarovsky's interviews, men

Table 4: Family roles and career conflicts

	Disagree	Uncertain	Agree
Ideally, a father and mother should spend an equal amount of time with their young children.	3%	13%	84%
In my household, I want all major decisions to be made mutually.	3%	7%	90%
As a matter of principle, a man and woman living together should do an equal amount of housework.	17%	25%	58%
When a man and woman are raising a family, the man should make the major decisions concerning finances.	68%	26%	6%
In a family situation, I feel it is the mother's responsibility to make major decisions concerning child care.	30%	52%	18%
The father should be the disciplinarian of the family.	58%	36%	6%
I feel I could learn to care for young children as well as their mother could care for them.	15%	23%	62%
There is no adequate substitute for a mother's care of young children.	34%	39%	27%
It is important to me that my salary alone be adequate to support by family.	58%	28%	14%

were less willing to endure discomfort felt when wives were working.

An affirmative answer to a proposition, "It is appropriate for a mother of a pre-school child to take a fulltime job," was, upon further questioning, conditioned by such restrictions as, "provided, of course, that the home was run smoothly, the children did not suffer, and the wife's job did not interfere with her husband's career."[5]

Though many men subscribing to egalitarianism in our survey were willing to relinquish their traditional role of bookkeepers, they were somewhat less willing to relinquish their traditional role as family disciplinarian. In a family context, 80% of the egalitarians disagreed that a man should make the major decisions concerning finances, but only 61% disagreed that the father should be the disciplinarian.

Men who feel they may not be able to care for their children as

	Disagree	Uncertain	Agree
CAREER CONFLICTS			
I do not want the woman with whom I live to work if it means the household is run less smoothly.	68%	21%	11%
A mother of a pre-school child should not take a full-time job outside the home if this means she spends less time with the child.	33%	39%	28%
A woman's profession should be secondary to the needs of her family.	38%	34%	28%
A man has a right to expect his family to adjust to the demands of his profession.	15%	46%	39%
I would not want the woman with whom I live to maintain a full-time job if it interferes with my career.	42%	39%	19%
REACTIONS TO CAREER WOMEN			
Generally speaking, a career woman is more likely to be an interesting conversationalist than a housewife.	21%	38%	41%
A career woman is less attractive as a potential marital partner than a woman who is less interested in a career.	73%	21%	6%

well as their wives may be more inclined to retain the more aloof and authoritarian role of disciplinarian. Support for this speculation may be found in the fact that among those who subscribed to the egalitarian ideal regarding child care, only 36% disagreed that there is no adequate substitute for a mother's care of young children. Komarovsky noted that in regard to occupational rivalry, "the expectation that the husband should be the superior achiever appears still to be deeply rooted."[6] Men who feel they must be better than their wives are not likely to willingly undertake responsibilities such as child care if they feel they are going to provide second-best care.

Very likely, another central dynamic in males' reluctance to assume responsibility for child care may be the fact that, "in sociological language, work has . . . been the main institutional anchorage or support for the adult male role."[7] The reward system of work is usually quite different from the rewards available in child care, and until men find the same satisfaction from child care as they do from "work," they are unlikely to find it desirable.

Apparently the existence of day care and nurseries for young children has not made much difference to many of the Oberlin men in terms of freeing mothers from young children to pursue careers. To the statement, "A mother of a pre-school child should not take a full-time job outside the home if this means she spends less time with the child," almost a quarter of the egalitarians agreed and another 39% were uncertain. Also note that the statement, "There is no adequate substitute for a mother's care," to which only 34% of our total sample disagreed, encompasses not only fathers' care but also day care and nurseries.

In her study, Komarovsky noted that "ambivalent attitudes manifested toward both the full-time housemaker and the career wife. The image of each contained both attractive and repellent traits."[8] Our study of Oberlin men revealed such ambivalences. Career women strike 41% of Oberlin men as generally more interesting conversationalists than housewives and 73% felt career women are at least as attractive as marital partners as women less interested in careers. However, 22% of these same men also felt a woman's profession should be secondary to the needs of her family and 31% were uncertain. Oberlin men tend to value highly an active career woman, but are ambivalent about whether family or career demands ought to be prior for her.

Surprisingly, and contrary to Komarovsky's findings, many Oberlin men expect that if they marry, their wives will help provide the family income. Komarovsky found most men in her study assumed "that a wife's paycheck would not be an economic necessity. The overwhelming majority were confident that their earnings would be adequate to support the family."[9] Fifty-eight per cent of our respondents, on the other hand, disagreed that 'it is important that their salaries alone be adequate to support their families. However, among these men who expected to share the breadwinner role, 36% maintained that a man has a right to expect his family to adjust to the demands of his profession, and 47% felt a woman's profession should be secondary to the needs of her family. The data are too limited and ambiguous to allow clear conclusions. But confusion, frustration and stress are predictable if a man expects part of the family's subsistence to be provided by the woman's occupation, while at the same time he expects the woman to adjust to the demands of his profession and to consider her family more important than her job. Some of our respondents may be advocating a shared breadwinner role while relegating the woman's career to a status inferior to his career and refusing to share those family and household tasks that traditionally have made it difficult for women to have time and energy to develop a career. This would not be increased sharing; rather the woman may have even greater responsibility, the man less. And the threats involved will cause great stress to both.

In summary, according to our data, Oberlin men are generally committed to egalitarian ideals regarding the maintenance of family life, and are quite willing to relinquish traditional male household roles, e.g., family bookkeeper. But they are anxious about their own abilities to assume traditional female household roles, especially regarding child care. And they are even more anxious regarding how egalitarianism, especially in terms of careers, might influence their own professional futures. Presumably spending more time with family and household responsibilities would provide less time for developing one's career, and there also may be less reward for pursuing solely one's career, at the expense of all else. As Komarovsky pointed out, these tensions may not presently "generate a high degree of stress, partly, no doubt, because future roles do not require an immediate realistic confrontation. In addition, there is no gainsaying the conclusion that human beings can tolerate a high degree of inconsistency as long as it does not conflict with their self-interest."[10]

Table 5: Sexual Responsibility

The relationship of sexual intercourse and conception has been complicated and obscured by the confluence of many recent social factors, including the relatively easy availability of contraceptives and the emergence of the so-called new morality with its sexual permissiveness. But a widely accepted social standard for determining responsibility in these matters has been slow in development. Response to several statements in our survey revealed several ambiguities and contradictions plaguing students' values and behavior regarding sexuality.

In the recent past the only commonly acceptable arena for sexual intercourse was the institution of marriage. That this is no longer the case among students at Oberlin is borne out by the fact that only 31% of our return sample said they had never had sexual intercourse with a female and 60% had experienced heterosexual intercourse several or many times. Furthermore, 51% said they had had sexual intercourse with two or more females; 36% with three or more females.

Increased sexual permissiveness carries with it concern about contraception. The wide range of contraception devices available for women as opposed to the very limited variety of contraception devices available for men underscores the extent to which contraception, conception and child-rearing traditionally have been the responsibility of women in our society. But in the context of more permissive sexual behavior, apparently some men are beginning to re-examine their responsibilities concerning procreation. Slightly more than 50% of the men in our sample disagreed that a woman is more responsible than a man for birth control, and only about 20% felt the woman is more responsible. At least at the level of this broad value statement, Oberlin male students are heavily subscribing to the notion that men are at least as responsible for contraception as women.

The response to whether a woman is more responsible for birth control predicted response to the statement, "I expect that any woman with whom I have sexual intercourse will be using some method of contraception"; 54% of the men who agreed that a woman is more responsible for birth control expected a woman to be using a contraceptive, and 48% of the men who disagreed that a woman is more responsible also did not expect a woman to be using a contraceptive. This statement was somewhat misleading for it did not make clear whether the man expected a woman to be using a contraceptive simply because he believed all women were primarily responsible for birth control, or because, after discussing contraception, he and the woman decided for any number of possible reasons that she would be using the contraceptive.

We intended to clarify this by posing this statement for response: "When I expect to begin having sexual intercourse with a female, I talk to her about our using some form of contraception." Response to whether a woman is more responsible for birth control was only slightly related to response to this statement, but response to whether one expected a woman to be using a contraceptive was statistically unrelated to whether the couple discussed contraception before beginning intercourse. The most alarming discrepancy is that of the 80% of the men who disagreed or were uncertain that a woman is more responsible for birth control, only 39% disagreed that they expect the woman to be using a contraceptive, and only 65% to the 80% talk about contraception when they are initiating heterosexual intercourse.

Apparently for many of our respondents there is little or no connection between responsibility for contraception and responsibility

Table 5: Sexual Responsibility

	Disagree	Uncertain	Agree
I feel the woman is more responsible for the use of birth control methods than the man.	51%	30%	19%
I expect that any woman with whom I have sexual intercourse will be using some method of contraception.	35%	31%	34%
When I expect to begin having sexual intercourse with a female, I talk to her about our using some form of contraception.	11%	24%	65%
I have no right to interfere with a woman seeking to abort a fetus I helped conceive.	36%	29%	35%
I feel it is the man's responsibility to pay at least part of the cost of an abortion.	7%	14%	79%
In marriage, it is primarily the wife's responsibility to decide whether to seek abortion of an unwanted pregnancy.	62%	25%	13%
I consider abortion a morally offensive means of birth control.	62%	16%	22%
I might feel less masculine if I had a vasectomy.	33%	42%	25%
When a vasectomy is reliably reversible, I will get one.	28%	43%	29%

for abortion. The statement concerning whether a woman is more responsible for birth control than a man contained the term, "birth control," rather than "contraception," in order to allow respondents to include abortion in their response. However, response to that statement did not predict response to the statement, "I have no right to interfere with a woman seeking to abort a fetus I helped conceive." In fact, among the men who disagreed that the woman is more responsible for birth control, 39% disagreed and 35% agreed that they had no right to interfere with an abortion.

Surprisingly, of the 36% of the men who felt they had no right to interfere in an abortion, 86% also felt responsible for paying at least part of an abortion cost. In one sense, these men have assumed partial financial responsibility for the cost of a decision in which they felt they had no right to participate. On the other hand, they have maintained some responsibility for the welfare of the woman, whose situation they helped create, and for the fetus.

In the context of marriage, many of the men in our survey reneged on their claim that the woman has a right to decide on abortion. In fact, the response to whether a man has a right to interfere in an abortion decision was a highly significant predictor of the response to whether, in marriage, it was primarily the wife's responsibility to decide whether to seek abortion of an unwanted pregnancy. Seventy-four percent of the men who felt that in general they had no right to interfere, in the more specific context of marriage, were either uncertain about their rights and responsibilities (30%) or completely reversed their stand about their right to interfere when the women were their wives. Yet presumably marriage does not change the right of a woman to make decisions about her own body and the existence of a fetus in it.

Apparently, our respondents saw little relation between the statement that a mother should be responsible for major child care decisions and the statement that in marriage it is primarily the wife's responsibility to decide whether to seek an abortion of an unwanted pregnancy. Response to the two were statistically unrelated.

As was expected, males displayed considerable uncertainty concerning vasectomies, though the statements themselves were highly speculative. With 43% of the response being uncertain, 29% of the respondents indicated that when a vasectomy is reliably reversible, they may get one. Though still with a very high percentage of uncertainty (43%), 33% disagreed that they might feel less masculine if they had a vasectomy, and 25% said they would feel less masculine.

Table 6: Heterosexual Experiences

The majority of the freshman respondents said that they had experienced heterosexual intercourse. Only 40% of the freshmen reported that they had never experienced heterosexual intercourse and 46% reported having had such experiences several or many times. Among the senior respondents, only 15% said they had never experienced heterosexual intercourse and 74% said they had had several or many such experiences. Because our survey was taken in early April, and we included no device for determining how many of our respondents experienced heterosexual intercourse before coming to college, we can only conjecture that though Oberlin College provides an atmosphere in which many males establish sexual relationships with females, it is likely that many of them had had such experiences before coming to Oberlin.

Tables 7 And 8: Homosexual Attitudes

Students and faculty members sometimes speculate that there might be an ethic among Oberlin students suggesting that "heterosexual people" are incomplete persons. The sometimes explicit suggestion is that men ought to be able to relate sexually in a comfortable manner to both men and women, and the same for women. The data from our survey show little support for the contention that this

Table 6: Percentage by religious groups of men experiencing heterosexual intercourse during Oberlin career

		Never had hetero-sexual intercourse		Several or many heterosexual intercourse	
Jewish	underclassmen	56%		28%	
			(39% diff.)		(45% diff.)
	upperclassmen	17%		73%	
Protestant	underclassmen	43%		61%	
			(18% diff.)		(6% diff.)
	upperclassmen	25%		67%	
Roman Catholic	underclassmen	33%		61%	
			(8% diff.)		(6% diff.)
	upperclassmen	25%		67%	

ethic is strong at Oberlin. Fully 70% of the respondents disagreed and only 9% agreed that they would be more complete persons if they developed sexual relationships with both men and women. On the other hand, two-thirds of our respondents disagreed that developing sexual relationships with men is morally wrong. Though few men felt homosexuality is morally offensive, 62% of our respondents agreed that they do not want anyone to think that they are homosexual.

In face of these attitudes concerning homosexuality among men, a

Table 7: Male homosexuality: attitudes

	Disagree	Uncertain	Agree
I am more complete as a person if I develop sexual relationships with both men and women.	70%	21%	9%
I feel that developing sexual relationships with men is morally wrong.	67%	20%	13%
I do not want anyone to think that I am a homosexual.	14%	24%	62%

Table 8: Male homosexuality: behavior

	Underclass Men	Upperclass Men	Total Sample
I have had sexual encounters with a male (not necessarily the same person):			
never	76%	80%	78%
once	7%	8%	8%
a couple times	6%	2%	4%
several times	6%	6%	6%
many times	6%	4%	5%
My last sexual encounter with a male occurred:			
never had one	73%	79%	76%
within the last year	17%	8%	13%
one to three years ago	4%	6%	5%
more than three years ago	6%	6%	6%
I have felt sexually attracted to a male:			
never	67%	51%	59%
once	3%	3%	3%
a couple times	10%	26%	18%
several times	11%	14%	12%
many times	9%	6%	8%

sizable number of Oberlin men have experienced at least one sexual encounter with another male. About 15% of the respondents reported having homosexual encounters since beginning their Oberlin careers. Over twice as many freshmen as seniors (17% vs. 8%) reported homosexual encounters within the last year. There is no way to know on the basis of our survey whether this fact has more to do with a new generation or the new freedom of one's first year in college. Overall, there was no significant difference between underclassmen and upperclassmen regarding the percentage of men who had had homosexual encounters at one time or another, but there was a large discrepancy between freshmen's and seniors' feelings of sexual attraction for other males, particularly in light of the similarity of the two groups' sexual behavior. Among men who had never experienced a homosexual encounter, 14% of the freshmen reported having felt sexually attracted to a male at least a couple times, whereas fully 51% of the seniors reported having felt at least two homosexual attractions.

These responses suggested that something happened to the majority of Oberlin males during the course of their Oberlin careers which led them to experience sexual attraction to other men, but these men gained no corresponding increase in willingness or opportunity to express such feelings sexually. In fact, the responses to our statements suggested that though many of these men felt that homosexuality was not morally wrong, they did not want others to think that they might be homosexual. Our survey did not suggest what caused the increased homosexual attraction and the contradictory unwillingness to express these feelings sexually.

Our brief and tentative survey indicates that more study of all these issues could provide a clearer picture of the precise nature of these various tensions and could lead to constructive conversation on how groups of men and women and the college itself can enable their resolution. Only as men begin to share their confusion and their clarity will they be able to support each other enough to make the adjustments needed for sexual equality. And only then can sexual equality mean not just liberation for women, but liberation for both men and women.

References

1. We mailed questionnaires to names and addresses selected from the February register of students in the Housing and Dining Office. Four ques-

tionnaires were returned to us because the campus mail service had no forwarding address for students who had moved, so our return rate was 211 of 296 questionnaires.

2. Pleck, Joseph, "Psychological Frontiers for Men," an unpublished talk given at the Sex Role Discussion Series, Brandeis University Student Center, Feb. 22, 1973.

3. Komarovsky, Mirra, "Cultural Contradictions and Sex Roles: The Masculine Case," *American Journal of Sociology*, Volume 78, Number 4 (January 1973) p. 873.

4. *Ibid.*, p. 874.

5. *Ibid.*, p. 878.

6. *Ibid.*, p. 881.

7. Pleck, *op. cit.*

8. Komarovsky, *op. cit.*, p. 880.

9. *Ibid.*, p. 878.

10. *Ibid.*, p. 884.

The Paradox of the Contemporary American Father: Every Day Is Mother's Day

By Myron Brenton

Comparisons between men and women on which sex has it rougher in this world are both onerous and pointless. Yet it is fair to say that in at least one area men face far more difficult problems than women. I refer specifically to the parental role.

It is no easier, of course, to be a mother than a father. The important difference is that while the mothering role has remained essentially the same throughout the ages, the father's role has been changing radically. The mother has always nurtured her children, exercised discipline over them, and involved herself deeply in their socialization, in seeing to it that they grow up more or less adjusted to the requirements of society.

The role of the contemporary American father, however, is inconsistent with the patterns of the past. Since he works outside the home and often has to travel a considerable distance to get to his place of employment and back again, today's father has little opportunity to be with his children or even to make his presence felt by them. The trend to the equality of the sexes is rapidly doing away with the external scaffolding of authority that used to structure him in the past. The shrinking of the wider family unit to its nuclear base focuses the

spotlight of paternal responsibility directly on him and this responsibility has enlarged in inverse ratio to his authority. In other words,
his duties have expanded while his rights have diminished. Today's
father no longer teaches his children his craft, as he did in rural
America. He no longer apprentices them to others. He no longer
controls their education, nor does he even have the illusion of doing
so. He has little, if anything, to say about their marriages. On the
other hand, he's expected to exhibit a wide range of fatherly responses. He's supposed to support his youngsters financially, as always;
support them all the way through college and even graduate school,
if possible; be firm with them but understanding; involve himself in
their problems; help his wife care for them physically; baby-sit with
them occasionally; discipline them effectively, but be a pal to them
as well; present an authoritative masculine figure that his girls will
admire and his boys will emulate; act as friend of and wise counselor
to his brood; be warm and affectionate with them; and be their link
to the wider community.

Countless books, magazine articles, speeches by childcare special-
ists, parent-training manuals, and pronouncements by psychologists
tell him of these responsibilities and make him feel guilty—or, more
likely, spur his wife on to make him feel guilty—about not meeting
them adequately. Advice and criticism have been coming in thickly
and heavily for the past decade or so. It seems that there's little he
does or can do right. If he moves his family from city to suburb, he's
placing them in a "manless" environment. If he concentrates on being
a pal to his son, he's evading his role as authority figure. If he has a
nurturing bent, some of the psychiatrists call him a motherly father.
If he doesn't do any nurturing to speak of, he's accused of distancing
himself from his children. If he's the sole disciplinarian, he takes on,
in his youngsters' eyes, the image of an ogre. If he doesn't discipline
them sufficiently, he's a weak father. If he's well off and gives his children all the material advantages he didn't have, he's spoiling them,
leaving them unprepared for life's hard knocks. If he's well off but
doesn't spoil them the way other fathers in the community do their
boys and girls, he gains the reputation of a latter-day Scrooge. If his
work keeps him away during the week and he tries to compensate by
spending extra time with his children on weekends, by doing special
things with them, this is also wrong. He's told either that he's making
himself into a goody-goody figure with them, while his wife has all the
dirty work of really bringing them up or that he'll eventually come to
resent the concentrated time he spends with them because he'd rather

be out playing golf. And, repeatedly, the accusing voices tell him that he has given up his rightful place as head of his family, as guide and mentor to his children.

If the advice is contradictory at times, and the criticism more so, it is in part due to the fact that the experts themselves have widely divergent opinions on the proper role of the father. So does the society in general. In fact, American society is somewhat schizoid in its attitude toward fatherhood. This is the result of another one of the innumerable ironies springing out of the patriarchal system. The Victorian mother might have shouldered most of the responsibility for the children's care and upbringing, but she gained in turn a powerful form of compensation: She was glorified. She was idealized. Her virtues were praised to the skies, and of faults she was deemed to have none. To an extent we have inherited this glorification of the mother. True, vituperation is often hurled at the possessive, castrating, domineering Mom that Philip Wylie first thrust into the spotlight some twenty years ago, and currently there are attempts by some neofeminist writers to downgrade the mother's importance. But theirs isn't a winning battle. The "cult of motherhood," as Wylie aptly described it, is still fairly potent. In fact, when sociologist Helena Lopata at Roosevelt University in Chicago asked more than 600 urban wives what a woman's most important roles are, in order of importance, the great majority of the ladies voted first for "mother." ("Wife" come in second; "homemaker," third.)

As for fatherhood, there is no cult. Nobody votes the father's role as the most important in a man's life (although it's highly questionable whether either sex should consider the parental role the most important in its life). Despite all the demands that contemporary society makes on the father, despite all the expectations it has regarding his performance, fatherhood in America is accorded remarkably little respect.

An anonymous saying goes, "God could not be everywhere, and so he made mothers." In a nation in which Mother's Day not only is a yearly ritual but also generates $1,500,000,000 worth of business, such an aphorism is devoutly believed. From the mother-child mysticism stem such clichés as "Nobody knows a child the way its mother does" and "A boy's best friend is his mother." There's some truth to them, of course. Why shouldn't there be, if Pop hasn't been around much and traits like sympathy and understanding are labeled feminine?

Orthodox psychoanalysis, which has had such a pervasive influence on American culture, tends to elevate the emotional response between mother and child to impossibly lofty heights—heights to which no mere father could aspire. Consider Dr. Marynia Farnham's declaration: "The special genius of women has always been that of nurture, for which man has no talent whatsoever."[1] Consider Dr. Erich Fromm's phenomenally successful analysis of love, "The Art of Loving," which states, "Mother's love is bliss, is peace, it need not be acquired, it need not be deserved. . . . It is for this altruistic, unselfish character that motherly love has been considered the highest kind of love, and the most sacred of all emotional bonds."[2] Consider Dr. Ashley Montagu's pronouncement in another work that has garnered a huge readership over the years, "The Natural Superiority of Women": 'The sensitive relationships which exist between mother and child belong to a unique order of humanity, an order in which the male may participate as a child, but from which he increasingly departs as he leaves childhood behind'.[3]

Even the nation's child custody laws prove how potent the cult of motherhood still is. In almost every state both the law and court practice give the mother a clear and almost insurmountable advantage in divorce cases in which there's a battle between mother and father over custody of the children. Unless, it can be shown that she's a distinct hazard to the health or welfare of her offspring—something very difficult to do—most courts in most states award full custody rights to the mother under the blanket assumption that a child needs to be with its mother. It is the case even when the father is just as willing and just as competent to raise the children as she is. In some courts it is the case even when the mother is obviously the less desirable parent from the standpoint of both morals and competence. It could be argued that men want it this way, that it precludes saddling them with the physical responsibility for the offspring. This may have been true at one time, but the frequency of child-custody battles shows that at least for some fathers times have changed. (Both lay people and legal authorities in some states are trying to correct the situation. Attempting to effect legal reforms in his state, for instance, an Ohio jurist, Judge Roy C. Scott, has observed that "a man's status in divorce cases and domestic problems is not an enviable one" and that "the father in many cases is just as well equipped to have custody since he, too, can hire a baby sitter.")[4]

It should be possible to acknowledge the vital role of love and nurture that a mother plays without giving it the inflated stress that borders on caricature, without making the father's role seem peripheral and inconsequential by comparison. But this has not been happening.

Not surprisingly, the "Thesaurus of Quotations" lists thirty-one "apt thoughts" and "felicitous expressions" for motherhood and a scant ten for fatherhood, the most felicitous of the sparse lot being the proverb, "It's a wise child that knows its own father." Not surprisingly either, psychiatrists and sociologists complain about the dearth of solid data on fatherhood, pointing out that the behavioral sciences have concentrated primarily on motherhood. Even the mass media, grown so critical of the American father, make their own intriguing commentary on the condition of fatherhood today merely by the way they present this criticism. The majority of articles pointing out what's wrong with the contemporary father appear in the women's magazines, which most men don't read. Speeches on the subject are frequently given by women—and to an audience of women. In 1965 a series of television programs on the problems facing the American male, including those concerning his role as parent, took place on a midmorning show whose viewing audience is composed primarily of housewives. The ludicrous conclusion one could come to is that fatherhood is somehow feminine!

A goodly portion of the professional literature that exists on fatherhood suggests that the best father is the one who has relatively tenuous emotional ties with his young ones. When the child is in infancy, according to this viewpoint, the father's primary role is to protect and support (both psychologically and financially) the new mother. As the child grows older, it's permissible for him to show love, provided that this love is exclusively conditional—that is, strictly earned, given as a reward for good behavior or accomplishment. Woe to the father's image if he diapers the baby, feeds the child, or displays in any way the kind of warmth we have come to associate with motherliness. His image, many psychiatrists still insist, will turn motherly. It goes without saying that in such patriarchal eyes the father who has a nurturing bent, who enjoys helping take care of the little ones, who doesn't withdraw love from his children even when he exercises discipline, and who gets considerable emotional gratification out of their love for him is somewhat lacking in masculinity—and will create unmasculine sons.

As psychoanalyst Irene M. Josselyn is frank to admit, a great deal of psychological literature "tends to minimize the significance of any possible psychological response specifically called fatherliness." Pointing to a definite psychological existence of fatherliness, she includes among its elements the child as a narcissistic extension of the father, as proof of the father's manliness, as rival, and as an object of "tender love." Dr. Josselyn adds, "Unfortunately, when this emotion acts as a cohesive force in men, it is too often considered evidence of the repressed femininity of the man."[5]

The very term "tender love" within the context of fatherhood still sounds somewhat strange, so seldom is it used. It is not that the contemporary father fails to display warmth and affection to his children. By and large he does, at least when they are young. We have come a long way from the nineteenth-century aloofness, when a studied coolness was the mode between father and child. Today there are warmth, laughter, and spontaneous affection. Today some fathers delight in sharing with mothers in the care of even very young infants.

Still lacking is a really basic awareness that a father can enjoy, wholly as a man, the give-and-take of psychic nurturing that we tend to associate primarily with mothers. Actually, the father who permits this give-and-take to occur finds his own scope widening as a result. As Dr. Milton R. Sapirstein has pointed out, this kind of participation allows the father to resolve his own "residual dependencies," affords him an opportunity for "fulfilling his creative drives," and helps him to open up emotionally, for "many a father has learned to be a healthy emotional human being only through contact with his children."[6] Despite scattered insights such as these, there is still little real intellectual crystallization of father love.

Furthermore, the most recent sociological studies on the subject show that the boys who see their fathers giving warm positive affection, as well as providing discipline, are more likely to identify with them than the boys who don't. Hence, these are the boys least likely to have problems with their masculine identity.[7] Important as these findings are (and they're beginning to be publicized), it certainly seems as important to stress the joys of fatherhood—emotional rewards it provides for the father—as to stress the duties and obligations the paternal role imposes on him. Too often the emphasis is on what the father must do, with little or nothing said about what he can receive. Then, too, unless he's profoundly involved with his children on an emotional level, today's father is apt to have ambivalent feelings about them, for unlike youngsters in a rural setting, they constitute economic liabilities, and he must work all the harder to provide for them than he would otherwise. If the involvement isn't there, he's likely to feel, if a bit guilty, "Is it all really worth it?" Here, then, is another reason for stressing the fact that fatherhood is potentially a two-way street, that it provides rewards, as well as imposes obligations.

References

1. Quoted by Sapirstein, *Emotional Security* (New York: Crown Publishers, 1948), p. 191.

2. Erich Fromm, *The Art of Loving* (New York: Harper & Bros., 1956), pp. 39, 50.

3. Ashley Montagu, *The Natural Superiority of Women* (New York: The Macmillan Co., 1952), p. 142.

4. Quoted by Don Oakley, *New York World-Telegram* (June 25, 1964). Lest it be thought Judge Scott is biased in favor of men, he has also championed the rights of women—particularly mothers—in Ohio.

5. Irene M. Josselyn, "Cultural Forces, Motherliness and Fatherliness," *American Journal of Orthopsychiatry* (April, 1956). The traditional view holds that the father should be the sole disciplinarian and the sole provider of conditional love, because it's his exclusive job to instill conscience. Thus, Fromm states (op. cit., p. 43) that "Father's love should be guided by principles and expectations," and although he insists that the father ought to be "patient and tolerant," rather than "threatening and authoritarian," the effect is nevertheless a distancing and lack of spontaneity between father and child.

6. Sapirstein, op. cit., p. 176.

7. Donald E. Payne and Paul H. Mussen, "Parent Child Relations and Father Identification Among Adolescent Boys," *The Journal of Abnormal and Social Psychology* (May, 1956). Also, Paul Mussen and Luther Distler, "Masculinity, Identification and Father-Son Relationships," *The Journal of Abnormal and Social Psychology* (November, 1959). Also, Charlotte Himber, "So He Hates Baseball," *The New York Times Magazine* (August 29, 1965).

Confessions of a Househusband

By Joel Roache

*M*any men are coming to realize that sex-role privilege inflicts enormous damage on them, turning half of humanity into their subordinates and the other half into their rivals, isolating them and making fear and loneliness the norm of their existence. That ponderous abstraction became real for me in what many men consider a trivial realm: housework.

Every movement produces its truisms, assumptions that very soon are scarcely open to argument. The Women's Movement is no exception, and one of its truisms is that the home is a prison for women, trapping them in housework and child care, frustrating and distorting their need for fulfillment as whole persons. Whatever reality lies behind many situation comedy stereotypes—the nag, the clinging wife, the telephone gossip—is rooted in this distortion. Only after I had assumed the role of househusband, and was myself caught in the "trap of domesticity," did I realize that the reality behind those stereotypes is a function of the role, not the person.

Two years ago, my wife Jan and I tried to change (at least within our own lives) society's imposed pattern of dependent servant and responsible master by deciding to share equally the responsibility of housework. We made no specific arrangement (a mistake from which I was to learn a great deal); it was simply understood that I was going to take on roughly half of the domestic chores so that she could do the other work she needed to do.

Ms., 1 (November, 1972), pp. 25-27. Copyright © 1972 by *Ms. Magazine.* Reprinted by permission of *Ms.*

There was something of a shock for me in discovering the sheer quantity of the housework, and my standards of acceptable cleanliness fell rapidly. It became much easier to see my insistence on neatness as an inherited middle-class hang-up now that I had to do so much of the work myself. One of the long-standing sources of tension between Jan and me was almost immediately understood and resolved. What's more, I enjoyed it, at first. When not interrupted by the children I could, on a good day, do the kitchen and a bedroom, a load of laundry, and a meal in a little over two hours. Then I'd clean up after the meal and relax for a while with considerable satisfaction. So I approached the work with some enthusiasm, looking forward to seeing it all put right by my own hand, and for a while I wondered what all the fuss was about.

But within a few weeks that satisfaction and that enthusiasm began to erode a little more each time I woke up or walked into the house, only to find that it all needed to be done again. Finally, the image of the finished job, the image that encouraged me to start, was crowded out of my head by the image of the job to do all over again. I became lethargic, with the result that I worked less efficiently, so that even when I did "finish," it took longer and was done less well, rendering still less satisfaction. At first I had intellectual energy to spare, thinking about my teaching while washing dishes; pausing in the middle of a load of laundry to jot down a note. But those pauses soon became passive daydreams, fantasies from which I would have to snap myself back to the grind, until finally it was all I could do to keep going at all. I became more and more irritable and resentful.

Something similar happened even sooner and more dramatically to my relationship with our three children. I soon found myself angry with them most of the time, and I almost never enjoyed them. Then I watched myself for a couple of days and realized what was going on. They were constantly interrupting. I had tried simply to be available to them in case they needed me while I went on reading, writing, cleaning, or watching television. But of course with a six-year-old, a four-year-old, and a one-year-old, someone would need me every five to 15 minutes. Just enough time to get into something, and up Jay would come with a toy to be fixed, or Matthew would spill his juice, or Eric would get stuck between the playpen bars and scream. In everything I tried to do, I was frustrated by their constant demands and soon came, quite simply, to hate them; and to hate myself for hating them; and at some level, I suspect, to hate Jan for getting me into this mess. My home life became a study in frustration and resentment.

I soon reached the conclusion that if I was going to keep house and take care of the children, I might as well give up doing anything else at the same time if I hoped to maintain any equilibrium at all. So I deliberately went through my housekeeping paces in a daze, keeping alert for the children but otherwise concentrating on whatever was before me, closing down all circuits not relevant to the work at hand. I maintained my sanity, I think, and I ceased to scream at the children so much, but neither they nor anyone else got the benefit of any creative energy; there just wasn't any. In half a day I could feel my mind turning into oatmeal, cold oatmeal, and it took the other half to get it bubbling again, and by then it was bedtime, and out of physical exhaustion I would have to go to sleep on whatever coherent ideas I might have got together in my few hours of free time.

Things went on this way for quite some time, partly because I couldn't think of an acceptable alternative, and partly because I was on a kind of guilt trip, possessed by the suicidal notion that somehow I had to pay for all those years Jan was oppressed. After a while I began to "adjust"; even cold oatmeal has a certain resilience. I began to perceive my condition as normal, and I didn't notice that my professional work was at a standstill. Then Jan became involved in community organizing, which took up more and more of her time and began to eat into mine, until finally I found myself doing housekeeping and child care from eight to 16 hours a day, and this went on for about eight weeks. The astonishing thing now is that I let this masochistic work load go on so long. I suppose my guilt trip had become almost equivalent to a woman's normal conditioning, in reducing my ability to resist effectively the demands of Jan's organizing. And the excitement of her newly discovered self-sufficiency and independence (after eight years of her struggle to make me recognize what I was doing to her) functioned in the same way as the normal assumption of the superior importance of a male's work as provider.

I can pinpoint the place in time when we saw the necessity for a more careful adjustment of responsibilities, defining duties and scheduling hours more precisely and adhering to them more faithfully. It was at a moment when it became clear that Jan's work was beginning to pay off and her group scored a definite and apparently unqualified success. I went around the house for a full day feeling very self-satisfied, proud of her achievement, *as if it were my own*, which was fine until I realized, somewhere near the end of the day, that much of that sense of achievement resulted from the fact that I had no achievement of my own. I was getting my sense of fulfillment, of self-esteem, *through her*, while she was getting it *through her work*. It had happened: I was a full-fledged househusband.

A similar moment of illumination occurred at about the same time. Jan had spent the afternoon with a friend while I took care of the children and typed a revision of the bibliography for the book I was trying to finish at the time, the kind of drudgery more prosperous authors underpay some woman to do. By the time Jan got home I was in a state of benumbed introversion, and when she began to talk about the substance of her afternoon's conversation, I was at first bored and finally irritated. Before long I was snapping at her viciously. She sat there looking first puzzled, then bewildered, and finally withdrawn. In a kind of reflexive self-defense she cut me off emotionally and went on thinking about whatever was on her mind. As I began to run down, I realized that what she had been trying to talk about would normally be interesting and important to me, yet I had driven her away. Then I looked at her and suddenly had the really weird sensation of seeing myself, my own isolation and frustration when I used to come home and try to talk to her. I realized that I was in her traditional position and felt a much fuller understanding of what that was. In that moment, on the verge of anger, an important part of what we had been doing to each other for all those years became clearer than it had ever been to either of us.

Another problem was suddenly clear to me also. The loneliness and helplessness I had felt before we traded responsibilities had been a function of my own privilege. My socially defined and reinforced role as *the* responsible party to the marriage had cut me off from Jan's experience; had made inevitably futile our attempts to communicate with each other from two very different worlds. Since she has a strong sense of herself as a responsible adult, Jan was bound to resist the limits of her role as dependent and (though we would never have said it) subordinate. When I found myself muttering and bitching, refusing to listen, refusing to provide any positive feedback on her experience in the outside world, I realized that her preoccupation, her nagging and complaining, her virtual absence from my psychic world, had not been neurotic symptoms but expressions of resistance to my privilege and to the power over her life that it conferred.

Jan's failure to force a real change in our life together for so long is a grim tribute to the power of socialization, and to my ability to exploit that power in order to protect myself from reality. When Jan realized how really minimal were the satisfactions of housework, there was also a voice within her (as well as mine without) suggesting that perhaps she was just lazy. If she began to hate the children, she knew that it was because they were helping to prevent her meeting real and legitimate personal needs, but the voices were always there hinting that the real trouble was that she was basically a hateful person and thus a poor mother. If her mind became sluggish, she knew at some level that she was making an adaptive adjustment to her situation, but those voices whispered in a thousand ways that she might be going crazy, or perhaps she was just stupid. And when she became sullen and resentful toward me, the voices were always there to obscure her perception that I had it coming. They even encouraged her to feel guilty, finally, when she did not feel my success as her reward, the payoff for all her drudgery. They kept her from realizing that such a payoff cost her a sense of her independent selfhood; that it was at best the pittance of exploitation: shit wages for shit work.

Those voices, within and without, kept reminding us both that Jan's real destiny was to keep me comfortable and productive and to raise "our" children. The feelings I'd come to experience in a few months had for years made Jan feel lazy, selfish, and egotistic; unable to empathize with the needs of the family (read: my need for success). Just as importantly, her knowledge that the sources of her troubles were not all within herself could not have received any reinforcement in the social world. I was her only link with that world; my affection and "respect" were her only source of assurance that she was real. To the extent that identity depends on recognition by others, she depended on me for that as surely as she depended on me for grocery money. The result was that she was afraid to share with me huge areas of her life, any areas which might threaten my regard for her. She could not afford, psychologically or economically, to challenge me overtly. And when she managed to make any suggestion that her discontent was a function of what was being done to her, it was battered down, by my recriminations, into a quagmire of guilt.

I had had some inkling of all this before I ever committed myself to cooking a meal or washing a single pair of socks (as my responsibility, rather than a favor to her). But at every stage of our experiment in role reversal (or rather our attempt to escape roles) my understanding of her position became more real. I had got a lot of domestic services but I had been denied real contact with a whole human being, and hard upon my guilt came anger, rage at what had been done to us both.

I don't have space here to go on and extend our experience into the world outside the family. It is enough to say that when someone has concrete power over your life, you are going to keep a part of yourself hidden and therefore undeveloped, or developed only in fantasy. Your identity becomes bound up in other people's expectation of you—and that is the definition of alienation. It did not take long for me to make connections between the alienating ways in which Jan had to deal with me in the early years of our marriage and the way that I was dealing with my "senior colleagues," the men and women who had power to fire me and did.

Our experience also helped me to understand the distortions of perception and personality that result from being the "superior" in a hierarchical structure. The nuclear family as we know it is one such structure, perhaps the crucial one. But the alienation which results from privilege pervades all our experience in a society which values human beings on the basis of sex, race, and class and which structures those standards into all its institutions. Housework is only a tip of that iceberg, but for Jan and me it has helped to make the need to fundamentally transform those institutions a gut reality.

"Growing Up Popular"

By A Men's Consciousness Raising Group

*P*robably the first real experience that I ever had with "the-difference-between-boys-and-girls" was playing doctor, a fairly short-lived period when I was about six. Janet and I would take turns being doctor and patient. I liked being the patient most—just passively lying back being "examined" and fondled. Being doctor got to be boring after the first few genital and anal examinations and probes. My curiosity was soon satisfied and it was just routine, tedious check-up work after that. But getting examined—that was always nice. I told Janet once that I wished she had 'real' tits. That would have been new and interesting. She sympathized with me. Although we did have to do our playing clandestinely, in the bushes or garages, the fear of being caught wasn't too great. We would only have been embarrassed, not really punished. We did hear, though, that a "patient" a few blocks away had to go to the hospital to have an "examination instrument," i.e., a stick, removed from his asshole. That was a chilling thought. I played doctor with one or two girls—maybe some boys, too—but I guess we all just got bored with it after a while. I think the whole period lasted only a year or so.

Three or four years later my curiosity must have been up again. While I was staying overnight with my cousin Bob, who was three years older than me, he told me about this magic powder which he

From the book *Unbecoming Men: A Men's Consciousness-Raising Group Writes on Oppression and Themselves.* Copyright © 1971 by Times Change Press, Penwell Road, Washington, New Jersey 07882.

took before going to bed at night. It would make him tiny, about fingernail high, so he could get into his girlfriend's bed while she was asleep and roam around over her breasts and between her legs. That really sounded fine to me. So I took some of his magic powder the next night, followed his advice to concentrate before falling asleep only on the promised wanderings, and floated off smiling.

The kids next door and I, during our period of drawing heavy war scenes—battleships, tanks, airplane dogfights, etc.—included a few Nazi torture scenes of women with their tits cut off and hot irons stuck up their cunts. Once my mother caught us, and once their mom did. It was embarrassing but we really only got frowns and minor reprimands.

Around fifth grade that word "girlfriend" began to take on some real meaning. On Valentine's Day, when we exchanged cards with our friends in school, I got a foot-high card from Nita. It included a picture of her dressed up in a cute cowgirl outfit. I was in Seventh Heaven. Boy, was I proud of that card and of the fact that I now had a girlfriend who really liked me. I liked her, too. She was cute and nice. Then my uncle called the house and said he had heard that I had a girlfriend. I proudly fired back, "Yeah, and we're married now and have four kids." He thought that was the funniest thing he had ever heard, told it to everybody, and would boisterously ask me about it, in front of all our relatives, whenever he saw me after that. I avoided him like the plague thereafter, and hated it whenever my parents made me go with them to his home. I never did understand what the whole scene had been all about, and it was frightening.

At a party during sixth grade, the mother of the kid who was having the party got us all into our first game of spin-the-bottle. Although slightly timid at first, I really got into the game and had a great time. All of us boys loved the mother's sexy kisses, as well as kissing the three or four girls who were the prettiest in our class. It was a thrilling night for me. Kissing those popular girls, getting "girlfriends," becoming a popular boy—I didn't want that night to end.

After that it was bye-bye Nita. She wasn't in the "In" set, and that's where all my energy was to be directed from then on out. The main girl I liked throughout the rest of grade school was Maggie, a queenpin of the In crowd. All in all, though, trying to get her to like me was seldom a rewarding experience. She was after bigger fish— mainly the boys a year or two older, or the ones from other schools. This pained me a lot, but I kept on trying. Almost every night after school, for two and a half years, I would be over at Maggie's, or at one of her girlfriends' houses, with three or four other guys, trying to get up kissing games, bugging the girls, showing off—mainly just nervous, anxious, adolescent "play."

At one point Maggie and the girls got into going out to the roller-skating rink, I guess to meet some older, new boys. So I started going, too, although it was frightening at first. I was anxious about not knowing any of the people there, about how tough all the guys were, and about the flirting Maggie was doing with them. I'd come home feeling depressed, thinking it was hopeless, but then, next Friday night, I'd be back out there trying to keep up.

The guys in our crowd were mostly active in sports, as well as generally tough. There was a lot of jocular, challenging, competitive "play" at this time. Steve, especially, was tough. And I was often the target of his bullying. Once he and the other guys thought it was hilarious to put my bike up in a tree. I tried to stop him verbally— I couldn't have done it physically. Although I didn't want my bike fucked-up and I didn't like always being the butt of the guys' jokes, I didn't try too hard to stop him. I didn't want to seem a drag or a baby. In this "good-natured" rough-housing, Steve would often have me in a painful hold, and I'd have to beg him to let go. That was humiliating. I'd always try to hold out as long as possible, hoping he'd just tire and stop. I hated always being helpless and at his mercy, but, on the other hand, I knew I couldn't get angry or protest too much. I didn't want to spoil the fun.

Actual sex-play with girls still didn't enter in too much yet. By the end of the eighth grade, though, Steve did fuck one of the girls who was sort of in our crowd. I knew she did it because she was losing favor with the crowd (she was a little fat), and she hoped that this would help her keep popular. I knew Steve was as brutal to her as he was to me, and that he was just showing off and being tough, only in a new way. I partially thought the whole thing was disgusting. (Also it frightened me because it meant I would soon have to fuck somebody in order to remain respected and popular.) But I was also in awe of Steve. I wanted, too, to be tough and to be able to fuck girls like he did, like the cool guys did. Part of me knew the whole thing stunk, but a bigger part of of me knew that I had to soon get into it myself, and that's what I began gearing myself for.

I felt pressure to date popular girls *and* to fuck. The popular girls generally weren't into fucking yet, so I had a conflict. I didn't solve it by dating the nice girls and fucking others; I felt I was above "just fucking whores." I wouldn't be seen with non-popular girls. (Besides, they scared me. I didn't know how to relate to those tough, more lower class girls.) I tried to solve the conflict by dating the popular girls and working toward fucking them, too. I soon got a reputation for being "fast." From the first date on, I tried ceaselessly to go as far as possible—parking, feeling the girls up, bare tits, into their pants, fingering, etc. I can see now how I never related to the person I was with. I didn't feel anything particular toward her, except the challenge; not even sexual excitement. My first goal was to go out with ever more popular girls; my second was to go as far as possible sexually.

During my first three years of high school I worked like hell on this, intensely, single-mindedly. Since I wasn't in sports and failed in my attempts to get on the prestigious newspaper and yearbook staffs, I got into the band so I could at least be *in* something, to have *something* after my name in the yearbook. There were two or three high school fraternities, and in my sophomore year I managed by hook and crook to become a pledge to the most popular one. I really felt good about this. The glory of pledging this number one fraternity more than compensated for the minor humiliations of obeying the members that pledge year. Also, I constantly sought out, began hanging around with, and finally worked my way into, progressively more popular crowds. I always dropped my earlier friends as I made my way up the social ladder. I had nothing to do with my old grade school friends, and even by late high school I had left behind my closest friends from freshman and sophomore years.

My obsession with sexual conquests was generally very frustrating. By the end of junior year I still hadn't fucked anyone. But there was always this ethic to insinuate that a guy had gone farther than he really had, although not to outright lie about it. Some friends would ask, "Hey, did you get your finger wet last night?" And I'd just give them the silent smile that said, "I'm not going to tell you, but, yes, I did." And then I'd see the envy in their eyes. There was also an ethic, very strong in me, to never go steady—not to be "pussy-whipped." No girl could ever hold me down. I wanted the freedom to fuck around with lots of girls. I was always looking for new territory to conquer. I thought masturbating was too lower class and crude. Also, it was an admittance of not "getting any ass." And I wouldn't admit that! I already had my father's superiority by then; beating off was beneath me. I had wet dreams a lot, and they were a little puzzling and embarrassing, my sheet and pajamas being wet and sticky in the morning. My older brother occasionally got hold of "eight-page Bibles"—tiny illustrated dirty stories—and I used to enjoy looking at them. And once, around this time, while rough-housing with some five-year-old neighborhood kids, I tried to put my finger up into one of the little girl's cunts. I don't know how I related to that afterwards. I think I never let myself think of it; it's still touchy.

By my senior year I finally felt I was secure enough, popularity-wise, to relax and enjoy myself a little. Things were much nicer that year. I could date almost anybody I wanted, and because of the security I had gained, I didn't have so much social and sexual anxiety. Pam had been a girl I had tried dating my sophomore year, but she had generally rejected me and I finally gave up on her. But then that senior year I got the word that she wanted to go out with me. So I asked her out. I had always liked her. She was pretty, lively, and straightforward. From that first date we really hit it off. I liked being with her and just goofing around together. And, sexually, things were right up front. She really liked me, figured we'd be going together, and so was completely uninhibited. She even initiated some sex-play herself. That blew my mind—a girl who liked me and who openly really enjoyed our playing around sexually! What a pleasant change. And, an even more pleasant change, I liked her. She was not a means to an end, but an end in herself. I just liked her and I liked myself. I felt relaxed. Early in our relationship we tried to fuck, both of us for the first time, but either my cock wasn't hard enough or her cunt was too tight, because we couldn't get it in. But that didn't bother either of us, and we just vowed to try again the next chance we got, and it worked out okay. While we were lying together resting after our first try, I asked Pam to go steady, much to her and my surprise. I had thought I would never break down and do that, but I loved Pam and felt great.

After a few months of going together I began to get restless. I felt boxed in, that Pam and I were too close together, that I had gotten *too involved.* I felt the need to get free and roam around loose again. I especially wanted to date a few of the girls I had never been able to date before. It would be my last chance before high school ended and we would all go our separate ways. So I dropped Pam. And I did just *drop* her. By then I was long past worrying about how that affected her or any of the girls I dropped. I was not at all in touch, anymore, with the pain I caused them. I had even learned how not to feel and definitely not acknowledge, my own pain. Pain was a weakness, and I wasn't about to be weak.

I went right on to college. There, too, being "popular"—dating the right sorority girls, moving with the coolest guys, becoming a B.M.O.C.—a big man on campus—was my full time orientation. I had been very successful at it in high school, and now it looked like my first year at college was off to a good start—studying engineering (it was "in" then) at a Big Ten University, and being in one of the top fraternities. But then reality came crashing down. In high school I had four years of hard work to build up my popularity and self-confidence. But the intense, highly-competitive fraternity-sorority social world at college was a whole new trip. At the early fraternity-sorority mixers I nearly stumbled over myself in the mad rush to grab the prettiest girls. I usually got pretty ones, and later circled their pictures in the semester sorority books, showing the fraternity brothers all the sharp dates I had. Seldom, though, would one of these women really go out with me on a date after being with me at mixers. I had just been too scared and uptight to be any fun. I remember once, on a night picnic mixer, around a fire, lying on a blanket beside a particularly fine "piece" I had managed to pair myself up with, not knowing what to say to her, trying to think of how to "snow" her, and being afraid to try necking with her for fear she'd refuse. Thinking she really ought to like me. Boy, would that impress the brothers. What should I do? If she only really had a chance to know me. I can't lose this one too. . . . But the next week she declined a date with me and was soon going out with one of my fraternity brothers.

This type of experience was soon getting all too common for me. To try to recoup my sagging popularity-rating, my own social survival and self-respect, I would mouth all the "in" sayings and phrases, would try to drink a lot of beer in the old frat tradition, even sang a little in a Kingston Trio-type group (always scared stiff), and put a lot of emphasis upon clothes—immaculate trench-coat and umbrella, expensive, newest-style sweaters, the sharpest sportcoats and suits, always of course with the right poses and expressions.

But all this wasn't saving me from my down-hill slide. One particular unfortunate incident occurred while riding in a crowded car on the way back from another outing with another just-met "partner" on my lap. Again I was feeling fear knowing she really wanted to be with one of the cooler brothers. We stopped at her sorority house before the whole group was to move on to another spot. While waiting in the uptight sorority lounge for the women to come back down, I began getting uneasy. Various sisters would look down over the banister, whispering to each other. Eventually everybody else's partners came down except mine. Finally an older sister coolly told me that my partner wasn't feeling so well. So I politely left alone, went back to the frat house, and went to bed depressed. It was just one more rejection. One more humiliation. A few hours later, however, when the brothers returned, a very serious delegation came up to wake me and interrogate me. My ex-partner had told everyone that I had felt her up in the car. . . . Were this true (it wasn't) it would have been a social shock and damaged the good name of our fraternity. Being a "loser" was already a drag on the frat, but now this was too much. Boy, the roof caved in then on whatever confidence I had left. All this on top of being a lowly freshman fraternity pledge and having to put up with, even believing in, all its sick, authoritarian bullshit—the paddle-beatings, senseless make-work, serving the members, the endless petty humiliations. And then, too, the constant threat of flunking out always hanging over my head. What a painful year! Never the less, I was still hoping and planning for the next year!!

Fortunately, however, a psych department "counselor" helped me see that I was on the whole engineering and fraternity trip just to gain approval in my father's eyes. This came on top of a more important break—I flunked out! That was hard to take at first, but the next year I got into a more relaxed school, began studying (and enjoying) philosophy and history, and became a beatnik. Hallelujah. An unconscious life/survival-force within me pulled me out of that bullshit death trip I was on when my consciousness was too fucked-up to do it for me.

So I woke-up, and although I was saved from the "straight-American-success-story," I found that the twenty years of conditioning for this end were not incompatible with the hip scene I later got into. But while I am now able to realize so much more of who I really am, sexism remains still so pervasive in the "alternative" culture that I have to struggle now much as ever to escape it.

Why Men Don't Rear Children:
A Power Analysis

By Margaret Polatnick

Introduction

The starting point for this paper is a simple fact of contemporary social life: In our society (as in most societies familiar to us), women rather than men have the primary responsibility for rearing children. Of course, fathers are not devoid of obligations vis-à-vis their off-spring, but the father who accepts the routine day-to-day responsibility for supervising his children and servicing their needs, at the expense of outside employment and activity,* is still a rare bird indeed.

In examining why this is so, I plan to steer clear of two potential pitfalls. First, I will make no attempt to unravel historical causes in pursuit of a primeval "first cause." Anthropological evidence about the origin of male and female behaviors is inconclusive and sheds little light on the contemporary situation, where the conditions of life are substantially different. This paper will deal only with current reasons why men don't rear children.

*Let this suffice as my definition of child-rearing responsibility, with the qualification that outside employment and activity is possible if children spend part of the day with babysitters, at day-care centers, in school, or alone.

Berkeley Journal of Sociology, 18 (1973-1974), pp. 45-86.
Copyright © 1973 by Margaret Polatnick.

Second, I have no intention of discussing individuals and their personal motivations. I am treating men as a gender and women as a gender, and my conclusions will be generalizations about groups and group relations.

Now, the choice of who rears a society's children and the implications of that choice for the whole social structure seem to me extremely fruitful subjects for sociological examination. Yet sociologists have shown little inclination to consider the allocation of child-rearing responsibility to women as a matter of social choice. Instead they have been surprisingly willing to lay things at nature's door and ask no more: Men don't rear children because women are the natural rearers of children.

For sociologists, of all people, to rest so content with biological determinist explanations is at best intellectually unproductive and at worst politically suspect. Part I of this paper will discuss in more detail how the use (primarily misuse) of "nature" arguments has obscured the sociological understanding of child-rearing as a social job.

My own explanation for why men don't rear children (Part II of the paper) rests upon a basic premise about male/female relations: In our society (as in most societies familiar to us), men as a gender enjoy a superior power position in relation to women as a gender. That is, they are in control of the major sources of societal power* (political, economic, social, physical), their superordinate position and the subordinate position of women buttressed by an ideology of male supremacy and female inferiority.** It is not my purpose here to "prove" the existence of an over-all power inequality between the sexes. By now there is a sufficient corpus of Women's Liberation literature that documents painstakingly the subordinate status of women in the various spheres of societal life.[2] If every new paper on the sociology of women must prove these fundamental assertions yet again, the field will remain mired in its A B C's.

I am interested instead in demonstrating how the assignment of

---

*"The general definition of 'power' is 'a capacity to get things done.' Either resources (rights in things) or authority (rights in persons) increases the ability of a person to do what he decides to do."[1]

**Modern democratic ideology requires that groups be defined as "different" rather than unequal, but the essence of a power relationship shines clearly through most of the basic decrees about male and female natures: women are soft, weak, passive, helpless, compliant, in need of care and protection; men are strong, active, assertive, commanding, suited for leadership and managerial roles.

child-rearing responsibility to women articulates with a general pattern of male domination of our society. My analysis will illuminate and illustrate certain aspects of the gender power dynamic, but those unhappy with the basic premise will simply have to suspend misgivings and come along for the ride.

If, as I will argue, the current allocation of child-rearing responsibility to women must be understood in the context of their subordinate position in society, then two different causal relationships suggest themselves:

(1) Because women are the rearers of children, they are a powerless group vis-à-vis men.

(2) Because women are a powerless group vis-à-vis men, they are the rearers of children.

The first proposal is of course wholly compatible with a biological determinist position. If those who regard females as the biologically designated rearers of children had at least examined the implications of this "fact" for the over-all societal status of women, I would already have an important ingredient of my "power analysis." Unfortunately, biological determinists have been largely associated with the "different but equal," "complementary," "separate spheres" school of thought about male/female relations, in which power is a foreign concept.

Women's responsibility for child-rearing certainly contributes to their societal powerlessness, but this is only one component of the total "power picture." It will be my contention in Part II of this paper that the second causal relationship is operative as well. Thus, the causal model that will inform my discussion in Part II can be represented best by a feedback arrangement:

Women are a powerless group vis-à-vis men

Women are the rearers of children

My task in the second part of the paper will be to explain, elaborate, and justify this "power analysis."

Two final words of caution are in order. First of all, the subordinate position of women is rooted in multiple causes and reinforced by many different institutions and practices. The causal model above is by no means intended as a complete statement about women's powerlessness; many other variables besides child-rearing responsibility would have to be included in the picture. Freeing women from child-rearing duties would not in and of itself eliminate the power differential between the sexes. For example, if domestic responsibilities didn't bar women from most influential jobs, discrimination in education, training, hiring, and promotion still would. When I isolate the effects of any one variable upon the position of women, keep in mind that there are many other variables left behind.

Second, I will be unable to do justice in this paper to the complexities of social class. The gender dynamic of male superordination/ female subordination operates across the entire range of socioeconomic status, but different realities and norms in each socioeconomic group produce variations in the basic pattern. Some of my specific statements, and some of the quotations I use, will be slanted toward middle-class realities. However, the essentials of my argument apply equally well to all social classes.

Part I. Sociologists and the Biological Imperative

There is, to be sure, a strong and fervid insistence on the "maternal instinct," which is popularly supposed to characterize all women equally, and to furnish them with an all-consuming desire for parenthood, regardless of the personal pain, sacrifice, and disadvantage involved. In the absence of all verifiable data, however, it is only common-sense to guard against accepting as a fact of human nature a doctrine which we might well expect to find in use as a means of social control.

Leta S. Hollingworth,
The American Journal of Sociology, 1916[3]

Of all the social "roles"* associated with the female sex, the one most firmly bolstered by references to nature, biology, and anatomy is undoubtedly that of mother. Assumptions that all women are possessed of a maternal instinct, that they innately want to raise children and have the ability to care for them, that children need to be "mothered" by a mother or at least a "mother substitute," or they will suffer from "maternal deprivation," are at the core of both popular and scientific thinking about child-rearing.

*The notion of males and females playing different "roles" does not fit well with a power analysis, since it implies a certain voluntarism (actors taking on parts) and ignores power differentials between actors and between "roles." One would not say that black Africans performed "the role" of the colonized, that proletarians are in "the role" of exploited workers.

The sociological (and psychological) literature is permeated with explicit and implicit statements about the "naturalness" of women rearing children. It is difficult to find a treatment of motherhood that so much as entertains the notion that women's caring for children might be a socially engendered rather than a biologically based activity. When social scientists do feel obliged to offer some evidence for the "naturalness" of mothering behavior, they resort most often to convenient ape analogies, with the underlying premise that "anything primates do is necessary, natural, and desirable in humans."[4]

Even feminist* literature tends to tread lightly when it comes to the subject of motherhood. Old-style feminist writers would typically suggest that women wanting careers could hire babysitters to supervise their children. New-style feminists frequently propose that mothers organize cooperative day-care centers. But challenges to the proposition that children are in any way more the responsibility of females than males are not as common as one might expect.

The corollary to these beliefs about the biological sanctity of motherhood is that there is no such elemental biological connection between father and child. Males are not endowed with a corresponding "paternal instinct," and fatherhood, as "emphasized by Margaret Mead and others, is a 'social invention.' "[5] Leonard Benson, in his comprehensive survey and synthesis of the sociological literature on fathers, finds "the feeling widespread that the basic psychosomatic make-up of men provides them with little aptitude for child-rearing."[6]

Biological Beliefs in Family Sociology

In examining the literature on the family, one can distinguish two main ways in which the message is conveyed that women are meant to rear children:

(1) Constant equation of "mothering" with child-rearing. Without explicitly invoking biology many family sociologists discuss mothering behavior as if it is an unbreakable rule of nature for females to tend children. Why men don't rear children does not become a conscious question; children are reared by mothers, period. This identity between mother and child-rearer is both:

   (a) Linguistic (i.e., use of "maternal care," etc. as generic terms for the child-rearing function).

*The term "feminist" can refer to any advocate of "women's rights" or to a specific ideological camp within the Women's Movement. I am using it only in the former general sense.

(b) Conceptual (reflecting the belief that mothers are innately, necessarily the child-rearers).

(2) Explicit biological rationales based on female nature. These consist primarily of:

(a) References to women's specific physiological equipment as determinative of their child-rearing responsibility.

(b) References to more general instinctual or psychosomatic factors as determinative of women's child-rearing responsibility.

(1) Child-Rearer = Mother

The use of terms derived from "mother" to denote caring for children is far too commonplace to require documentation. The activity called "mothering" involves tending children, servicing their needs, and supplying the tender concern vital to healthy personality development. There is no effort to separate these functions semantically from the female person who typically performs them. These things constitute "maternal care," and the implication is that, *ipso facto*, they can only be provided by a female.

Consider the different meanings brought to mind by the following statements: The child was mothered by X; The child was fathered by Y. The first sentence suggests tender loving care, while the second implies mere physical paternity.

In the introduction to their standard anthology on the family, Norman Bell and Ezra Vogel write that "severe personality problems in one spouse may require the wife to become the wage-earner, or may lead the husband to perform most maternal activities."[7] Although "wage-earning" tends to be the job of fathers, the term is not sex-specific. But when a father takes on child-tending responsibilities (because of "severe personality problems" or some other awful eventuality), the job can never be rightfully his, for "pater" just isn't "mater."

So far I have been speaking as if this were all a matter of semantics. But sociologists don't just happen to *say* "mother" for "child-rearer," they *mean* it. Identity in word reflects identity in thought.

The linguistic/conceptual equation of child-rearer and female parent is most pernicious, from a feminist perspective, when it appears in statements about the needs of children. Experts on child development ought to tell us simply that a child needs loving care, but what they proclaim instead is "a child needs a mother."

Let one example suffice: Anna Freud and Dorothy Burlingham,

in their study of war-time children's relocation centers, state that a growing child's basic requirements include "intimate interchange of affection with a maternal figure."[8] Are we to conclude that men are incapable of providing this affection? Is their affection biologically not the right sort? Must we refer to those men who do exchange intimate affection with growing children by an exclusively female term?

The term and concept "maternal deprivation" presents similar difficulties. Can a child receive loving care only from a woman? Is it possible for a man to be a "mother substitute"? Are males constitutionally impotent when it comes to "maternal love"?

It might be argued that all these female-specific words for intensive "parenting" are merely *descriptive*, since in the societies familiar to us, women *are* almost exclusively the providers of "maternal care." Nonetheless, there exist a few societies and some individual men in our society that do not conform to this pattern. And the constant use of female terms for the rearing of children becomes obviously *prescriptive*. With messages like this omnipresent—

. . . when deprived of maternal care, the child's development is almost always retarded—physically, intellectually, and socially . . .[9]

—few mothers will reject the primary parenting role (and few fathers will give them the opportunity to do so). For anyone seeking fresh perspectives on the sexes and the social structure, the very language in which child-rearing is discussed is already blatantly biased. In both the terminology and the thinking of most family sociologists, child-rearing stands defined as inherently women's work.

(2)(a) Wombs and Breasts

One of the ways in which social scientists rationalize their assumption that mothers must be the child-rearers is by reference to women's specific physiology. For instance, in a chapter entitled "Family Organization and Personality Structure" in Bell and Vogel's anthology, one reads that "the feminine role derives from the woman's biological structure and is related to nurturance of children and the maintenance of a home."[10]

It is certainly indisputable that two fundamental biological factors connect women to children: women bear babies, and they are equipped with breasts to feed infants. Of course, the former function may well become an anachronism at some point in the future,[11] and the latter endowment was undercut some time ago by the advent of the bottle.* However, what I find objectionable is not the existence of these two biological capabilities in women, but the conclusion, blithely drawn by lay people and academics alike, that therefore women have a biologically decreed responsibility to raise and care for children. Where is the compelling logic in either of these connections?:

Embryos grow in women's bodies, *ergo* women must have primary responsibility for taking care of children.

Women are able to nurse babies, *ergo* women must have primary responsibility for taking care of children.

Yet sophisticated versions of these same *non sequiturs* roll smoothly from the tongues of reputable social scientists.

With reference to the first of these two assumptions, Ethel Albert has noted that "biological maternity is not correlated very neatly with psychological or social aptitude or liking for motherhood. Having babies is one thing, raising them another."[13] Nonetheless, Erik Erikson informs us that a woman's "somatic design harbors an 'inner space' destined to bear the offspring of chosen men, and with it, a biological, psychological, and ethical commitment to take care of human infancy."[14] Erich Fromm proclaims that the mother/child attachment

begins before the moment of birth, when mother and child are still one, although they are two. Birth changes the situation in some respects, but not as much as it would appear. The child, while now living outside of the womb, is still completely dependent on mother.[15]

Because mother was the one the child depended on in the womb, she must also be the one to meet the infant's needs after birth.

Sometimes the connection is more attenuated, but childbearing still suggests child-rearing. Take Talcott Parsons:

. . . a certain importance may well attach to the biological fact that, except for relatively rare plural births, it is unusual for human births to the same mother to follow each other at intervals of less than a year with any regularity. It is, we feel, broadly in the first year of life that a critical phase of the socialization process, which requires the most exclusive attention of a certain sort from the mother, takes place.[16]

*The rubber nipple was patented in 1845; the first good formula was developed about 1860.[12]

In other words, nature, by the very spacing of childbirths, has decreed who should attend to infants.

The second physical function in women directly linked to motherhood, producing milk for nursing infants, can easily be broadened into a wider social responsibility for children through a blurring of the two meanings of the term "nurturant." To nurture in the specific sense is to provide food or nourishment, but it also means "to raise or promote the development of; train; educate; rear."[17] Thus, from being the parent endowed with the physical capacity to nurse, the mother becomes, according to Benson's book on *Fatherhood*, "the crucial parent for maintaining the basic essentials of a nurturant family life."[18]

Let's consider a somewhat subtle transition from nursing to "nurturing." Morris Zelditch, Jr., a collaborator with Parsons on *Family, Socialization and Interaction Process*, writes that

... a crucial reference point for differentiation in the family ... lies in the division of organisms into lactating and nonlactating classes. Only in our own society (so far as I know, that is) have we managed to invent successful bottle-feeding, and this is undoubtedly of importance for our social structure. In other societies necessarily—and in our own for structural reasons which have *not* disappeared with the advent of the bottle—the initial core relation of a family with children is the mother-child attachment. And it follows from the principles of learning that the gradient of generalization should establish "mother" as the focus of gratification in a diffuse sense, as the source of "security" and "comfort."[19]

The "gradient of generalization" indeed! Mother becomes the source of security and comfort because she *provides* security and comfort: she "cleans and clothes the infant, ... soothes it with her voice and cuddles it with her body."[20] Who would be the "focus of gratification" if mother merely offered her breast now and then and father provided all the other ingredients of loving care? Wet nurses once fed the infants of mothers who couldn't or wouldn't nurse;* who then was the source of security and comfort?

Zelditch invokes "structural reasons" when he has to explain why bottles haven't freed women from child-rearing responsibility, but

*According to W. Kessen's study of *The Child*: "Perhaps the most persistent single note in the history of the child is the reluctance of mothers to suckle their babies. The running war between the mother, who does not want to nurse, and the philosopher-psychologists, who insist she must, stretches over two thousand years."[21]

otherwise his argument is biological: because mothers produce milk, they are the child-rearers.

The landmark experiments of Harlow and associates with infant monkeys[22] (if I may be permitted to draw upon *reputable* ethology) suggest that the critical aspect of "mothering" is not the providing of food but of warm, comforting physical contact (cuddling, stroking, soothing). This led Harlow to observe that "the American male is physically endowed with all the really essential equipment to compete with the American female on equal terms in . . . the rearing of infants."[23] But this has not caused most sociologists to stop assuming that she who can nurse must also be the nurturant one. Benson concludes his comments on Harlow's work thusly:

> Among humans, too, it appears that there are alternatives to the mother's feeding function, but no alternative to the sustained physical presence of a mothering one in the life of the infant. There is no evidence that the father's physical contact with the child provides any special "paternal" quality. . . .[24][!!!]

Causal arguments from breast-feeding to child-rearing often have an intervening variable of "convenience": since women had to be around to breast-feed anyway, it was "convenient" that they take on the other tasks of child care. The question, of course, is convenient for whom? For the mother who doesn't want having children to interfere too much with her activities outside the home? Or for the father who doesn't want having children to interfere too much with *his* activities outside the home? Convenience is a *social* consideration; in many cases it has been "convenient" for humans to circumvent the "givens" of biology. Anyhow, with the easy accessibility in our society of bottles and formulas, such arguments are only of historical interest.

(2)(b) Maternal Instinct

If all biological determinists invoked only wombs and breasts to explain why women are the rearers of children, their position could be easily defeated. However, the more sophisticated "nature" advocates base their arguments upon less clearly defined instinctual or psychosomatic factors. Thus, a "maternal instinct" or something similar predisposes women toward child care, whereas men have no such natural bent. (It might be noted that men also lack a biological "lawyer instinct," "junior executive instinct," "dockworker instinct," etc., yet perform these jobs admirably well.)

Confronting this more general formulation of the biological determinist hypothesis involves us in a classic "nature-nurture" controversy. Such controversies have always been difficult to resolve conclusively in the absence of a feasible, acceptable process for raising "nurture-free" children. In order to demonstrate that certain female and male behaviors are not the result of innate sex differences, one has to pursue two indirect lines of approach. First, one can attempt to prove that there is indeed little rigorous empirical evidence for the "nature" argument. Particularly vulnerable to such scrutiny are the psychologists and psychiatrists who have based their pronouncements about female "nature" almost solely upon subjective clinical experience.

The second line of attack is to accumulate an impressive array of evidence that gender behavior is socially produced. The mere existence of biologically normal individuals who don't conform to expected male/female behavior patterns undermines a strict biological determinist position. However, a more persuasive presentation demands detailed study of the effects of socialization (the inculcation of attitudes and values through formal and informal education processes) and social control (the external enforcement of prescribed behavior through a system of punishments and rewards).*

Another important source of evidence in favor of the social nature of gender behavior is the study of other societies (especially "primitive" ones) in which male/female behaviors are significantly different from or even totally the reverse of our contemporary pattern. And a final promising direction of "nurture" research falls under the rubric "sociology of oppression." The attempt here is to show how the experience of oppression (powerlessness) produces similar behaviors in different "out" groups, fully explainable by their position in the social structure.

All of these lines of investigation can contribute relevant evidence for refuting the biological argument about "maternal" behavior. My purpose here has been simply to map out the *modus operandi* for such a refutation. Thus I will touch only briefly upon some individual points of interest in the "nurture" case.

Here again, the research of Harlow and his co-workers provides a key finding about "mothering" in monkeys (who *can* be raised in "nurture-free" isolation cages). Female monkeys brought up without

*Under the broad category of social control I would include structural factors (e.g., what options exist for employment, education, living arrangements, etc.) which limit people's possibilities.

monkey mothers and without social experience with other monkeys
proved to be "totally inadequate" mothers: they "ignored, rejected,
and were physically abusive to their infants." The researchers are not
willing to discard completely the notion of an innate component to
maternal behavior in these monkeys, but they do conclude that "inadequate early social learning can block the expression of the normal
maternal pattern."[25]

In his report on *The American Male* (1966), Myron Brenton as-
serts that, whatever the maternal propensities of female apes, human
maternal behavior must be viewed "in the context of a learning
process."

> A woman is, as Morton M. Hunt has pointed out in his balanced explora-
> tion of the subject, a human being and is therefore "born almost completely
> unequipped with rigidly patterned instincts." . . . A human mother . . . must
> "*learn* how to be kind and loving, and how to want and to care for a child."
> . . . The learning process . . . begins, as the result of countless cultural clues
> . . . from infancy on.[26]

Despite these "countless cultural clues," and the overt motherhood training girls receive, many women embark on motherhood
with remarkably little knowledge about infant care, but, because it's
"their responsibility," they learn fast enough. As Harriet Rheingold
has stressed, the infant "teaches [parents] what he needs to have them
do for him. He makes them behave in a nurturing fashion."[27] We
know which "parent" must attend to the lesson.

There is a prevalent tendency, in "nurture" explanations of female behavior, to stress the effects of socialization (women, because
of their training, want to be child-rearers) and to neglect the influence
of social controls (women are forced to be child-rearers, whether they
want to or not). "While affirming the essential nature of woman to be
satisfied with maternity and with maternal duties only, society has always taken every precaution to close the avenues to ways of escape
therefrom."[28] Two obvious roadblocks are the lack of adequate institutional child-care facilities and the lack of husbands willing to
rear children. Even if a husband *is* willing to rear the children, financial considerations militate against such an arrangement. Economic
discrimination provides males with a substantial edge in earning
power, thus making it difficult to break the pattern of male bread-
winner/female child-rearer.

The choice for women (to the extent that they have a choice) is thus essentially: (a) have children and rear them,* or (b) don't have children. The latter option has been physically possible for hetero-sexually active women only since effective birth control became ac-cessible, and is still infrequently realized (for reasons of both socializa-tion and social control).

Another weakness in current "sociology of gender" research, as noted by Marcia Millman, is its tendency to focus "heavily on women (the implication being that it has to do only with women). . . ."[29] Boys, too, undergo a significant learning process about parenthood: they learn that they *don't* have to take care of children. "They see—in their own homes—that fatherhood either assumes narrow dimensions or is more or less irrelevant."[30] "Nurturance," they discover, is not regarded as a suitable ingredient of masculinity or male identity. If they dis-play any fondness for dolls or any "mothering" behavior toward younger children, they are negatively sanctioned. Before long, most boys pick up the appropriate cues about how to act around babies: they become practiced in that clumsy, self-conscious manner of han-dling infants which insures that some female will quickly step in and take over.

Reflecting the societal estimation of who's going to be doing the job, "parenting" information aimed at males "is remarkably scarce compared to the literature of advice, instruction, and edification for women." As Benson remarks:

Fatherhood is a pastime that does not call for training, discipline, or high-priority effort. Pressures upon men to take stock of themselves as fathers are fitful and unorganized at best.[31]

As for the social advantages to men of avoiding child-rearing re-sponsibility, these will be elaborated in the second part of the paper. All in all, it is hardly a surprise that most males develop neither en-thusiasm nor ability for child care.

One can continue indefinitely to demonstrate social factors con-tributing to the definition of women as child-rearers and men as non-child-rearers, but at what point has one accumulated sufficient ev-idence to convert a stalwart believer in at least *some* biological basis? Probably never, until biochemists are able to resolve the issue directly.

Be that as it may, the lack of a definitive conclusion to this debate does not constitute a serious stumbling block to my proposed "power

*Rich women, of course, can delegate some child-rearing tasks to em-ployees.

analysis." There is certainly enough evidence of a social component to parenting behavior to make a strict biological determinist position disreputable and a "social structure" analysis highly instructive.

A belief that women's responsibility for child-rearing *first arose* as a result of biological factors is not incompatible with a belief that this responsibility is now socially generated and socially alterable. The question of the origin of certain social behaviors can be profitably separated from the question of how and why those behaviors are currently maintained: What are the mechanisms by which the behavior pattern is perpetuated? What interests and uses does that perpetuation serve?*

Explaining mothering versus fathering responsibilities in the context of a whole social system brings into sharper focus how these responsibilities are interrelated with other dimensions of the gender dynamic. Benson, in his overview of the literature on fatherhood, takes occasional account of this theme. On the subject of mothers he says at one point:

> "Mothering behavior" is not simply the product of the mother's nature, but is influenced by her relationships with father, her marital frustrations, and by the father's attitudes toward the children. Mothering is as much a function of the woman's position in the family structure as it is an expression of her personality. . . .[34]

> *This perspective is not very far from the theoretical position of functionalism. Functionalists "interpret data by establishing their consequences for larger structures in which they are implicated."[32] As Alvin Gouldner has pointed out:

>> The functionalist's emphasis upon studying the *existent* consequences, the ongoing functions or dysfunctions of a social pattern may be better appreciated if it is remembered that this concern developed in a polemic against the earlier anthropological notion of a 'survival.' The survival, of course, was regarded as a custom held to be unexplainable in terms of its existent consequences or utility and which, therefore, had to be understood with reference to its consequences for social arrangements no longer present.[33]

> Both feminists and functionalists might wish to show, accordingly, how the pattern of differential parenting responsibilities for males and females ties in to existing institutions, structures, and processes in the society. But the crucial difference between the two perspectives would lie in the value orientation of each toward the integrated, static system such an investigation tends to suggest. One of the main critiques of functionalist analysis has been that it slips imperceptibly into an affirmation of the status quo. Feminist analysis is surely not characterized by *that* shortcoming.

But Benson never develops the full implications of these remarks, because the scope of his thinking (and the thinking in the literature he reviews) is limited by the persistent assumption that child care is inherently the work of women.

For the further purposes of this investigation, then, I will treat the assignment of child-rearing responsibility as the prerogative of society, not biology. Staunch support for biological determinist explanations of gender behaviors can be a convenient rationalization for ignoring their larger social ramifications. By regarding beliefs about proper mother and father duties as ideology rather than eternal verity, I can consider questions of function, utility, purpose, and interest. A number of influential Women's Liberation writings have popularized the policy of viewing personal and social relationships between the sexes as "political"—that is, involving group conflict of interest in which resources of power and leverage are brought to bear.[35] The rest of this paper will be an attempt to apply this framework to the allocation of child-rearing responsibility.

Part II: Social Advantage: the Power Analysis

Having addressed the argument that men don't rear children because of "biology," I can now present and defend the central thesis of this paper: men (as a group) don't rear children because they don't *want* to rear children. (This implies, of course, that they are in a position to enforce their preferences.) It is to men's advantage that women are assigned child-rearing responsibility, and it is in men's interest to keep things that way.

I should emphasize at once that I have no intention of measuring the "inherent worth" of child-rearing as compared to other pursuits. On some "absolute" scale of values, child-rearing would probably rank higher than many a work-world job. But my topic is not "the good life," it is power advantages. Thus my view of child-rearing must be unabashedly pragmatic: Will it get you ahead in the world? Does it even get you power in the family?

I will discuss the undesirability of the child-rearing job under two general categories: (1) the advantages of avoiding child-rearing responsibility (which are, primarily, the advantages of breadwinning responsibility); (2) the disadvantages attached to child-rearing responsibility.

Breadwinning Beats Child-Rearing

Full-time child-rearing responsibility limits one's capacity to engage in most other activities. However, the most important thing, in power terms, that child-rearers can't do is to be the family breadwinner.* This is the job that men prefer as their primary family responsibility. It offers important power advantages over the home-based child-rearing job.

MONEY, STATUS, POWER

First of all, and of signal importance, breadwinners earn money. "Money is a source of power that supports male dominance in the family. . . . Money belongs to him who earns it, not to her who spends it, since he who earns it may withhold it."[37]

Second, occupational achievement is probably the major source of social status in American society. As Parsons has noted, "In a certain sense the most fundamental basis of the family's status is the occupational status of the husband and father." The wife/mother "is excluded from the struggle for power and prestige in the occupational sphere," while the man's breadwinner role "carries with it . . . the primary prestige of achievement, responsibility and authority."[38]

Even if one's occupation ranks very low on prestige and power, there are other tangible and intangible benefits which accrue to wage earners, for example, organizational experience, social contacts, "knowledge of the world," feelings of independence and competence.

The resources that breadwinners garner in the outside world do not remain out on the front porch; breadwinning power translates significantly into power within the family. This is in direct contradiction to the notion of "separate spheres": the man reigning su-

---

*Many women work during some of the child-rearing years, but if they have husbands, they are very rarely the principal breadwinner. The U.S. Department of Labor reports the following figures for the median percentage of family income earned by wives in 1966:

Family income	Percentage
under $2,000	6.0
$2,000-$2,999	12.2
$3,000-$4,999	14.4
$5,000-$6,999	15.8
$7,000-$9,999	23.0
$10,000-$14,999	28.1
$15,000 and over	22.9

preme in extrafamilial affairs, the woman running the home-front show. (I'll discuss this theme more later.)

The correlation between earning power and family power has been substantiated concretely in a number of studies of family decision making (Blood, 1958; Heer, 1958; Hoffman and Lippitt, 1960; Middleton and Putney, 1960; Nye and Hoffman, 1963).[39] These studies show that the more a man earns, the more family power he wields, and the greater the discrepancy between the status of the husband's and wife's work, the greater the husband's power. When the wife works too, there is a shift toward a more egalitarian balance of power* and more sharing of household burdens.

Lois Hoffman has proposed four explanations for the increased family power of working wives, which convey again some of the power resources connected with breadwinning:

1. Women who work have more control over money, "and this control can be used, implicitly or explicitly, to wield power in the family."
2. "Society attaches greater value to the role of wage earner than to that of housewife and thus legitimizes for both parents the notion that the former should have more power."
3. "An independent supply of money enables the working woman to exert her influence to a greater extent because she is less dependent on her husband and could, if necessary, support herself in the event of the dissolution of the marriage."
4. "Working outside the home provides more social interaction than being a housewife. This interaction has been seen as leading to an increase in the wife's power because of: (a) the development of social skills which are useful in influencing her husband; (b) the development of self-confidence; (c) the greater knowledge of alternative situations that exist in other families; and (d) the more frequent interaction with men, which may result in the feeling that remarriage is feasible."[40]

Not only does the woman's working modify the power relation between husband and wife, it also affects the gender power distribution in the whole family:

Boys become more dependent and obedient when the mother works, and the masculine side of the family reflects a generally diminished status (L. Hoffman, 1963). By contrast, daughters of working mothers are more independent, self-reliant, aggressive, dominant, and disobedient; in short, they act more like little boys (Siegel, Stolz, *et al.*, 1963).[41]

*This should not imply, however, that women who earn more than their husbands necessarily have superior power, since the subordinate position of women stems from multiple causes.

POWER STRUCTURE OF THE "NORMAL" FAMILY

It is worth noting, in this connection, how sociological definitions of the "normal" family situation and "normal" personality development for sons versus daughters sanction the status quo of male power and female powerlessness. Healthy families are those which produce strong, independent *sons*, ready to take on strong, independent "masculine roles." (Strong, independent daughters are not a goal; they're a symptom of deviance.)

For the proper "masculine" upbringing, boys must have "male role models." What little importance academics have attached to fathers' playing a greater role in child-rearing has been largely motivated by this concern. Boys, brought up by "nurturant" mothers, should have strong male role models available lest they develop "nurturant" personalities. These male role models should be close at hand, but not too actively involved in child-rearing, for

a child whose father performs the mothering functions both tangibly and emotionally while the mother is preoccupied with her career can easily gain a distorted image of masculinity and femininity.[42]

Precisely.

MEN WANT TO BE THE BREADWINNERS

Men have good reason, then, to try to monopolize the job of principal family breadwinner much as they may appreciate a second income). Husbands' objections to wives working ". . . stem from feelings that their dominance is undermined when they are not the sole or primary breadwinners."[43] There is also

. . . the feeling of being threatened by women in industry, who are seen as limiting opportunities for men, diminishing the prestige of jobs formerly held only by men, and casting a cold eye on masculine pretensions to vocational superiority.[44]

These feelings are quite justified; as Benson so neatly understates it, "The male fear of competition from women is not based solely on myth."[45]

Where outright forbidding of the wife to work is no longer effective, the continued allocation of child-rearing responsibility to women accomplishes the same end: assuring male domination of the occupational world. Should all other barriers to economic power for women suddenly vanish, child-rearing responsibility would still handicap them hopelessly in economic competition with men.

Of course, children are not just a handy excuse to keep women out of the job market. Most people—male and female—want to have them, and somebody has to rear them. Men naturally prefer that women do it, so that having children need not interfere with their own occupational pursuits.

Since housewife and mother roles are preferred for women, it is considered distasteful and perhaps dangerous to upgrade their occupational status. Apparently there is a fear of mass defections from maternal responsibility. Perhaps there is also a hidden suspicion that the woman's employment is symptomatic of a subversive attitude toward motherhood.[46]

Both these motives, therefore,—the desire to limit females' occupational activities, and the desire to have children without limiting their own occupational activities—contribute to a male interest in defining child-rearing as exclusively woman's domain.

Thus,

. . . there has been consistent social effort to establish as a norm the woman whose vocational proclivities are completely and "naturally" satisfied by childbearing and child-rearing, with the related domestic activities.[47]

One of the controls operating to restrict women's breadwinning activities is the social pressure against mothers who "neglect their children." Where financial need compels mothers with young children to work, their absence from the home is accepted as a "necessary evil." (Welfare departments, however, will generally support mothers of young children without pressuring them to seek work.) In the middle classes, sentiments about male/female responsibility are less obscured by immediate economic considerations:

. . . some public disapproval is still directed toward the working mother of young children and the mother who devotes her primary attention to a career; the feeling persists that a mother who creates a full life for herself outside the home may be cheating her children, if not her husband.[48]

Fathers, on the other hand, have public license (in fact, a veritable public duty) to devote primary attention to job or career. Sandra and Daryl Bem have illustrated the existent "double standard" of parental responsibility with the example of a middle-class father who loses his wife:

> No matter how much he loved his children, no one would expect him to sacrifice his career in order to stay home with them on a full-time basis—even if he had an independent source of income. No one would charge him with selfishness or lack of parental feeling if he sought professional care for his children during the day.[49]

MEN WANT WOMEN TO BE THE CHILD-REARERS

By propagating the belief that women are the ones who really desire children, men can then invoke a "principle of least interest": that is, because women are "most interested" in children, they must make most of the accommodations and sacrifices required to rear them. Benson says that "fatherhood . . . is less important to men than motherhood is to women, in spite of the fact that maternity causes severe limitations on women's activities."[50] My own version would be that fatherhood is "less important" to men than motherhood is to women *because* child-rearing causes severe limitations on the child-rearer's activities.

In a discussion of barriers to careers for woman, Alice Rossi cites some very revealing findings about which sex advocates a more rigid standard of "mothering responsibility."

> On an item reading "Even if a woman has the ability and interest, she should not choose a career field that will be difficult to combine with child-rearing," half of the women but two-thirds of the men agreed. Again, although half the women thought it appropriate for a woman to take a part-time job if a child was a preschooler, only one-third of the men approved. A quarter of the men, but only 14% of the women, thought a full-time job should not be taken until the children were "all grown up."[51]

Women too imbibe the ideology of motherhood, but men seem to be its strongest supporters. By insuring that the weight of child-rearing responsibility falls on women's shoulders, they win for themselves the right of "paternal neglect." As Benson observes, "The man can throw himself into his work and still fulfill male obligations at home, mainly because the latter are minimal." Men have "the luxury of more familial disengagement than women."[52]

Of course, men as family breadwinners must shoulder the *financial* burden involved in raising children: they may have to work harder, longer hours, and at jobs they dislike. But even factory workers enjoy set hours, scheduled breaks, vacation days, sick leave, and other union benefits.

To the extent that men *can* select work suited to their interests, abilities, and ambitions, they are in a better position than women arbitrarily assigned to child-rearing. As to the extent that breadwinning gains one the resources discussed earlier (money, status, family power, etc.), financial responsibility is clearly preferable, in power terms, to "mothering" responsibility.

CHILD-REARING RESPONSIBILITY HANDICAPS WOMEN

From the perspective of women—the more affluent women faced with "mother/career conflict," the poorer women faced with "mother/ any job at all conflict"—men possess the enviable option to "have their cake and eat it too": that is, to have children without sacrificing their activities outside the home.

A woman knows that becoming a parent will adversely affect her occupational prospects. "For a period, at least, parenthood means that... whatever vocational or professional skills she may possess may become atrophied."[53] During this period of retirement the woman

... becomes isolated and almost totally socially, economically, and emotionally dependent upon her husband. . . . She loses her position, cannot keep up with developments in her field, does not build up seniority. . . . If she returns to work, and most women do, she must begin again at a low-status job and she stays there—underemployed and underpaid.[54]

It is not just during the period of child-rearing that women become economically or professionally disadvantaged vis-à-vis men. Most women's lives have already been constructed in anticipation of that period. "Helpful advice" from family, friends, and guidance counselors, discriminatory practices in the schools and in the job market, steer women toward jobs and interests compatible with a future in child-rearing.

With the assistance of relatives, babysitters, or the few day-care centers that exist, women can hold certain kinds of jobs while they're raising children (often part-time, generally low-status). Women without husbands, women with pressing financial needs, women who can afford hired help, may work full-time despite the demands of "mothering."* But to an important extent, occupational achievement and child-rearing responsibility are mutually exclusive. A 40-hour work week permits more family involvement than a 72-hour work week

*In 1960, 18.6% of mothers with children under six years old were in the labor force in some capacity; 11.4% were working 35 hours or more per week.[55]

did, but it's still difficult to combine with primary responsibility for children (given the lack of institutional assistance). Furthermore, the higher-status professional jobs frequently demand a work-week commitment closer to the 72-hour figure. Men can hold these jobs yet also father families only because they can count on a "helpmeet" to take care of children and home. Thus it is said that the wages of a man buy the labor of two people. Without this back-up team of wife/ mother's, "something would have to give."

Alice Rossi has suggested that the period of women's lives spent at home rearing children is potentially the peak period for professional accomplishment:

> If we judge from the dozens of researches Harvey Lehman has conducted on the relationship between age and achievement, . . . the most creative work women and men have done in science was completed during the very years contemporary women are urged to remain at home rearing their families. . . . Older women who return to the labor force are an important reservoir for assistants and technicians and the less demanding professions, but only rarely for creative and original contributors to the more demanding professional fields.[56]

The woman who tries to work at home while raising children finds that this is not too practicable a solution. As writer/critic Marya Mannes notes with regard to her own profession:

> The creative woman has no wife to protect her from intrusion. A man at his desk in a room with closed door is a man at work. A woman at a desk in any room is available.[57]

MAINTAINING THE STATUS QUO

If working hours and career patterns were more flexible, if child-care centers were more widely available, and if "retired mothers" re-entering the work force got special preference rather than unfavorable treatment,* child-rearing wouldn't exact quite so heavy a toll on women's occupational achievement. Because men benefit from the status quo, they ignore, discourage, or actively resist such reform proposals. Alternative arrangements for rearing children, for balancing work commitment with family commitment, are not pressing concerns for men; the structural relegation of women to domestic service suits their interests very well.

*Consider how the re-entry of veterans into the work force is eased by special benefits and preferential treatment.

Women's responsibility for children in the context of the nuclear family is an important buttress for a male-dominated society. It helps keep women out of the running for economic and political power. As Talcott Parsons states:

> It is, of course, possible for the adult woman to follow the masculine pattern and seek a career in fields of occupational achievement in direct competition with men of her own class. It is, however, notable that in spite of the very great progress of the emancipation of women from the traditional domestic pattern only a very small fraction have gone very far in this direction.* It is also clear that its generalization would only be possible with profound alterations in the structure of the family.[58]

*   *   *

I have chosen to focus upon breadwinning (economic activity) as the most important thing, from a power perspective, that child-rearers can't do. However, other activities—educational,** political, cultural, social, recreational—suffer as well when one's life becomes centered around children and home. The "on call" nature of "mothering" responsibility militates against any kind of sustained, serious commitment to other endeavors. A full-time mother loses

> ... the growth of competence and resources in the outside world, the community positions which contribute to power in the marriage. The boundaries of her world contract, the possibilities of growth diminish.[59]

While women are occupied with domestic duties, men consolidate their resources in the outside world and their position of command in the family. By the time most women complete their child-rearing tenure, they can no longer recoup their power losses.

Child-Rearing: Not An Equal Sphere

By my explicit and implicit comparisons of breadwinning with child-rearing, I have already asserted that the former is the more desirable "sphere" of action. Now I will discuss more directly the disadvantages of the child-rearing job.

*One might well inquire what this "very great progress" is, if "only a small fraction" of women are actually involved.

**Here again, there's been little effort, for the sake of *female* child-rearers, to develop more flexible programs of higher education and professional training.

MONEY, STATUS, POWER

Once again, let's begin with the simple but significant matter of money. Money is a prime source of power in American society, and tending one's own children on a full-time basis is not a salaried activity. Margaret Benston has elucidated most effectively the implications of this fact:

> In sheer quantity, household labor, including child care, constitutes a huge amount of socially necessary production. Nevertheless, in a society based on commodity production, it is not usually considered "real work" since it is outside of trade and the market place. . . . In a society in which money determines value, women are a group who work outside the money economy. Their work is not worth money, is therefore valueless, is therefore not even real work. And women themselves, who do this valueless work, can hardly be expected to be worth as much as men, who work for money.[60]

Performing well at the job of child-rearer may be a source of feminine credentials, but it is not a source of social power or status. According to Parsons, of all the possible adult roles for females, "the pattern of domesticity must be ranked lowest in terms of prestige," although "it offers perhaps the highest level of a certain kind of security."[61] When a woman bears and raises children, therefore, she is fulfilling social expectations and avoiding negative sanctions but she "is not esteemed, in the culture or in the small society of her family, in proportion to her exercise of her 'glory,' childbearing."[62]

The rewards for rearing children are not as tangible as a raise or a promotion, and ready censure awaits any evidence of failure: "if the child goes wrong, mother is usually blamed."[63] Thus the male preference for the breadwinner role may reflect (among other things) an awareness that "it's easier to make money than it is to be a good father. . . . The family is a risky proposition in terms of rewards and self-enhancement."[64]

FAMILY POWER

If child-rearers don't accumulate power resources in the outside world, do they at least win some advantage in the family balance of power? I have already cited the evidence that family power is directly related to earning power. Not surprisingly, researchers have also found that the wife's power declines with the arrival of children; an inverse relationship exists between number of children and the wife's power vis-à-vis her husband (Heer, 1958; Blood and Wolfe, 1960; Hoffman and Lippitt, 1960; Campbell, 1967).

There are two major theories of conjugal power which suggest explanations for this effect. Blood and Wolfe's "resource theory" (1960) posits that "power will accrue to the spouse who has the more imposing or relevant resources, and thus has the greater contribution to make to the family."[65] If one considers occupational status and income as the most imposing of resources, then this explanation is little different from the "earning power equals family power" thesis. However, Blood and Wolfe don't illuminate why breadwinning should be a "greater contribution" to the family than child-rearing.

David Heer's "exchange value theory" (1963) postulates that "the spouse who could most likely marry another person who would be as desirable as or much more desirable than his (her) present spouse"[66] enjoys the superior power position. When a woman has children and becomes a full-time child-rearer, she grows more dependent on her husband, her opportunities to meet men decrease, and her prospects for remarriage decline. The husband thus possesses the more promising alternatives outside the marriage, and his power increases.

The woman's power is at its lowest point during the "pre-school" period, when child-rearing responsibilities are most consuming.

When her children start school, the mother can be more autonomous and exercise more power because she is better able to handle outside employment; the children can now take care of themselves in many ways and are supervised to a greater extent by the school and other community agencies (Heer, 1963). The mother's gradual resumption of a position of independent influence coincides with her re-emergence from the ceaseless responsibilities of mothering (Blood, 1963), and children do report father as "boss" of the family less often as they grow older (Hess and Torney, 1962).[67]

CHILD-REARING: NOT A SEPARATE SPHERE

Despite the empirical evidence that women lose family power when they become mothers, one is still tempted to believe that by leaving child-rearing to women, men have surrendered a significant area of control. This belief is based on the erroneous notion that women preside over child-rearing as a separate sovereign domain. On the contrary, men's authority as family provider/family "head" carries right over into child-rearing matters. Men may have surrendered the regular responsibility and routine decision making, but they retain power where important decisions are concerned (including what the routine will be).

In a sample of adolescents studied by Charles Bowerman and Glen Elder

(1964), the father was reported to be the dominant parent in child-rearing matters as often as the mother, in spite of the fact that mother does most of the actual work; apparently she often finds herself responsible for doing the menial chores without having the stronger voice in "child-rearing policy."[68]

Constantina Safilios-Rothschild (1969) found that American men delegate to their wives many of the minor decisions related to rearing children and running a home—"those decisions, the enactment of which involves time-consuming tasks." This suggests to her that

American husbands do not wish to take on "bothersome" decisions which are not crucial . . . and take too much of the time and energy that they prefer to dedicate to their work or leisure-time activities.[69]

Fathers may default from the daily child-rearing routines, but, much like male principals supervising female teachers, they still tend to wield the ultimate force and the ultimate decision making power. Consider these statements of Benson's on the nature of paternal authority:

The father as threatener is superimposed upon the mother's more basic pattern and is therefore more likely to appear as a terrorizing intruder, but one who speaks as authority and therefore ought to be obeyed.
Family members can foresee his judgments and are constrained to act correctly according to their conception of his wishes.
Even the social pattern that mother establishes is typically legitimized by the larger, more insistent parent lurking in the background. . . . Father is the embodiment of a basic form of social control: coercive power. . . . Father is an agent of both internal and external control, and the child responds to him in terms of both his respect for the man and his respect for the man's power.
But when order breaks down or is openly challenged the need for a new approach assumes an immediate, deliberative significance, and father is customarily expected to help meet the crisis. In fact, it is common for him to take charge. . . .[70]

Taking care of children, therefore, does not provide women with any real power base. Men can afford to leave child-rearing *responsibility* to women because, given their superior power resources, they are still assured of substantial child-rearing *authority*.

THE NATURE OF THE JOB

Child-rearing, I have argued, is not a source of money, status, power in the society, or power in the family. The child-rearing job is disadvantageous in terms of these major assets, but there are also draw-backs inherent in the nature of the work itself. The rearing of children "involves long years of exacting labor and self-sacrifice," but

the drudgery, the monotonous labor, and other disagreeable features of child-rearing are minimized by "the social guardians." On the other hand, the joys and compensations of motherhood are magnified and presented to consciousness on every hand. Thus the tendency is to create an illusion whereby motherhood will appear to consist of compensations only, and thus come to be desired by those for whom the illusion is intended.[71]

The responsibilities of a child-rearer homemaker are not confined to a 40-hour work week. Margaret Benston estimates that for a married woman with small children (excluding the very rich), "the irreducible minimum of work . . . is probably 70 or 80 hours a week."[72] In addition to the actual hours of work, there is the constant strain of being "on call." Thus, another consideration in why the husband's power is greatest when the children are young "may be the well-described chronic fatigue which affects young mothers with preschoolers."[73]

Furthermore, women are adults (assertions that they have "child-like" natures notwithstanding), and they need adequate adult company to stimulate their mental faculties.

. . . , A lot of women become disheartened because babies and children are not only not interesting to talk to (not everyone thrills at the wonders of da-da-ma-ma talk) but they are generally not empathic, considerate people.[74]

Although interaction with young children is certainly rewarding in many ways, child-rearers can lose touch with the world outside their domestic circle. In addition, American society segregates the worlds of childhood and adulthood; adults who keep close company with children are *déclassé*.

Since the "less-than-idyllic child-rearing part of motherhood remains 'in small print,' "[75] new mothers are often in for some rude shocks. Betty Rollin, in the Skolnick and Skolnick anthology on the family, quotes some mothers interviewed in an Ann Arbor, Michigan study:

Suddenly I had to devote myself to the child totally. I was under the illusion that the baby was going to fit into my life, and I found that I had to switch my life and my schedule to fit *him*. . . .

You never get away from the responsibility. Even when you leave the child with a sitter, you are not out from under the pressure of the responsibility. . . .

I hate ironing their pants and doing their underwear, and they never put their clothes in the laundry basket. . . . Best moment of the day is when all the children are in bed. . . . The worst time of day is 4 p.m., when you have to get dinner started, and the kids are tired, hungry, and crabby—everybody wants to talk to you about *their* day. . . . Your day is only half over.

Once a mother, the responsibility and concern for my children became so encompassing. . . . It took a great deal of will to keep up other parts of my personality. . . .

I had anticipated that the baby would sleep and eat, sleep and eat. Instead, the experience was overwhelming. I really had not thought particularly about what motherhood would mean in a realistic sense. I want to do *other* things, like to become involved in things that are worthwhile—I don't mean women's clubs—but I don't have the physical energy to go out in the evenings. I feel like I'm missing something . . . the experience of being somewhere with people and having them talking about something—something that's going on in the world.[76]

AVOIDING THE JOB

When women are wealthy enough to afford it, they often hire nurses and governesses to relieve them of the more burdensome aspects of child care. They can then enjoy the children's company when they want to, be active mothers when it suits them, but have the constant responsibility and the more unpleasant parts of the job (diapers, tantrums, etc.) off their shoulders.

The relationship between rich mother and governess resembles in significant respects the relationship between average father and average mother. The father "hires" the mother (by providing her with support), in the expectation that she will relieve him of the major burdens of child-rearing. (However, even a rich mother is expected to pay a lot more personal attention to her children than any father is.)

From the perspective of an ambitious person, taking fulltime care of your own children is rather like baking your own bread: it might be nice if one had the time, but there are more important things one needs to be doing. Thus you pay for the service of having someone else do it, increasing your financial burden, but freeing yourself of a time-consuming task.

Fathers, with full social support, can buy a significant degree of freedom from direct family responsibility. They have a category of people at hand—women—constrained by social forces to accept that responsibility. Women have no such convenient group to whom they can pass the child-rearing buck. For mothers, the price of escape from child-rearing—financial, social, psychological—is usually too high.

"MOTHERLY SELFLESSNESS"

A final relevant feature of the child-rearing job itself is that mothers are obliged to subordinate their personal objectives and practice "selflessness"—putting the needs of others first, devoting themselves to the day-to-day well-being of other family members, loving and giving "unconditionally."* Such domestic service may be deemed virtuous, but it isn't a path to power and success. Males primed for competitive achievement show no eagerness to suppress their personal ambitions and sacrifice their own interests to attend to others' immediate wants.

Furthermore, men desire from women the same services and support, the same ministration to everyday needs, that mothers are supposed to provide for children. ("I want a wife to keep track of the children's doctor and dentist appointments. And to keep track of mine too. . . . A wife who will pick up after my children, a wife who will pick after me."[77]) "Mothering" behavior is not very different from "feminine" behavior. By grooming females for "nurturance," men provide a selfless rearer for their children and an accommodating marriage partner for themselves. Thus:

> Evidence clearly indicates that the wife is more likely than the husband to subordinate her personal desires to family goals (Bowerman, 1957). The woman is called upon to adapt to her husband's life pattern: to the man, his work schedule, where he works, what he does, and to the general proposition that she is a helpmeet. It is the wife, not the husband, who finds marriage accommodation a primary life task (Burgess and Cottrell, 1939). Since we still define the woman as keeper of the family retreat, she develops an accommodative pattern in her relationship with her husband and becomes the expressive, compliant member of the family (Stuckert, 1963).[78]

Several movies and television serials have been constructed around the situation of a father/widower with a son or two, all in need of a "nurturant" woman to take care of them. The fact that children and fathers "compete" for similar services from the mother may explain why the Oedipus Complex is more pronounced than the Electra Complex (if these concepts still have any credibility).[79]

*Erich Fromm, in *The Art of Loving*, waxes eloquent about mothers' "unconditional" love.

Margaret Adams has discussed the negative effects of this obligatory "selflessness" upon women, under the title of "The Compassion Trap":

> Both family and professional commitments incorporate the insidious notion that the needs of others should be woman's major, if not exclusive, concern. Implicit in the role that derives from this notion is the supposed virtue of subordinating individual needs to the welfare of others and the personal value and supposed reward of vicarious satisfaction from this exercise. . . . Women must abandon the role of the compassionate sibyl who is at everyone's beck and call, because being permanently available to help others keeps women from pursuing their own chosen avocations with the concentration that is essential for their successful completion.[80]

Men have a stake in insuring that women remain unable to "abandon the role of the compassionate sibyl." They derive double benefit—as husbands wanting wifely services, as fathers wanting child-rearing services—from the "emotional indenture"[81] of women.

MORE EVIDENCE THAT MEN DON'T WANT THE JOB

Despite all the disadvantages of child-rearing responsibility, men often protest that they'd love to be able to stay home with the kids. However, there are two additional sources of evidence that men don't really find the job desirable.

The first relates to the widely noted phenomenon that boys who behave like girls draw stronger negative reactions than girls who behave like boys. A "sissy" playing with dolls elicits unmixed scorn, while an adventurous "tomboy" (as long as she's not too old) gets a certain amount of approval. In over-all social estimation, female activities and traits are not as worthy or desirable as those of males. "The fact that . . . both sexes tend to value men and male characteristics, values, and activities more highly than those of women has been noted by many authorities."[82]

All of this suggests the essential hypocrisy of men who laud female achievements as "different but equal," or who claim they'd gladly switch. Studies have consistently shown that far fewer men than women wish they had been born the opposite sex. The work of women, including most prominently the "nurturing" of children, is socially devalued, and a miniscule number of men have actually taken it on.

The second source of evidence relevant here is the attitude of men toward working with children as a salaried job. The overwhelming majority of people in occupations involving close interaction with children (elementary school teachers,* day-care and nursery school personnel, child welfare workers, etc.) are women. Students of male/female occupational distribution (Bird, 1968; Epstein, 1971) have noted that men monopolize the jobs most desirable in terms of prestige, power, and salary, leaving the residue to women. Judging by the statistics, men have not chosen working with children as suitable employment for their sex.

However, as Caroline Bird found in her "Sex Map of the Work World," the "most striking boundary of all is occupational *status.*"[83] Thus, men are willing to enter such "female" fields as children's education at the upper echelons. In 1968, 78% of elementary school *principals* were male.[84] Men dominate the top of the profession of child study[85] and dispense highly professional advice on child-rearing to the actual rearers of children ("Dr. Spock Speaks to Mothers").

Thus, working with children might not be such an unattractive prospect for males, if the rewards (money, status, power) could be made commensurate with their expectations. In fact, there seems to be a current trend toward increased participation of males in elementary education. This development is probably the result of a few different causes: a tight job market; the effect of the draft on male occupational choice; a new concern that men be present in schools as "male role models"[86]; and a general societal shift toward evaluating early childhood as a crucial learning period, and early education as a more important business. If the last factor is the predominant one, then it's possible that the occupation of elementary school teacher could undergo a sex change, with the improvements in salary, benefits, job conditions, etc. that result when males move into female occupations. But even with a radical change in the status of salaried work with children, it is doubtful that unsalaried rearing of children will ever attract many males.

Conclusion

The allocation of child-rearing responsibility to women, I have argued, is no sacred fiat of nature, but a social policy which supports male domination in the society and in the family.

Whatever the "intrinsic desirability" of rearing children, the con-

---

*The closer children approach to adulthood, the higher the percentage of males teaching them.

ditions of the job as it's now constituted—no salary, low status, long hours, domestic isolation—mark it as a job for women only. Men, as the superordinate group, don't want child-rearing responsibility, so they assign it to women. Women's functioning as child-rearers reinforces, in turn, their subordinate position. Thus we come back again to the causal model of my Introduction—

Women are the rearers of children

Women are a powerless group vis-à-vis men

—one of the vicious circles which keeps male power intact.

Notes

1. Arthur Stinchcombe, *Constructing Social Theories* (New York, 1968), p. 157.

2. See, for example: Caroline Bird, *Born Female;* Cynthia Fuchs Epstein, *Woman's Place;* Kirsten Amundsen, *The Silenced Majority;* Simone de Beauvoir, *The Second Sex.*

3. Leta S. Hollingworth, "Social Devices for Impelling Women to Bear and Rear Children," *The American Journal of Sociology,* XXII (July, 1916), p. 20.

4. Naomi Weisstein, "Psychology Constructs the Female," in Michele Hoffnung Garskof, *Roles Women Play* (Belmont, Calif., 1971), p. 77.

5. Myron Brenton, *The American Male* (New York, 1966), p. 144.

6. Leonard Benson, *Fatherhood: A Sociological Perspective* (New York, 1968), p. 7.

7. Norman W. Bell & Ezra F. Vogel, eds., *A Modern Introduction to the Family,* Rev. ed. (New York, 1968), p. 32.

8. Anna Freud & Dorothy Burlingham, *Infants Without Families* (New York, 1944), p. ix.

9. John Bowlby, *Maternal Care and Mental Health* (Geneva, 1952), p. 15.

10. Bell & Vogel, *op. cit.,* p. 580.

11. See Shulamith Firestone, *The Dialectic of Sex,* on test-tube babies.

12. Robert F. Winch, *The Modern Family,* Rev. ed. (New York, 1964), p. 451.

13. Ethel Albert, "The Unmothered Woman," in Garskof, *op. cit.,* p. 29.

14. Erik H. Erikson, "Inner and Outer Space: Reflections on Womanhood," in Robert Jay Lifton, ed., *The Woman in America,* 2nd ed. (Boston, 1965), p. 5.

15. Erich Fromm, *The Art of Loving* (New York, 1956), p. 41.

16. Talcott Parsons, Robert F. Bales, *et al., Family Socialization and Interaction Process* (New York, 1955), p. 18.

17. *Webster's New World Dictionary* (New York, 1957), p. 1009.

18. Benson, *op. cit.*, p. 249.

19. Parsons, Bales, *et al., op. cit.*, p. 313.

20. Benson, *op. cit.*, p. 65.

21. Quoted in Arlene S. Skolnick & Jerome H. Skolnick, *Family in Transition* (Boston, 1971), p. 12.

22. See bibliography listings under Harry F. Harlow and Bill Seay.

23. Harry F. Harlow, "The Nature of Love," *The American Psychologist,* XIII (Dec., 1958), p. 685.

24. Benson, *loc. cit.*

25. Bill Seay, Bruce K. Alexander, & Harry F. Harlow, "Maternal Behavior of Socially Deprived Rhesus Monkeys," *Journal of Abnormal and Social Psychology,* LXIX (Oct., 1964), p. 353.

26. Brenton, *op. cit.*, pp. 146 & 145.

27. Harriet L. Rheingold, "The Social and Socializing Infant," in David A. Goslin, ed., *Handbook of Socialization Theory and Research* (Chicago, 1969), p. 783.

28. Hollingworth, *op. cit.*, p. 24.

29. Marcia Millman, "Observations on Sex Role Research," *Journal of Marriage and the Family,* XXXIII (Nov., 1971), p. 773.

30. Brenton, *op. cit.*, p. 146.

31. Benson, *op. cit.*, pp. 5-6.

32. Robert K. Merton, *Social Theory and Social Structure* (Glencoe, Ill., 1957), pp. 46-7.

33. Alvin Gouldner, "The Norm of Reciprocity," *American Sociological Review,* XXV (April, 1960), p. 162.

34. Benson, *op. cit.*, p. 120.

35. Kate Millett, *Sexual Politics;* Pat Mainardi, "The Politics of Housework"; Susan Lydon, "The Politics of Orgasm"; Ti-Grace Atkinson, "The Politics of Sexual Intercourse."

36. U.S. Women's Bureau, *1969 Handbook on Women Workers,* p. 35.

37. Reuben Hill & Howard Becker, eds., *Family, Marriage, and Parenthood* (Boston, 1955), p. 790.

38. Talcott Parsons, "Age and Sex in the Social Structure," in Coser, Rose Laub, ed., *The Family: Its Structure and Functions* (New York, 1964), pp. 258, 261-2.

39. For a full report, see Benson, *op. cit.*, pp. 297-305.

40. Lois Wladis Hoffman, "Effects of the Employment of Mothers on Parental Power Relations and the Division of Household Tasks," *Marriage and Family Living,* XXII (Feb., 1960), p. 33.

41. Benson, *op. cit.*, pp. 302-3.

42. Bell & Vogel, *op. cit.*, p. 586.

43. Phyllis Hallenbeck, "An Analysis of Power Dynamics in Marriage," *Journal of Marriage and the Family,* XXVIII (May, 1966), p. 201.

44. Helen Mayer Hacker, "The New Burdens of Masculinity," *Marriage and Family Living,* XIX (Aug., 1957), p. 232.

45. Benson, *op. cit.*, p. 293.

46. *Ibid.*

47. Hollingworth, *op. cit.*, p. 20.

48. Benson, *op. cit.*, p. 292.

49. Sandra L. Bem & Daryl J. Bem, "Training the Woman to Know Her Place," in Garskof, *op. cit.*, p. 94.

50. Benson, *loc. cit.*

51. Alice S. Rossi, "Barriers to the Career Choice of Engineering, Medicine, or Science Among American Women," in Jacquelyn A. Mattfeld & Carol G. Van Aken, eds., *Women and the Scientific Professions* (Cambridge, Mass., 1965), p. 87.

52. Benson, *op. cit.*, pp. 132 & 134.

53. Winch, *op. cit.*, p. 434.

54. Dair L. Gillespie, "Who Has the Power? The Marital Struggle," *Journal of Marriage and the Family*, XXXIII (Aug., 1971), p. 456.

55. U.S. Bureau of the Census, *Statistical Abstract of the U.S.: 1971*, Table 332, and *U.S. Census of Population: 1960, Subject Reports: Families*, Table 11.

56. Rossi, *op. cit.*, pp. 102-3, 107.

57. Quoted in Betty Rollin, "Motherhood: Who Needs It?" in Skolnick & Skolnick, *op. cit.*, p. 352.

58. Parsons, *op. cit.*, pp. 258-9.

59. Gillespie, *loc. cit.*

60. Margaret Benston, "The Political Economy of Women's Liberation," in Garskof, *op. cit.*, p. 196.

61. Parsons, *op. cit.*, p. 261.

62. Judith Long Laws, "A Feminist Review of Marital Adjustment Literature," *Journal of Marriage and the Family*, XXXIII (Aug., 1971), p. 493.

63. Benson, *op. cit.*, p. 12.

64. Brenton, *op. cit.*, p. 133.

65. Benson, *op. cit.*, p. 149.

66. Constantina Safilios-Rothschild, "The Study of Family Power Structure: A Review 1960-1969," *Journal of Marriage and the Family*, XXXII (Nov., 1970), p. 548.

67. Benson, *op. cit.*, p. 152.

68. *Ibid.*, p. 157.

69. Safilios-Rothschild, "Family Sociology or Wives' Family Sociology?" *Journal of Marriage and the Family*, XXXI (May, 1969), p. 297.

70. Benson, *op. cit.*, pp. 14, 18, 50-2, 59.

71. Hollingworth, *op. cit.*, pp. 20-1, 27.

72. Benston, *op. cit.*, p. 199.

73. Hallenbeck, *op. cit.*, p. 201.

74. Rollin, *op. cit.*, p. 353.

75. *Ibid.*, p. 349.

76. *Ibid.*

77. Judy Syfers, "Why I Want a Wife," in *Notes From the Third Year* (New York, 1971), p. 13.

78. Benson, *op. cit.*, pp. 134-5,

79. See Firestone, *The Dialectic of Sex*, for an excellent analysis of these Complexes in power terms.

80. Margaret Adams, "The Compassion Trap," *Psychology Today*, V (Nov., 1971), pp. 72, 101.

81. *Ibid.*, p. 100.
82. Jo Freeman, "The Social Construction of the Second Sex," in Garskof, *op. cit.*, p. 126 (references included).
83. Caroline Bird, *Born Female* (New York, 1968), p. 101.
84. Cynthia Fuchs Epstein, *Woman's Place* (Berkeley, Calif., 1971), p. 10.
85. Bird, *op. cit.*, p. 102.
86. See Patricia Sexton, *The Feminized Male.*

References

Adams, Margaret. 1971 "The Compassion Trap." *Psychology Today,* V Nov., p. 70 ff.
Albert, Ethel. 1971 "The Unmothered Woman." in Garskof, Michele Hoffnung. *Roles Women Play: Readings Toward Women's Liberation.* Belmont, Calif.: Brooks/Cole Publishing Co., pp. 25-38.
Bell, Norman W., Ezra F. Vogel, eds. 1968 *A Modern Introduction to the Family.* Rev. ed. New York: The Free Press.
Bem, Sandra L., Daryl J. Bem. "Training the Woman to Know Her Place: The Power of a Nonconscious Ideology." in Garskof, pp. 84-96.
Benson, Leonard. 1968 *Fatherhood: A Sociological Perspective.* New York: Random House.
Benston, Margaret. "The Political Economy of Women's Liberation." in Garskof, pp. 194-205.
Bird, Caroline. 1968 *Born Female: The High Cost of Keeping Women Down.* New York: David McKay.
Blood, Robert O., Jr. 1958 "The Division of Labor in City and Farm Families." *Marriage and Family Living,* XX May, pp. 170-174.
Blood, Robert O., Jr., Donald M. Wolfe. 1960 *Husbands and Wives: The Dynamics of Married Living.* New York: The Free Press.
Bowlby, John. 1952 *Maternal Care and Mental Health.* Geneva: World Health Organization.
Brenton, Myron. 1966 *The American Male.* New York: Coward-McCann.
Campbell, Frederick L. 1967 *Demographic Factors in Family Organizations.* Unpublished Ph. D. dissertation, University of Michigan.
Ehrlich, Carol. 1971 "The Male Sociologist's Burden: The Place of Women in Marriage and Family Texts." *Journal of Marriage and the Family,* XXXIII Aug., pp. 421-439.
Epstein, Cynthia Fuchs. 1971 *Woman's Place: Options and Limits in Professional Careers.* Berkeley: University of California Press.
Erikson, Erik H. 1965 "Inner and Outer Space: Reflections on Womanhood." in Lifton, Robert Jay, ed. *The Woman in America.* 2nd ed. Boston: Houghton Mifflin Co., pp. 1-26.
Firestone, Shulamith. 1971 *The Dialectic of Sex: The Case for Feminist Revolution.* Rev. ed. New York: Bantam Books.
Freeman, Jo. "The Social Construction of the Second Sex." in Garskof, *op. cit.*, pp. 123-141.

Freud, Anna, Dorothy Burlingham. 1944 *Infants Without Families: The Case For and Against Residential Nurseries.* New York: Medical War Books, International University Press.

Fromm, Erich. 1956 *The Art of Loving.* New York: Harper and Row.

Gillespie, Dair L. 1971 "Who Has the Power? The Marital Struggle." *Journal of Marriage and the Family,* XXXIII Aug., pp. 445-458.

Gouldner, Alvin. 1960 "The Norm of Reciprocity." *American Sociological Review,* XXV April, pp. 161-178.

Hacker, Helen Mayer. 1957 "The New Burdens of Masculinity." *Marriage and Family Living,* XIX Aug., pp. 227-233.

Hallenbeck, Phyllis N. 1966 "An Analysis of Power Dynamics in Marriage." *Journal of Marriage and the Family,* XXVIII May, pp. 200-203.

Harlow, Harry F. 1959 "Love in Infant Monkeys." *Scientific American,* CC June, pp. 68-74.

Harlow, Harry F. 1958 "The Nature of Love." *The American Psychologist,* XIII Dec., pp. 673-685.

Harlow, Harry F., Margaret Kuenne Harlow. 1962 "Social Deprivation in Monkeys." *Scientific American,* CCVII Nov., pp. 136-146.

Heer, David M. 1958 "Dominance and the Working Wife." *Social Forces,* XXXVI May, pp. 341-347.

Heer, David M. 1963 "The Measurement and Bases of Family Power: An Overview." *Marriage and Family Living,* XXV May, pp. 133-139.

Hill, Reuben, Howard Becker, eds. 1955 *Family, Marriage, and Parenthood.* Boston: D. C. Heath.

Hoffman, Lois Wladis. 1960 "Effects of the Employment of Mothers on Parental Power Relations and the Division of Household Tasks." *Marriage and Family Living,* XXII Feb., pp. 27-35.

Hoffman, Lois Wladis, R. Lippitt. 1960 "The Measurement of Family Life Variables." in Mussen, P. H., ed. *Handbook of Research Methods in Child Development.* New York: Wiley.

Hollingworth, Leta S. 1916 "Social Devices for Impelling Women to Bear and Rear Children." *The American Journal of Sociology,* XXII July, pp. 19-29.

Laws, Judith Long. 1971 "A Feminist Review of Marital Adjustment Literature: The Rape of the Locke." *Journal of Marriage and the Family,* XXXIII Aug., pp. 483-516.

Merton, Robert K. 1957 *Social Theory and Social Structure.* Glencoe, Ill.: The Free Press.

Middleton, Russell, Snell Putney. 1960 "Dominance in Decisions in the Family: Race and Class Differences." *The American Journal of Sociology,* LXV May, pp. 605-609.

Millman, Marcia. 1971 "Observations on Sex Role Research." *Journal of Marriage and the Family,* XXXIII Nov., pp., 772-776.

Nye, F. Ivan, Lois Wladis Hoffman, eds. 1963 *The Employed Mother in America.* Chicago: Rand McNally.

Parsons, Talcott. 1964 "Age and Sex in the Social Structure." in Coser, Rose Laub, ed. *The Family: Its Structure and Functions.* New York: St. Martin's Press, pp. 251-266.

Parsons, Talcott, Robert F. Bales, *et al.* 1955 *Family, Socialization and Inter-action Process.* New York: The Free Press.

Rheingold, Harriet L. 1969 "The Social and Socializing Infant." in Goslin, David A., ed. *Handbook of Socialization Theory and Research.* Chicago: Rand McNally, pp. 779-790.

Rollin, Betty. 1971 "Motherhood: Who Needs It?" in Skolnick, Arlene S., Jerome H. Skolnick, eds. *Family in Transition.* Boston: Little, Brown, pp. 346-356.

Rossi, Alice S. 1965 "Barriers to the Career Choice of Engineering, Medicine, or Science Among American Women." in Mattfeld. Jacquelyn A., Carol G. Van Aken, eds. *Women and the Scientific Professions.* Cambridge, Mass.: The M.I.T. Press, pp. 51-127.

Safilios-Rothschild, Constantina. 1969 "Family Sociology or Wives' Family Sociology?: A Cross-Cultural Examination of Decision Making." *Journal of Marriage and the Family,* XXXI May, pp. 290-301.

Safilios-Rothschild, Constantina. 1970 "The Study of Family Power Structure: A Review 1960-1969." *Journal of Marriage and the Family,* XXXII Nov., pp. 539-552.

Seay, Bill, Bruce K. Alexander, Harry F. Harlow. 1964 "Maternal Behavior of Socially Deprived Rhesus Monkeys." *Journal of Abnormal and Social Psychology,* XXIX Oct., pp. 345-354.

Sexton, Patricia. 1969 *The Feminized Male.* New York: Random House.

Skolnick, Arlene S., Jerome H. Skolnick, eds. 1971 *Family in Transition.* Boston: Little, Brown.

Stinchcombe, Arthur. 1968 *Constructing Social Theories.* New York: Harcourt, Brace, and World.

Syfers, Judy. 1971 "Why I Want a Wife." in *Notes From the Third Year: Women's Liberation.* New York.

U.S. Bureau of the Census. 1971 *Statistical Abstract of the U.S.: 1971.* Washington, D.C.: U.S. Government Printing Office.

U.S. Bureau of the Census. 1963 *U.S. Census of Population: 1960, Subject Report: Families.* Final Report PC(2)-4A. Washington, D.C.: U.S. Government Printing Office.

U.S. Women's Bureau. 1969 *1969 Handbook on Women Workers.* Washington, D.C.: U.S. Government Printing Office.

Weisstein, Naomi. "Psychology Constructs the Female, or the Fantasy Life of the Male Psychologist." in Garskof, pp. 68-83.

Winch, Robert F. 1964 *The Modern Family.* Rev. ed. New York: Holt, Rinehart, and Winston.

The History of a Short Unsuccessful Academic Career

By Michael Silverstein

*T*he usefulness of a history is to show the operation of process. In this case, the process is the development of an identity. By using my experiences as an example, I hope to show the experiential reality of the one-dimensionality of this society in determining an individual's identity. This is done through the key institution of sex roles. What I must grow up to be, what it must mean to me to be a male human being, was presented to me as inevitable and unquestionable. Masculinity was defined for me by the social world I was a part of as a set of personal characteristics that must become a part of my identity. I believe I can illustrate how I, like all male children, was taught that my value as a person depended on my power over others. I was taught that I must compete for personal power, and that to be successful I must conceal feelings of weakness, tenderness, and dependence, and present myself to other men as self-sufficient and insensitive.

In spite of the all-pervasiveness of this lesson, I finally found myself in full rebellion against manhood. The source of this rebellion was something that appeared to me as entirely external to the reality of the world I was taught about, the fact of my Gayness. To those of us who identify ourselves with the Gay Liberation movement, Gay-

The Insurgent Sociologist, 1972, pp. 4-19. Reprinted by permission of *The Insurgent Sociologist* and the author. An abridged version of this article was published in *The Journal of Applied Behavioral Science,* Vol. 8, No. 5, copyright © 1972.

ness has come to mean far more than the original fact of our homosexuality. The description of how I came to reject the definition of myself as a man, will at the same time be a description of how I came to understand the concept of Gayness, by coming to an understanding of the political reality of the psychological characteristics of manliness.

But our lives are lived in the context of social institutions. In my case, these processes worked themselves out in the context of academia. This was not accidental. I found myself in academia because of its peculiar embodiment of the masculine role. I had sought it out because it had been presented to me as a less masculine milieu than most social institutions, yet ultimately it turned out that success in this sphere was as much dependent on those personality traits defined as male as in any other part of the society. Thus in describing the history of my academic career, I believe I can show how the social needs men are taught to act upon, are essential to the functioning of even the less masculine-appearing social institutions.

Ultimately, this leads to the assertion that the masculine personality, the man's learned drive for interpersonal dominance, is the psychic engine required for capitalist society to function. Those with real power, ruling class males, in order to perpetuate the existing social structure, and thus insure their continued control, must use their control of the educational, communicational, entertainment, and religious institutions to create men who seek a positive self-image in their power over others. Thus they have at their disposal middle class men motivated to operate the organizational machinery of capitalism by a desire to achieve power, and working class men that can be reconciled to their real powerlessness by an experienced personal power over their women, and the possibility of successfully competing for personal power with rivals of their own class. In addition white working class men are given at least a vicarious power over third world peoples. Similarly those in power also require women who learn to evaluate their self-worth by their success in emotionally and materially supporting a man in his struggle for power, rather than acting as competitors themselves. The present paper doesn't attempt such an ambitious argument, but leads in that direction by illustrating how the masculine drive for power is the essential motivating force in the functioning of academic institutions.

But these abstractions can only define the argument, they can never advance it. My experiences aren't abstractions to me, my life depends on them. Manhood appears to me not as a sociological concept, but as a Procrustian bed the society would force me into, and my struggle against it is a struggle to keep from being mutilated out of all human shape. My academic career appears to me as a life and death struggle I just barely survived. It is the reality of this struggle I want to communicate. It was well under way by the time I was ten years old.

By the time I was ten, the central fact of my life was the demand that I become a man. By then the most important relationships by which I was taught to define myself, were those only with other boys. I already knew that I must see every encounter with another boy as a contest in which I must win or at least hold my own. School was the major arena of this contest, especially the playground, and P.E.: this was always the major lesson that school taught. But the same lesson continued everywhere, after school, even in Sunday School. My parents, relatives, teachers, the books I read, movies I saw, all taught me that my self worth depended on my manliness, my willingness to stand up to the other boys. This usually didn't mean a physical fight, though the willingness to stand up and fight like a man always remained a final test. But the relationship between us usually had the character of an armed truce. Acceptance as an equal depended on the maintenance of a front of being just as tough, strong, big, as the other guys. Girls weren't part of this social world at all yet, just because they weren't part of this contest. They didn't have to be bluffed, no credit was gained by cowing them, so they were more or less ignored. Sometimes when there were no grown-ups around we would let each other know we liked each other, but most of the time we did as we were taught.

So I knew what I had to do to be a man. There was no alternative. One could only succeed at establishing his manliness or be a failure, a sissy, someone who couldn't stand up and fight. One didn't choose to be a sissy, a loser, one lost. Since manliness was of course what everyone would want, the unmanly must be those who were too weak to make it as a man.

By the time I was in Junior High I defined myself and was defined by the other boys as a loser, as the class sissy. Largely this meant that I saw myself as a failed man, too weak to be the only thing worth being. Yet the beginning of my Gayness was the beginning of my attempt to choose to be what I was. I began to redefine myself positively, to redefine what it was not to be a successful man, and in so doing I was moving outside of the social reality I had been born to.

My first attempt at self-affirmation was to insist to myself that I didn't really want to be a man anyway. Much of this was sour grapes of course, and I knew it. But there was something else there. There really was a part of me that, in opposition to everything I had been taught, really didn't want to be a man. This was my Gayness. I didn't know anything about homosexuality then, I didn't even know about sex. But from the time I was five years old, I had wanted to touch and hold the bodies of other boys, and when I had done so I had felt warm and comfortable, and affectionate toward them. By the time I was eight or nine I had learned how bad and dirty, how unmanly, this was, and I was so scared of being caught at it that I stopped. But the desire remained, a gigantic thing always there. It was totally outside the reality of what it was to be a man. Yet it was so real, so undeniably a part of me, that it forced me to see myself as outside the world of all the other boys I knew. It was not just that I couldn't be a man, it was also that I knew about this part of me that could never be satisfied by manhood, because it wanted something that no man would ever want. For the reward of success as a man is power over other men, and I understood that this need I had could never be satisfied by power. I wasn't sure exactly what I wanted, what I actually wanted to do with another boy. But I knew that whatever it was, it required that we both want it, that it was only itself if given freely. All sorts of fantasies were going on in my head, completely dominating my consciousness. They were all rather vague, but they all involved relating to other boys in very unmanly ways, ways that had nothing to do with power.

So I did try to be a man. But there was always something half-hearted about my attempts. I could never entirely put my heart into a contest, when the reward for success seemed incompatible with what I really wanted. This may seem rather abstract for a 13 year old, but I believe I understood the reality of the world far better at 13 than I did for a long time thereafter. It was at this time that I set out to find an alternative to manhood, something else I could grow up to be. Ultimately this would lead to the goal of Gayness, the rejection of the whole dimension of masculinity-femininity as a scale on which people find their proper status and the attempt to create a new concept of peoplehood. But that would come later. I didn't feel ready yet to take on the world in Junior High, so I started looking around in the world as it had been presented to me to find a place for myself. One choice I could have made was to decide that since I wouldn't be a man, I would be like a woman instead. Many young Gay males have made this choice. They'll have to tell their story, what their decision has meant to them. I thought I saw another alternative, something else I could be, that was a recognized part of the world I knew, yet wasn't a man. In fact this alternative would turn out to be a twenty year long detour into a blind alley, the blind alley of an academic career. But at the time I thought I saw an escape route, I would grow up to be a Brain.

Brains were a little weird group of people I had heard about for a long time, in comic books, television shows, and from my family. I remember "the Absent-Minded Professors" in the comic books. They wore Caps and Gowns and were bare-foot, and while other men were the heroes of the story—did the fighting—they did all sorts of funny unreal things, like asking how the world worked, that didn't really matter because such interests didn't lead to any power. They were small and pot-bellied and comical, no match for the heroes. But they did seem to be having fun. Looking around for something other than a man I could be, I seized on them as the most unmanly males visible. So I set out to be a Brain.

In the next few years I learned more about what being a Brain meant. About this time dating started replacing sports as the most important medium of competition among men. Instead of fighting with our own bodies we were now supposed to fight over the bodies of women. It was the guys who were already established as toughest and strongest who won the most girls, of course, and since I had already decided I wasn't going to be like them, I wouldn't fight here either. It never occurred to me that this had anything at all to do with the physical need I felt . . . (there isn't any word available to let me describe what seems to me to be such a simple and basic feeling: to mutually and physically show affection with another person. It's simpler, less dramatic, than "making love," nothing climactic, or special, just comfortable, mundane, one of the best parts of the day to day living of a life.) Anyhow, it never occurred to me that this had anything to do with the way big guys used girls. What I wanted was something you did with your friends, and the real winners, the real men, made it clear they didn't even regard women as people. But being a Brain got me out of this too. Because by now I had learned about Brains. They were sexless. In fact they were all but bodiless. They never caught girls, they didn't even chase them. So as a Brain I had an excuse why I didn't chase girls. (By now I needed an excuse very badly, I was terrified they'd think I was queer.) I didn't chase girls because I never did anything with my body at all. If people assumed I didn't want to touch anybody, they'd never suspect the dirty, nasty truth. So I started pretending my body wasn't there. I was fat, and dirty, and sloppy, and wore "out-of-it" clothes.

By high school I was firmly established as The Brain, a junior scientist, good in the classroom, lousy on the sports field, and sexless. By now I was perfecting my role on a more sophisticated level; I was an Intellectual. This meant making plans for what I wanted to do when I grew up, and my family taught me that the least manly of all Brains were my old friends the college professors. Their reasons were quite convincing. For them, an adult shows his manliness by his success in supporting his wife and children. College professors go to college as long as doctors and lawyers, but they don't support their families nearly as well, and knowing this they waste all that time in school anyway. No real man would act like that. That decided me. Brains didn't fight like men; they didn't fuck like men; they didn't even work like men. If I wanted to grow up into something other than a man, the best way I could do it was by being a Brain, a college professor. Of course, this still wouldn't allow me to love people, but I didn't see any possibility for that anywhere in the world. I felt I had to settle for whatever rewards could be found in the world as I was taught to see it.

Entering college, my act was pretty well down. My self-image and sense of self-worth was based on my conception of myself as an intellectual, an ascetic, and an aesthete. Art, literature, "things of the mind," these were both my major source of pleasure, and the basis of a sense of myself as superior, more sensitive, more moral, than real men. Of course, the pleasure was largely a consolation for loneliness, and the self-worth contained much self-hate as well, especially of my body. But I saw no alternative, so I clung to it. I never planned to have any sex or let anyone know I wanted to. The only physical pleasure I allowed myself was food. People seemed to buy the act, and I found I could relate to them in a friendly enough way as long as we kept our distance. But now something strange started to happen. I continued as always, great in the classroom, lousy on the playing field. But now the playing field started to fade out and what replaced it was so unexpected that it took me years to understand what was happening.

Intellectual abilities and attainments had always been presented to me as essentially unmasculine, something a real man wouldn't take seriously, because they weren't practical, that is they didn't lead to power. Thus they appeared to me as an escape from masculinity into a sexless asceticism, and they could be the source of the only positive self-image I could imagine. I had hoped that by graduate school, with the Big Men On Campus off to the professional and graduate business schools, that I might find myself among other people like myself, and that as unmanly intellectuals, we might find some new way to relate to each other.

Instead, now that all the Big Men were gone, it seemed like all the other Brains wanted to play at being men. Only now they'd play their way. But their way was my way. My sanctuary from manly competitiveness had become another of its arenas. And the weapons being used, words, were something I was accomplished in the use of. For the first time in my life I could be a Big Man, a winner. Moreover, I started doing this without even knowing it. I just went on like I always had. Suddenly I started myself being proclaimed a winner in a contest I never knew I had entered.

The Graduate Sociology Department at UCLA was as masculine as any locker room. The female graduate students were self-effacing, weren't taken seriously in the competition, and didn't seem to take themselves seriously. (Of the three exceptions I can remember to this, two are now Radical Feminists, and the third killed herself.) But I didn't recognize the games being played, because the main way I recognized them was from the perspective of a loser. Suddenly finding myself in the middle of the same game as a winner, I didn't know where I was for quite awhile. But I knew that I was one of the bright young men of the department. I was awarded a Special Research Training Fellowship of the National Institute of General Medical Sciences. I talked more than anybody else in all the seminars and could keep the other men from getting in a word edgewise. And I found myself enjoying the hell out of doing it.

For the first time in my life I had some taste of power over others. While I still appeared to my teachers as rather naive and erratic, nonetheless I was finally treated like a man. Even my family decided that college professors did pretty well after all. For the first (and last) time in my life, my family regarded me as a success. I just forgot about being the Sissy of my Junior High, and I started believing that I had just been a late bloomer, now I was coming into my manhood at last.

Except that I knew that none of it was real. I knew I was just pretending to be a man, because by this time I knew what it meant that I was a homosexual, that the most I would ever be capable of

was a facade of manliness. Even in academic circles, being a successful man means more than just success as an academician. The successful academician doesn't just succeed in his career; he uses that
success to buy himself manly success, to win all the rewards common
to a successful man. This requires that he achieve recognition as a
prominent member of his community. And part of this is being a
householder, the head of a family. Even an academician has to get
himself at least one woman and a child or two. I was still an outsider to this world. I felt neither the desire nor the ability to become
the head of a household. Thus although I had access to masculine
power for the first time, I still didn't want what this power must be
used to purchase if it is to be actualized in this society. And I was
sure that as soon as this became apparent, people would realize that I
wasn't really a man after all. While I could get some gratification out
of being super stud of the advanced seminar on alienation, I knew
as much as I had always known that it could never lead to the kinds of
gratification that I still felt were the only things that would ever
really give meaning to my life.

    Thus the power I started to attain in the academic world never
meant the same thing to me as it would to a heterosexual man. I
believe this power was typical of that wielded by "successful" homosexuals, in that I experienced it as essentially defensive. It was not a
weapon to win for myself the masculine prize I still didn't want, but
a shield to hide my failure from public view. As time went on I
came to value this power highly, because it seemed necessary to use
it to defend myself, hide myself, but it never became a positive thing.
No matter how powerful I might appear to others, the most I could
ever hope from this power was security, safety, never gratification. If
this is true of apparently powerful homosexual men, then no matter
how much they appear a part of and committed to the society, their
attachment is based on fear and defensiveness, and their only hope
of gratification lies in abandoning such power and abandoning their
commitment to the society in which it is the greatest possible gratification.

    But what could I do? If academia wasn't an escape from mascu-
linity, I could see no such escape anywhere. So I set out to be a success after all, not because it seemed positively desirable, but for want
of anything better to do. Academia might just be another masculine
cage, but at least was one where I found myself on one of the higher
perches. Just to be confident that I could pass for a man, especially

with my family, was something to be grateful for. I had even picked out a specialty, I hoped to make it as the big man in Alienation Theory.

But now, just when I was ready to play at being a man, and strive for success, the game changed again. As I reached the end of graduate school, and started looking for a job, the most important arena of competition moved from the polemics of the classroom, to the use of entrepreneureal and managerial skills within the bureaucracies of academic departments. Success now was determined by the sale of your products and future products, writings and research projects. These were to be sold to academic departments, publishers, and agencies that funded research grants. While the polemic skills that let me argue successfully for the correctness of my analysis of things was relevant to this kind of competition, other skills were more important, such as the ability to write long, formal, highly-structured, and bureaucratically sound research proposals. I first ran into this new set of required skills in applying for fellowships. Then came applying for a job. And I was already getting scared by the prospect that a successful career required a concentration on these things. I could do them if I had to, but they didn't bring even the spurious gratification of power in the classroom. They didn't seem to be any fun, only drudgery, alienated labor. They were the means to a successful career, but the end had never seemed worth it.

By this time I had gone to my first Sociology Convention, and any hope I had left that I might find some other non-Men around was smashed by the sight of all the bustling young executive types, drinks in hand, button-holing each other to sound out prospects. No wonder my family had decided that it was all right to be a college professor.

II

Nevertheless I got a job at C.C.N.Y., and that was the peak of my academic career.

Arriving in New York, in the fall of 1967, I had a whole personality ready for presentation, down to a bushy beard. By now I knew that as long as I kept things on an abstract and intellectual level—and we Men kept them there—I could be articulate to the point of glibness, and self-confident to the point of smugness. I was distantly friendly and impersonally cheerful to everyone. I was pretty sure I could pass as a man now. But I still knew that passing as a man wouldn't help. And thus the dirty, ugly, angry city of New York pounded into me every day I spent in it—I was too lonely to give a shit about making it, too lonely to take anything as meaningless as a successful academic career seriously. I'm still grateful to New York for this. When I got there and felt what it was like, I needed people so badly I wanted to die most of the time. This forced me to get down to the real business of living, and start finding out how to get in touch with other people, and myself.

So, once in New York, my most urgent need was other people, and looking around me, I saw two groups of them, my colleagues, and the students. Since my colleagues, my peers, were the group from which I was supposed to draw my friends, I turned to them first. What I found shouldn't be surprising; they weren't as different from me as I had thought. But somehow the differences were such that they made the similarities between us barriers.

A lot of my colleagues looked as if they had been pretty lousy at sports as kids, and had had a hard time hustling up a date. And I wasn't the only one who had read about the "Absent-Minded Professors". Plenty of them had ended up in the academy for reasons similar to mine, but they were still very different from me, most importantly because as adults they had finally found that they could make it as Men, if they worked at it, and they certainly were working at it. As straight men the rewards of manliness were real goals for them.

But a more obvious difference was also more paradoxical. Many of them seemed less "manly" than I did. They hadn't done nearly as well as I had in the word games of graduate seminars. I could talk rings around most of them. They had finally found their arena of successful competition just where it went past me. They were the entrepreneurs, the letter writers, the applicants for grants, the hard-working serving time on committees. Their scholarly writing is largely the ability to do the academic drudgery of devising complicated and highly structured formulae, that they could then follow precisely in defining, selecting, analyzing, and interpreting data; this being the central activity of American sociology. The same skills served for structuring a text, a series of classroom lectures, or the agenda of a committee meeting. And, as they and I both knew, these are the skills that lead to as much success and masculine power as are available to the academician. But even though the interpersonal skills of polemic discussion are objectively less valuable, nevertheless, they are still seen as an immediate expression of manly power. On a personal level, such academicians are still intimidated by men who talk better than they can. Most of my colleagues were personally withdrawn and somewhat shy. They were virtually all married, and generally related closely only to their wives.

In spite of these personal characteristics, they were very much men in their fascination with power. They were awed by those with more power than they had, and extremely jealous of their own power, though it was often trivial or fictitious. This became obvious as I got involved in faculty politics. The chairmen of about half the departments (the Liberals) as well as some "junior faculty" were meeting every week to work out an elaborate scheme to emasculate the President by appointing one of their own as Provost under him. The plot failed amidst infighting and bumbling. Later in the Faculty Senate (where I was a Junior Senator) incredibly elaborate debates were held between the same Liberal faction and the administration supporters over the exact wording of elaborate resolutions recommending how the college should deal with its adversaries, the students. All the resolutions were as meaningless as the earlier plot. The whole phantom of faculty power was like the court intrigue of the Jugoslavian government in exile, it meant nothing at all. All the real power had always rested with a Board of Higher Education appointed by city politicians. The college administration was answerable above not below, and the only access the faculty had to real power was by promotion from above into the administration, in return for services rendered. The professors were powerless after all. The real men, with real power just didn't have to take them seriously. In the final score, however, the only men with real power are the small elite of the ruling class. But within the artificial little worlds of academic departments, these Absent-Minded Professors with all their timidity and insecurities are the men with power.

There weren't many women on the faculty, and aside from a few exceptional women, they were mainly junior partners to husbands who were higher ranking academics or other professionals. The only independent professionally-minded, unmarried woman in our department was widely rumored to be a "bull-dyke". (I was afraid to associate with her for that reason.)

Not all the professors fit into this pattern of course. Some of them, especially the younger, "hipper", radical, professors were also quite good at talking, and like me had established their manliness in the polemics of the intellectual arena. I could enjoy talking to them and we shared a similar perspective politically, as well as feeling closer to, and less intimidated by students. The friends I made among the faculty came from this group. But here too there were real barriers. Both categories of faculty were straight men. The reason this is important here is that it means that the academy could offer them more of a real reward than it could ever offer to me. For them a "successful academic career" would enable them to buy all the accessories of what passes for a successful life—a wife, children, place as an influential member of the community. This gave even the more radical of them an attraction to conformity that I never had. I knew that no matter how successful I seemed I would always be an outsider, and as an outsider, I never entirely trusted the men who could be a part of the system if they chose to.

Also, in some ways I found the young, hip, radical faculty even less trustworthy than their more conventional senior colleagues. They were the Big Men on Campus now, if not in terms of real power, at least in terms of interpersonal relationships. And they knew it and showed it. From being the ones most likely to be playing around with "the girls", to making no secret of their opinion of the administration and its faculty allies as a bunch of "cocksuckers". In fact in personal encounters these young studs weren't at all above bullying the old "queers" some, whether on an intellectual level, making them feel like inarticulate ignoramuses, or just by overwhelming them with the masculinity of their come-ons. I knew I was accepted by the radicals, more or less, as one of the real men, out to get the bunch of "faggots" running the place.

But I understood that after all they believed real men are entitled to power over non-men, women, and failed men, faggots. They called themselves radicals and socialists and called for an end of the oppression of the third world and of the white poor. But in their own lives, their behavior toward other women and men, they showed that they still believed in the right of the strong to rule the weak. They still used their power to control people, and they still judged themselves and others by the criteria of relative power. They want to redistribute power, but are committed to it as the measurement of personal worth.

In some ways I learned that there was some power I did want, the power to rule my own life. I decided that I must have the power to free myself from those with power over me. So I stopped thinking of myself as an anarchist pacifist, and started thinking of myself as a radical Marxist. But I do not want power over others, and I will not trust as an ally any man who rests his sense of self-worth on the extent of his personal power. I trusted the hip, radical faculty men then, no more than I trust the big men of the movement, now.

And what about other Gay teachers? They were in hiding of course. Only as I was leaving did I find out who some of them were. Generally they were the most invisible, innocuous people on the faculty. They had been around long enough to learn that the first law of survival for a Gay person is never to call attention to oneself. It is not for me—and certainly not for straights—to judge their behavior. They were doing what they had been taught they had to do to survive.

So I turned to the students. My first encounter with them had been the first morning of the semester. At 8 A.M., I found the first of three groups of 80 people staring at me. As a promising graduate student, I had been continually groomed to do research, and to define myself as a researcher. Teaching was a minor chore I'd pick up on the side. Consequently, I had never been in front of a class before in my life, and I was very scared. I stammered through the first day, but made it somehow. By the end of the week it was much easier, though there were occasional flashes of panic. The second week I was starting to get into it, and by the end of a month, I was home. The endless, effortless flow of words that had made me the terror of the pro-seminar still would turn the trick. In a class of thirty graduate students I could keep the other men from getting in a word edgewise, with undergraduates, inexperienced and already accepting my right to speak as much as I wanted, it was all my show. This was just the opposite pattern of most of my colleagues. Since they tended to shy away from verbal encounter and argument, from masculine competition on that level, they were generally intimidated by any direct contest with students. Their ability to compete was at a distance by paper proxies, their victories were in endurance contests in the production of paperwork evaluated by weight. They were particularly afraid of young people, since they represented such an enigmatic and possible hostile force to them. They knew them so little that they feared they were on the edge of revolution. Besides this, in the "Social Sciences," there's an additional reason for defensiveness. The faculty believed that many of the students doubted the validity of the discipline they were supposedly being taught. They suspected the students regarded both the ideas of the social sciences and the methods by which they are arrived at, as trivial and irrelevant to an understanding of the real world around them. Thus the legitimacy of the faculty member's authority as expert is also called into question. Most students regard the kind of concepts and analysis found in social science texts as an obtuse and pretentious load of bullshit. (The students are right.)

Consequently, most of the faculty needed to use their power as teachers to force students to acknowledge the legitimacy of their authority as experts, and thus the truth of the conceptual system within which their expertise lies. This is how our system of higher education works. All the requirements, texts, tests, papers, are designed so that the student's success or failure depends on her ability to understand, interpret, and work within the teacher's definition of reality. Of course academic freedom requires that the student have the right, be encouraged in fact, to evaluate the ideas herself. But only after understanding the official interpretation thoroughly. And given the pressure of requirements, students usually can't budget any time to do anything more than understand the teacher's ideas well enough to pass. Moreover the amount of effort invested in understanding the official line, gives the student some commitment to accepting its reality. Thus with all the academic freedom in the world, all the power is on the side of the teacher. And his own insecurity in dealing with students on any other than a power basis assures that he'll use it.

This is how the connection that men learn to make between self-esteem and power works as the psychological underpinning in the operation of such capitalist institutions as the educational system. Even the most independent student can only be on the defensive, since she has to work within the teacher's conceptual world, and the teacher has not the slightest obligation to understand her perspective at all. The most independent response most students can make is a sullen resentment, and an anti-intellectual skepticism denying the relevance of any abstract analysis, while meeting requirements as superficially as possible. In fact this describes the attitude of most of the students I've known.

After a while, especially at the better colleges, some of the more experienced teachers develop enough virtuosity in presenting their ideas to become almost professional entertainers. They are generally considered the real pros, since they are more often amusing than boring, and that's the only realistic way for students to evaluate teachers. I didn't have to resort to any of this. I didn't need to use my formal authority to have power over my students. First of all, I didn't find them particularly intimidating. As a vicarious hippie, and a vicarious radical, for years, I understood the youth culture as only an envious outsider could. (Neither hippies nor radicals had much use for queers.) Most importantly, I didn't see students as an outside threat to an establishment of which I was a part. I saw myself as far more` outside it than they were. I was not defending either a system of analysis in which I believed—I'd considered the practice of American sociology garbage for quite some time—or my authority as an expert in the understanding and teaching of these concepts. In fact my real power over students lay just in my ability to give up formal authority. By abdicating my sole right to define the situation, I seduced the students to speaking up, presenting their own ideas, disagreeing with me. Then I'd smash them. I put on quite a show. I was intimidated by students too (male students at least. I was just starting to see women as people); I was intimidated by them as men, usually men who were bigger, stronger, better-looking than I was. But here they were on my home grounds. I was more than eager to give up all external power, professional authority, and fight on a man to man basis—here. I was finally getting back at the same kind of man who always beat the shit out of me. This was far better than just making them study hard for tests.

And on top of all this I was loved. For I could afford to be generous. I didn't actually humiliate students. I just wanted a general acknowledgement that I was smarter than they were. The atmosphere was one of easy informality, with an undertone of benevolent paternalism, typical of the classroom of the "radical" teacher. And since this is about the freest atmosphere any student is likely to find in a classroom, I was appreciated. Within a few months I had a reputation as one of the grooviest of the hip, young, radical, teachers. By the second year, I could depend on all the big Radical Men of the school being in my classes, considering me an ally, even something of a guru.

This was the closest to real manly power I had come in my life, and the closest to satisfying human relationships. Is it any wonder that it became more and more central to me?

Soon, most of my close friends were students, former students, and other people I met through them. They were generally younger than I was, poorer than I was, and didn't have their lines down nearly as well as I did. I was guru, father-figure, and host. My apartment was a meeting place for young, hip radicals. Usually a few of them were crashing there. In my office or the cafeteria, I usually had an entourage of half a dozen students or so.

(Right while I was writing this, and feeling bitter over the inauthenticity of all my old friendships, the phone rang. It was a former student of mine, a middle-aged Black woman. She called just to say that she had been talking with some other former students of mine, and they missed me and wondered how I was doing. Some of it was real after all, it called up on the phone to tell me so. There are people who I love, and who love me, that I met while I was teaching, both former students and former colleagues. Some of them I'm still in contact with. We've talked about these things and hopefully gone on to more authentic relationships. To dismiss the four years of experiences I've just come from is not only unfair to myself, but to many other good people. In spite of everything there was some real human contact, some authentic friendship, some little love.)

But there was so much game playing, so many power trips, I came so close to being a man after all. And, finally, with all the gratification, victory, power, recognition, it still wasn't real, I still couldn't believe in it. For what I got from people still depended on the power I had over them—that was all the society would ever offer to me as a professional success, and it wasn't enough. I still knew that the only thing that really mattered to me was what people would give me freely. Away from the classroom, alone with another person, someone I had met as a student, his power as a straight man re-asserted itself. I could make it as a teacher, guru, advisor, but I never believed I was any of these things; they were never real enough to satisfy me. Outside of these roles, my friends, straight men, would never give me what I really wanted from them. Sex was part of it, of course. In fact at the time I believe I experienced it as the major part, since I lived in a seemingly eternal state of sexual tension, and sexual frustration. The whole atmosphere of the milieu I'd built up for myself reeked with sublimated sexuality. But looking back on it (from the perspective of having had a lot of sex, and finding out that didn't help much either) the real reason I couldn't settle for the kind of life and relationships I had was less direct. My friends were the most important part of my life. But for them, no matter how much they liked me, no matter how much they looked up to me even, their relationships with me were of secondary importance. Their most important relationships were with women, wives or girlfriends. Our time together was when they didn't have a date, or when their wife had something else to do. Or I was a guest of the family, or being dragged along on a date.

This wasn't due to any personal failure either on my part or theirs. They are part of a society in which a man's real intimacy and commitment can only be expressed toward a woman. That is, he can only reveal himself and make himself emotionally dependent on someone who is not a potential rival, but his inferior in terms of power, someone who has been trained to be emotionally supportive of men, rather than competitive with them, and to expect a position of dependency. Before another man, a rival, such a display of emotional commitment would be an indication of weakness. Masculine solidarity is a real phenomenon in this society among straight men. But it is a coalition of equals against inferiors for the maintenance of power. The personal relationships within such coalitions are a grown up version of the armed truce that has existed among men since boyhood. Such relationships are satisfying to straight men who are interested in maintaining power, and can turn to subservient women for emotional support, but they were not satisfying to me at all. And they were the only kind of relationships with other men that my straight male friends were really comfortable with. I needed close emotional relationships with other men, my straight friends did not. In fact straight men find the thought of intimate, emotional relationships with men revolting, because they are so threatening to the masculine facade of self-sufficiency. This is behind much of the straight man's revulsion with Gayness. Even the best intentioned, most liberal straight male friend is not going to place the same value on a friendship with a Gay man, that the Gay man places on it.

So as I got over being grateful for what I had, I started to panic at the thought that this was the best I could ever expect, if I continued to live my life the only way that seemed right to me. The best I could look forward to within the straight world, was to be a friend of the family, to depend for my emotional needs on people for whom I was a pleasant, but superfluous relationship. When I finally realized this, I finally realized that I had to have the opportunity to be at the center of a relationship—I had to come out.

Until then everything I had been taught about Gay men had made it totally unthinkable for me to openly accept myself as one of them. Ever since their existence had been admitted to me, I had been taught increasingly sophisticated reasons why they were not to be taken seriously as people. For years the only knowledge I had of the category of people in which I was included was through dirty jokes. Later I learned that they were to be pitied as cases of arrested development. The message that finally came across was that they were pitiful, crippled, tormented creatures always good for a laugh. But in all cases Gay people could not be taken seriously, and since it was tremendously important for me that I take myself seriously, I was completely unwilling to see myself as part of a group that was depicted either as vain, frivolous, child-like, fools, or tormented, mutilated metaphors for human loneliness.

My fear of this image was so great that it prevented me from having any real contact with Gay people that might have shattered the image. The only way I saw open to me to avoid self-hate was to tell myself I must be different from the rest of those fairies. Thus the image of the homosexual presented in this society not only teaches all men to be afraid of, hide their own Gayness, it teaches those of us who cannot hide our Gayness from ourselves to nevertheless avoid and be contemptuous of other Gay people. Even when our sexual needs bring us together there is often a mutual distrust and contempt based on our early internalization of the society's stereotypes, and this works against any real solidarity between us. Then the isolation of Gay people from each other can be pointed to by the society that creates it as evidence of the neurotic inability of homosexuals to relate to one another.

This describes my life up to my twenty-eighth year. But I was desperate enough now so that very little was necessary to break me out of this pattern. That was supplied by Gay Liberation. The Gay Liberation movement is a very complicated thing: it requires extensive analysis. But for me, in 1969, there was nothing complicated about it at all. I went to the November Peace March in Washington, and I saw five Gay men with a Gay Liberation banner. I don't think I can ever communicate how important a thing that was for me. Nothing would ever be the same again. I saw five people with a Gay Liberation banner. People. They didn't look ridiculous, silly, grotesque. They were talking to each other like friends, they didn't seem tormented, lonely, miserable. They were people, like me, at a peace march, and proud of being Gay. They looked like people I could talk to, about serious things, about my life.

Nothing happened right away. It took me until the following January to get up the nerve to go to a Gay Liberation meeting. But I started becoming a different person, and the world started appearing to me as a different kind of place. Before, my homosexuality had made me an outsider, alienated from society. But the social reality I had been taught still gave me the terms in which I defined myself. I was a tiny isolated satellite revolving around an immense social universe. Now I had contacted other people out here, and suddenly it all appeared as a lie. What I had been taught about such people wasn't true, there were people like me, and I didn't have to be isolated. I didn't understand at first why I had been lied to. But now that I could talk to others like myself it gradually appeared to us that the lie was essential for the ruling class to keep America running. Men have to believe that anyone who chooses not to be a man is a failure or a fool, if they are to be driven to function by a need to prove their masculine power. As we understood this, all the self-hate of our isolation started to turn outward into a growing torrent of rage. I had never really hated anything before—except part of myself. Now I began to hate this society, and I began wanting to destroy all of it. It was this wave of rage that finally broke through the conditioning of a lifetime, and what had seemed true and unalterable before, now appeared as something monstrously evil that must be destroyed. I hated what this society had done to me, then what it had done to us. And that led me to really see what it had done to others. I had always been against racism from the usual liberal perspective of paternalistic altruism. Now I could connect it to my own experience in having been taught that I was less than human. This didn't make me sympathetic toward Black people; it made me look to them and the rest of the third world as people who might be willing to join with me in the destruction of America. I was able to listen to women now and understand something of what they are saying. All oppressed peoples, all the people who the ruling class have defined as incapable of determining their own lives, share the same need to destroy the present reality of this society, if they are to assert their right to determine how they will choose to live. But this is getting ahead of myself, because all of this happened gradually, in fact it has just begun. But this is the process that the Gay Liberation Movement set in motion for me. Gay Liberation is the assertion by Gay People of their humanity, and the inevitable result of this assertion is to totally change the way we see the world, to create a new reality for us in which this society appears as an oppressor we must destroy. For me all of this became inevitable when I saw five Gay men carrying a banner in a Peace March. More and more of us are coming to this assertion.

Meanwhile, my academic career was quietly dying of neglect. The focus of all my energies was my emotional life. Teaching was very much a part of this; the rest of the package wasn't. I applied for no grants, set up no research projects, and served on no committees in more than a perfunctory way. The only thing that still meant anything to me aside from teaching was writing. But as my conception of sociology got more subjective and problem-oriented, it got harder and harder to write about something that didn't touch on my personal experience as an extremely alienated closet Gay and I wasn't ready for that yet. I rewrote several theoretical papers for my dissertation ("Alienation as an Ideology Among Intellectuals") but didn't put the necessary effort into either rewriting them enough to make them academically acceptable, or more important getting out there and selling them. More and more, I felt detached from the motivational system that was supposed to keep me functioning in the academic context.

By the third year the only part of an academic career I cared about was teaching. Now I was up for tenure, and the alternative to tenure was dismissal. The sociology department faculty committee, much to my surprise, recommended me for tenure. Perhaps it was because they wanted one "experimental teacher" around, with rapport with students. Also I believe they liked me, since I was the least manly of the radical teachers. I didn't try to bully them personally, and I wasn't trying to take over power in the department. I was seen as radical, but not personally threatening. Like the radicals, they perhaps sensed they didn't have to take me seriously as a man. However, the real Big Man of the department voted against me, and ultimately higher authority supported him, and I was fired. The reasons, as tradition dictates, were kept as obscure as possible, but one official suggested to the student newspaper that my behavior was "unprofessional" which was quite perceptive of him. Quite a number of radical faculty were fired that year, eight in the sociology department alone. I got to be one of the Sociology 8, and a building was taken in our honor and held for several hours. In any case I was out.

III

My academic career was now drawing to a close. I had finally stopped being a Brain and had become a Gay person working at being a teacher. I was out of the closet and working actively with the Gay Liberation Front. But being a "good teacher" still seemed meaningful, and was still an important source of gratification for me. And I still felt too isolated, too cut off from the support of a community, to live without a job. So I looked around for another place to teach. Several senior colleagues who liked me, or for various reasons, helped me. I wanted to stay in New York, to continue working with G. L. F., but I could not work it out.

So in the fall of 1970, I found myself starting the second, and last job of my academic career, at California State College, Hayward. But

academia would never again be the central feature of my life. For
three years my life had centered around a college and the relationships that originated there. Now my life centered in the Gay community of Berkeley, where I lived, and I had a job in Hayward. This
was fortunate; I don't think I could have survived Hayward otherwise.

Hayward is one of the new mass produced suburbs thirty miles
southeast of San Francisco, and Cal State, Hayward, is one of the new
mass produced colleges, with a mass produced faculty, and mass produced students. It's a second rate place, and everyone knows it. Even
the architecture is second rate. It ranks higher in the status system
than the Community Colleges, but at some of the Community Colleges, especially in the bay area, there's a certain spirit of defiance
against the ranking system. Perhaps because the communities they
serve tend to be third world, a place where defiance is really catching
on. But the mood at Hayward, among faculty especially, was resigned
acceptance of second-class status. C. C. N. Y.'s faculty were largely
New York intellectuals, and this put them somewhat outside the
mainstream of the American educational system. There was at least
a patina of cultural taste and intellectual perspective, even in the
sociology department. Hayward, on the other hand, is much more
representative of the wave of the future. Its faculty the products of
the newest and most efficient educational plants, unencumbered by
the dysfunctional vestiges of a humanist education. It is the true home
of the highly educated barbarian, the academician as pseudo-tech-
nocrat. In being prepared for their positions, the bureaucrats of Hayward never encounter the idea that "I was only doing my job" isn't
the only possible professional ethic.

But I lived in Berkeley, now, not Hayward, emotionally more than
physically. The main focus of my life was to find, or help create Gay
counter-culture that would give me the support I needed when I
finally left the social milieu of school, the only environment I had
successfully functioned in since I had been a kid. I never got as involved with students as I had at C. C. N. Y., and I didn't have much
to do with the faculty. I went to one faculty party, bringing two rather
militant friends as dates, and that was the last of my socializing. After
my first few faculty meetings, I found it was hard even to be around
my colleagues without getting profoundly depressed. There was an
almost metaphysical air to the pristine unreality with which they
viewed the world. They were equally out of touch with the social
and historical events proceeding around them, and with their own
emotions, desires, and weaknesses as human beings. To be in the

same space with several of them was to be sealed in a crystalline cap-
sule, out of time, out of space, where all of the world for all eternity
was precisely determined by clearly specified guidelines set down by
the appropriately designated authorities. They draw about them a
world without passion, without creativity, without morality.

I didn't last long. I knew I was living on borrowed time, but I still
wasn't ready to make a break; I wanted to draw things out as long as
possible. In order to have a couple of years to prepare myself, I was
ready to compromise as much as I could, and retreat into the background. It didn't take long to figure out that it would require quite
a retreat. Two events in my first week there set the pattern. The chairman called me in and explained that Sociology was going to upgrade
its image in the college. This was going to be done by downgrading
the students. From now on they would expect less A's and B's to be
given, especially to students insufficiently prepared for college work
(Blacks and Chicanos), a higher proportion of C's and D's would earn
the department more respect. For the last two years students in my
classes had graded themselves. But I said yes, sir, and decided to compromise as much as I could in good conscience (that phrase itself gives
away how much I was slipping back into a "professional orientation").
I went back to tests and grading, explaining to the students that I had
to keep the job, and I hoped they wouldn't take this shit any more
seriously than they had to. But it was too late; I could sell my soul,
but I didn't know how to stay sold anymore. One of the quasi-official
reasons for my eventual firing was that I gave too many A's and B's.

Also in the first week, my officemate, advising me as a newcomer,
suggested that I not let myself be intimidated by the Big Buck Niggers
around the place. Somehow this remark got back to the Black Student
Union, my officemate found himself in some trouble (though eventually he was promoted at the same time that I was fired), and I was
called on the carpet for unprofessional conduct in discussing the remarks of a colleague with students.

It should be noted in passing, that the chairman at Hayward, like
the chairman at C. C. N. Y. was a front man. Both chairmen were
typical of the academics I've described, shy, insecure, clinging desperately to formal authority in any encounters with other men. Both had
sought to be chairmen to avoid teaching classes. They both seemed to
really be perfect tools for the real men, in both cases senior professors,
with a long list of publications, seldom seen by junior colleagues,
hardly ever seen by students, these Big Men mixed mainly with Senior
administrators. Also in both cases, the Big Men not only came on as

more sophisticated and cynical, but as less desperately committed to bureaucratic procedure. They had enough real power so that they didn't have to depend on bureaucratic authority to prove their manhood.

I hated being in the room when my officemate gloried in the begging and pleading of a student—a big buck—for a chance to make up a test, and thus not be flunked out of school and drafted. But it's easy to feel revulsion at the spectacle of a weak man glorying in his professional authority. It's far more important to understand that this is no exceptional case; it's an archetypical example of the systematic use of masculinity to keep the system functioning. Male teachers, aware of their own real powerlessness, and needing to re-establish their sense of self-worth are enabled to do so by the power they are given over the life of students. And in so doing they further train the students to the same equation of power over others with self-esteem. This is part of the educational system whereby places like Cal State, Hayward, produce a new generation of functionaries. And it's only the weakest man within the system, in this case the teacher, who must dirty his hands with such crude expressions of power.

All of this was mostly justified by the ideology of professionalism. One of its most depressing features was the "professionalization" of those of the junior faculty who were graduate students at Berkeley, and had been part of the Free Speech Movement. They confided in me how they were perfecting their professional sneers in dealing with student requests, advised me that treating students as people was all very well, but you had to keep a tight grip on the requirements, since they would always get away with whatever they could. Soon they would be taking the same delight as the senior faculty in making a coed fly back from her honeymoon to take a final (an ultimate proof of masculinity, stealing the bride from her man, on her wedding night).

At C. C. N. Y. the faculty lived in a constant fantasy of rebellion. The plots, cabals, scheming, and endless talk of faculty power at least represented a wish for autonomy, however unreal. At Hayward the air was permeated with resignation and defensiveness. Professors are a glut on the market now, and in Reagan's California there is not even a facade of academic freedom any more. People just want to keep their jobs, to be left alone. The power of the administration is more naked and is wielded more nakedly. People just follow orders to survive.

The students, on the other hand, compared favorably to those at C. C. N. Y. They included many less budding intellectuals and junior aesthetes of course, but their grasp of the reality of their situation and the opportunities open to them was much clearer. The faculty lived in a world of illusions, the students had few of them. Overwhelmingly, they saw their "education" as something meaningless and worthless in its own right. They were there because they knew that after getting diplomas they could get better paying, if no more meaningful, jobs than they could get without them. This perspective is as true for the large number of middle-aged women returning for teaching licenses, as for the young "with-it" hippies. In the year I was at Hayward, I encountered no students, from middle-aged women to Jesus freaks, who defended the administrative procedure they were subjected to as legitimate or just. The general mood of the student body was cynicism and embittered resignation. At C. C. N. Y. the administration was afraid that the students were on the edge of rebellion; at Hayward the administration constantly congratulated itself on its success in maintaining an air of law and order among the inmates. But there comes a point when despair passes beyond resignation into something that no longer resembles submission. Perhaps the Hayward administration has more to worry about.

Naturally there weren't many radical students around. But the few who were there took themselves quite seriously. I doubt if many of them are going to settle down to regular life after a few years as freaks. I especially doubt if the women among them will ever be willing to go back to the roles this society requires of decent women.

Well, given all this, I only lasted a year this time. I couldn't compromise enough on grades, couldn't keep the correct social distance from students. And finally once I had come out, I couldn't stuff myself even part way back in the closet. Once you've got out of the habit of cringing and hiding, its hard to pick it up again. I thought I could be active in Berkeley but cool it in Hayward. But a month after I arrived the Radical Student Union invited Berkeley Gay Liberation to speak as part of Political Education Week. The speakers would be my friends. I could pretend not to know them, or join them. I joined them. After that I figured what the hell, and set out to start a Gay Student Union. At Hayward that wasn't easy, but the effort continues without me. So there were stories about me in the school paper, and my name was on leaflets all over campus. The response of my colleagues was typical of how they dealt with the world around them, nobody ever said a word about it, as much as possible they pretended I wasn't there. Given their power to define the reality of the college, I took this to mean I wouldn't be there long.

So my academic career, the last of my life as a Brain, was almost over, but one barrier remained, one illusion still had to be shattered before I would be really reconciled to giving up manhood for good. That happened in Berkeley. In Berkeley, I was becoming part of a Gay community, getting to know Gay men on a really intimate basis for the first time. They were the kind of people who didn't know I was a college professor, or if they knew, didn't give a shit. They would relate to me as a friend, a brother, a lover, but that's all. They would not accept me as their teacher, their father, their guru, their patron. And I found I didn't know how to relate to them. I still hadn't learned to relate to others as an equal. Even here I continued to try to be a teacher, a good benevolent, paternalistic, teacher, because it was the only thing I knew, and I drove all my friends away. I found myself alone again, this time with a kind anguish and despair that seemed much worse than that I had been used to when I was resigned to being alone. Again I had to change to survive, and again it hurt very much but it was a good pain because it made me grow. I haven't finished here, I still have a long way to go before I can trust myself enough and trust others enough to know some of what must be done. And it's been a long time since I've thought of being a "good teacher" as a legitimate career. When I realized this I no longer wanted even a period of grace. Long before I lost the job I knew I would make no attempt to get another one.

I don't know if I can ever teach again. It would only be possible for me in the context of a teacher-student relationship where the teacher has no power over the student. And I see no educational in-stitutions now existing within this society where this is the case. Per-haps they are being created in the free schools and free universities. But in any case my academic career is over for good.

IV

Well, where does that leave me now? Trying to get back to where I was when I was ten, coming out of the blind alley of academia I had been led into by my error in not seeing the Brains turn out to be men after all. Back then I decided I didn't want to be a man. I never entirely gave up that decision. Defensiveness, a desire for security, and the surprising fact of my masculine competence in an academic setting, all of this led me into being a Male impersonator for far too long, and I got so used to it that it is very hard to stop. But I am not now, nor have I ever been a man. But what I really wanted to be when I grew up hadn't been invented yet. It does not—cannot—exist within the capitalist social system. Those of us that are now trying to create it call it Gayness. Being Gay means relating to other people without a need for power over them, or a fear of revealing yourself to them. Therefore it is the ability to love equals, such as other men, or women defining themselves as equals, without being humiliated by the exhibition of unmasculine interdependence. It is revolutionary because it requires the end of capitalist society and the creation of a society in which Gay people can live.

The concept of Gayness has come a long way from homosexuality, but it grows out of the efforts of people defined by this society as homosexual, to redefine and recreate themselves. What Gay people will really be like none of us know yet. We have had to survive in America and that has made it impossible to be really Gay. We cannot even entirely renounce power yet. We must have the power to defend ourselves against a society that will increasingly attack us as it comes to perceive the danger we are to it. Thus we talk about Gay Power, the power of the people. But this must not be power for its own sake. We must not define ourselves in terms of power. The first step we can take toward Gayness, the first concrete thing Gay people can do now, is relate to each other without a reliance on power.

That's the theory, it only becomes reality as it becomes a real part of one's life. Right now my life is learning what it means to be Gay. This means that at the moment I'm living in a big old house in Oakland, California, with five other Gay men. We've been living together for a year now, supporting ourselves with savings and various odd jobs, and trying to learn to relate to each other. We are breaking up soon. We didn't make it. We were still too frozen in the old patterns, still too much men. But we learned something in the process. Two of us are working at setting up a new collective, and we'll try again. There's no turning back; there's only a void behind us. And what's ahead of us only begins to exist as we create it.

I also have to decide what to do with all the knowledge and skills I've learned in my life in the straight world. Now that I don't define myself as an intellectual, I have to come to terms with intellectualism. As a Brain things of the mind were the source of my sense of self-worth and a consolation for loneliness. Now I have other, less alienated sources of self-worth, but it will be a long time if ever before I can live without such consolation. Later as an academician I learned to use ideas as weapons to establish my power over others. Now I reject a self-concept based on power. Yet I am involved more than ever in a struggle against all the power of this society, and in this struggle, it is only through the use of ideas that I can feel that I am fighting back against my oppressors. Thus this paper.

Finally I have no answers. I don't know where I am going, only the direction in which I must proceed. I still often feel alone and isolated in this journey, but that is changing. Slowly, with many false starts we are coming together. We are frightened because we are leaving all of the world we knew behind us, with whatever security it provided. And it is still very hard to trust each other with our lives. But there is no going back, and we are building the future as we go. We must create a new world, if we are to be able to go on living. We are determined to live, so the future is ours.

Afterword Concerning Objectivity

I became a sociologist because I wanted to understand the world I found myself in. Why did I seem so separate and apart from other people, how could I come to know them and stop being lonely? I was taught that the only way to understand the reality of the social world was through the scientific method, empirical observation, dispassionate analysis, the quantitative investigation of empirically defined phenomena. I was also presented with an image of social reality that was supposed to have been constructed in such investigations.

In this objective scientifically observed world I was taught to believe in, the questions that had always motivated me could not be asked, they were meaningless. Everything that was really important to my life was dismissed as having no objective reality. But I believed in an objective, scientific understanding of the world, because I had never encountered the idea that there was any other way of understanding acceptable to a rational person. In accepting the truth of this view I denied my own reality. I believed in a world in which I could not be.

Nevertheless I searched for a place within this social reality where I could find myself. So I became a specialist in theories of alienation as a social phenomenon. But this is still part of a different reality than the one I actually lived in as a painfully alienated person desperately trying to understand myself.

In reading about alienation, however, I discovered other intellectual traditions, embodying different world-views that seemed closer to my own experience. I learned about the outsider, the stranger, the marginal man, whose very alienation allowed her/him to see society more insightfully. For the first time I had a role, a perspective with which I could identify. It ranged from the romantic notion of the artist-visionary, superhuman in his inexplicable uniqueness, to the almost sociologically respectable notion of the "free-floating intellectual" detached enough from the social structure to be free of its distortions of perspective. For many years my self-image as a person and a sociologist was based on my desire to see myself as such an intellectual outsider. It never quite worked though. Because one of the characteristics of such an outsider, that provides him with his Olympian detachment, is his freedom from the common human needs of his society. To really exist the detached intellectual would have to be virtually ego-less. I attempted the pose, but my own awareness of the crude desperation of my needs never allowed me to believe it. One of the things I hope this article will demonstrate is the extent to which the misfit, just to the extent he is an outsider, is not outside the values of society, but is totally imprisoned by them, even though it is not in the conventional way. In my own case, at least, any insight I might have into the workings of society are derived not from any sense of detachment, but from an intense desire to attach myself to something. I don't believe there are any free-floating intellectuals; I don't believe there is anyone not anchored firmly to a predefined set of values, goals, and indicators of self-worth, that he can free himself from only by a difficult struggle. In my case, and I believe in many others, the motivation for this struggle is nothing mystical or unique, but the very real fact that I felt needs that it was impossible for me to ever satisfy in the world I was born and raised to live in. It was the concrete fact of Gayness that made me an outsider.

Only in Marxism did I finally find a perspective on the world that not only allowed me to experience my own personhood, but explained to me why that had so far been impossible. It taught me that the social reality of the world is defined by the ruling class, who among their other possessions own the institutions of communication, education, and religion, and means by which reality is defined. Their definition is one that serves their interest, and one of the ways it does this is by defining as unreal, meaningless, the interests that any other group experiences that conflict with the interest of the ruling class. I further learned that those outside the ruling class can never come to meet their own needs until they discover for themselves a new world-view in which the question of how they are to satisfy their needs is no longer meaningless. Marxism has not supplied all the answers, because it cannot tell me why I am separate from the class I spring from. In a Marxist context I am middle-class. I know I am not part of the middle-class world: I am a stranger there. This is why I believe I need a Gay perspective to understand who I am. I am still in the process of discovering it. Part of that process is described in this paper.

For the first time, though, I had a vantage point from which to judge the whole system of academic sociology that which I had learned was the only perspective from which social judgments could be made. For the first time my own experience of it makes sense. It had been a trap. The whole intellectual apparatus that led from the academic concept of sociology, to the empirical-rational model of sociological procedure, to the actual social structure of the academic world, all of this had led me to try to find personal salvation in professional expertise. For me this was an absurd grotesquery. For the ruling class it is a way of channeling the needs of unsatisfied people, into satisfying their requirements for professional experts. Academic sociology, academia as a whole, the bureaucratic, professional corporate organizations that are swallowing all the people of this country, all of them are justified in terms of the same worldview where reality is something to be understood by the properly trained experts, truth is determined by scientific techniques beyond the grasp of most, and human needs are therefore what the proper authorities tell you they are. This is the human meaning of the world of scientific sociological objectivity, and it appears to me as a vast collection of human squirrel cages, each with its exercise wheel. Each individual is led to an appropriate cage (one is given a choice of several) by the almost infallible process of never being allowed to suspect that anyplace else exists. The way forward is defined as running as hard as possible on the exercise wheel. One never gets anywhere but all the spinning wheels provide the energy that makes the whole giant engine operate as its owners want it to. Eventually the individual gives up all hope of realizing the promises that have been made to him but he keeps running until he dies: What else is he to do?

This is not an objective analysis of society. It springs directly from my own experience in society trying to get my needs met. By definition it could never have been arrived at by objective observation. Therefore if I restricted myself to objective observation I would blind myself to my own needs. Thus I must reject objective observation as a device which blinds me to my own condition. I am not a scientist. I can't even claim to be a scholar. There are no footnotes in the paper. I didn't give credit to the proper sources. The only authorities I recognize are those who are of help to me, who provide me with insight into my own condition. To the extent that they have done so their insights have become part of my thinking. There are many cases where this has been true. I learned about the social nature of reality from Durkheim. Simmel told me of the stranger, and Mannheim of the free-floating intellectual. Marx taught me how the ruling class manipulates social reality to its own interests and Marcuse showed how in our society it operates by making alternatives to the status quo literally unthinkable.

Yet after all this is said, the act remains to give the final meaning to reality. I cannot in the face of my act, deny that I am making some claim to objectivity. What it finally comes to is that act of faith on which all attempts at human communication are based. It is this faith that must underlie all attempts to create a sociology, to understand people's relationships with each other. It is that since the social world is made up of people and the way they treat each other, the understanding of it can be formed from an understanding of ourselves and how we relate to others. That we can not only learn from our own experiences, but that enough communication is possible so that we can give and receive from others understanding based on what each has learned in the adventure of living. I believe the readers of this retelling of my experience can understand something of me and the world I live in, and decide for themselves if there is any truth in it.